HUNTER'S FEN

Illustrated by
John Paley and Dave Parfitt

John Humphreys

HUNTER'S FEN

DAVID & CHARLES
Newton Abbot   London   North Pomfret (Vt)

I dedicate this book to the memory of the late James Wentworth Day, a romantic and a romancer; a writer and shooter who first brought the magic of the fen country and its wild people, fish, birds and beasts into a million suburban lounges.

·Contents·

Thanks to Ian Holmes of Spalding
for the loan of contemporary photographs

British Library Cataloguing in Publication Data

Humphreys, John 1939–
  Hunter's fen.
  1. Fens (England) – Description and travel
  I. Title
  914.26'04858   DA670.F33

  ISBN 0-7153-8761-8

Typeset by Typesetters (Birmingham) Ltd
Smethwick West Midlands
and printed in Great Britain
by Butler & Tanner Limited Frome & London
for David & Charles Publishers plc
Brunel House Newton Abbot Devon

Published in the United States of America
by David & Charles Inc
North Pomfret Vermont 05053 USA

·Preface·

This is a book I have long wanted to write. The misty miles of the wild fens have always held for me a peculiar fascination. Strangers passing through may see only straight roads, soot-black fields, rows of waving poplars and lowering, desolate skies. They may accelerate and hurry on to more homely, undulating country, having had no time to see the distant speck of a hen harrier, a savage relic of Hereward's Fen, hanging on the wind. They might not hear the rusty clashing of the cutlass blades of the reeds nor the reeling of the sedge-warbler's song; their urban eyes will not, perhaps, see the line of mallard, etched black against the sky. Scanning the speedometer and electric clock on the dashboard they may well overlook a blood-orange sun sinking in the western sky, slashed with every colour on an artist's palette.

They may not be aware that the very road they hurry to leave behind was once part of the bed of a great mere, a sheet of winking ripples where coot and moorhen clanged, bitterns boomed and wildfowl in great flocks rose with a sound like thunder. Romans, monks, blond Saxons, Vikings and mailed Normans boated over it; Flemish traders sailed its blue distances while the large copper and the swallowtail flickered over the reeds. In winter came the boom of the stanchion guns as the old punters took a toll of the fowl; when it froze they fixed bone skates to their punts to slide over the ice, or they abandoned the work altogether and took to their fen runners on which they flew like swallows over the crackling ice.

That humpy bridge, so quickly passed by a car, once saw endless strings of barges towed by patient horses while, beneath, the water's green depths concealed shoals of slab-sided bream, pike to frighten a modern angler and eels as thick as a man's arm. The speeding car is too fast for its occupants to see the remains of the old pumping mills, coprolite pits, and the heaps of bog-oak, last remnants of those ancient forests in which stalked bears, wolves and beavers. The curious, protracted and often bloody battles of the drainers – those dour Dutchmen who, 300 years ago, took the first important step of wresting from Nature what will ultimately always be hers – are now easily overlooked.

What can a 'furriner' know of the Black Winter of '47 when 'she' broke out, burst the banks and drowned the land, together with its cattle, pigs, crops and people? How may he know of the wild men who lived here, the fowlers, dyke diggers, reed cutters, fishermen, marsh shepherds, skaters, drinkers and fighters who survived flood, famine, ague, invasion and grinding penury to come to terms with their harsh environment? Uncouth and unlettered they may have been, but they had mastered the hardest art, that of survival.

The car hurries on, back to cosy civilisation, leaving me to lean on the white-railed bridge, cough in exhaust fumes and watch the receding tail light, a dimming, distant, red firefly which rounds the bend by the Upware pumping engine and vanishes: the silence rushes back.

A latter-day fen fisher and gunner, I feel something of what those old-timers felt, although incomparably more easy is my life than theirs. In the evening hush, their robust and cheerful ghosts crowd round and whisper to me from the sedge fen. A barn owl cries; something rustles deep in the elder thicket and another string of mallard, barely visible now against the final, orange sash across the west, goes on whickering wings with a burst of staccato chattering — who knows where?

The book is not exclusively about shooting, geography, history, people, fishing or places, but it contains elements of them all. No learned scholar will scan its pages for reference, but possibly those who feel that desolate, sad and remote places are not there merely to be accelerated through but worth lingering in with companions no more demanding than a fishing rod and a gun, will stay with me long enough to read these pages before rushing on and back to the hurly burly of life at the hectic end of the twentieth century.

John Humphreys
Bottisham

·Gunner's Dawn·

It lacked an hour to dawn. The frost did more than hold, it gripped with the icy fist of chainmail. Sheets of thin pack-ice drifted down the flooded washes, meeting other floes, joining them or separating to slide slowly on. Any of them could have been broken with the pressure of a finger, but a 20yd sheet of it broadside on to the punt would have carried us away downstream with an awful, irresistible power, and possibly dashed us against the pillars of the river bridge a mile below. A vessel with an inch of freeboard, 20ft long and 4ft wide, calls for careful handling in the ice.

To our right loomed the hairy slope of the flood bank, its crown a jumble of Norfolk reed, teazles and the dry sword blades of reeds which rustled and clashed peevishly in the mean, pre-dawn breeze, a far too soft word to describe a breath from the Arctic which cut through clothes as sweetly as a razor. Lying along the punt was The Gun, a weapon of stupendous firepower throwing 1½lb of large shot in a pattern as wide as a bed sheet. The recoil of such a monster untethered would have been enough to decapitate the gunner, so it was held in check by a breeching rope 2½in thick. The muzzle protruded black and gaping ahead, nosing between the ice floes, as though sensing its way upstream. We gauged our speed by marking the stealthy creeping past of the bank, here a stunted willow, there a ruined gatepost, next a jumble of frost-welded bottles and cans, flotsam from the easy days of summer.

Somewhere up ahead were the wildfowl. The ice had crept in on them from the banks, pushing them daily into a smaller area of open water, until every bird on the marsh was packed into a 20-acre lagoon, hemmed in by ice and linked to the main river by a tiny neck of open water, a neck which we now approached. My companion was Will Kent, a fen gunner of the old, tough school, a man who kept his watch in a lozenge tin packed with cotton wool, an old 'navigator's' trick used by men who led rugged lives. Will's arm was over the side of the punt, feeling for bottom with his 6ft weighted pole or sprit, fumbling for a grip and pushing the punt steadily, but imperceptibly forward. He lay on his thin belly, his stubbly jaw pressed into a bundle of sacking, his gasping breath beading wetly on the coarse fibres. Beneath his grubby, off-white smock, a small muscle in his forearm near the elbow flexed and tensed, swelled and sank with each movement. That muscle comes only after a lifetime of working gunning punts.

I lay ahead of him, one boot either side of Will's head, my own white smock and white woolly hat blending with the stone white of the punt, the same colour as the horizon or the hue of a gull which seems to vanish when it flies along that indefinable line where sky and water meet. To duck on the water or on a low mud bank we would not appear a threat so long as we approached them head on, for the slight movements of the punter's arm were hidden by the widest part of the beam of the punt, and the fowl were used to swans and pieces of flotsam creeping up on them − provided they did not creep too quickly.

We reached the point on the bank which was level with the neck of open water which led to the lagoon. The landmark was a ruined willow, browsed by bullocks each time it ventured forth a shoot, so it had put its energies into thickening its trunk and there it crouched, a shock-headed river watcher, summer perch for kingfishers and shelter for human anglers. I hissed a direction to Will, and slowly he swung our bows from south to east and, a foot at a time, we began to cut down the distance between us and the fowl. Their cries had accompanied us since we began an hour before: the silver whistling of cock wigeon, the growling of the hens and strident quacking of mallard. Now the sound was louder, amplified by the water, the cold and the stillness of the air.

We had been out many times that season, Will and I, and had fared badly. Puntgunning is a hard way to make a bag, for the birds might see you too soon, a low-flying falcon or aeroplane can put them up, as can a distant shore-gunner with his pop-pop of a double shot; or the fowl, being by nature restless creatures, might simply decide to move on elsewhere. Even with the big gun you need to be within seventy yards of your birds for a shot, and then they have to be tightly bunched and of sufficient numbers to make a 'pull' worthwhile. With shoulder guns we could have bagged a sackful at flight, but restricted to the punt and gun, had come home empty handed.

It was vital to hit the opening in the ice: a few yards too far to left or right and we would have ground to a halt in the pack, from which to extricate ourselves would have put every duck in the county on the wing. By keeping a line on the tip of Orion's sword low ahead in the heavens I was able to guide us through with no more than a silken rustle and delicate tinkle as the filigree edges of the floating ice caressed our pointed bows, and slid safely away to either side.

Now we were nearer to a good shot than we had been for four seasons. A careless tap with a pole on the woodwork, a head poked up too far, a careless swing broadside on and that great army would be gone, leaving us alone and disconsolate. The sounds grew in volume until, to our fevered senses, they seemed to fill our heads with a buzzing, whistling, quacking cacophony. Dawn was approaching: it was not so much growing lighter as simply becoming less dark. A pale-pink slash across the eastern gloom showed where dawn was levering the lid off the night.

We drew nearer with a dreadful stealth. Crushed fragments of reeds passed slowly as we inched along until the dibbling of a thousand bills and the shouting of a thousand birds, each one saluting the dawn, sounded a few feet away rather than a hundred yards. Surely some of the outriders to that mighty gathering were near enough for us to touch with the long pole. On and on we went, left a bit, right a bit, as I peeped alongside the breech of the gun at the dense, black line on the grey water ahead. We were just about in range; a few more yards to make sure.

Then the birds grew suspicious. With the suddenness of the turning of a switch, that mighty army fell silent, a thousand pairs of eyes and ears of the most alert birds that fly were concentrated on us. I reached for the lanyard, tipped the stock as with a roar like a mighty waterfall they were up and crying, and at that moment I aimed just above the thick and pulled the cord.

The roar of the departing birds was dwarfed by the thunder of the puntgun. It was the loudest bang in the world, a drum-shattering, throaty roar accompanied by a yard of orange flame, a shower of red sparks and a gout of acrid black powder smoke. The punt heaved back in the water, pushed gently but firmly by a giant hand; had we not seized our paddles she would have been shoved back to the neck of the lagoon.

The smoke cleared, drifting in ragged scarves across the ice and we saw that we had several birds down. Most were dead, although here and there an orange paddle waved feebly, there a wigeon furrowed the water in an attempt to escape. We pulled out the cripple-stopper from under the deck and working inwards in a large circle we dealt with the runners and then collected the dead birds. The departing army had fled noisily and completely, leaving behind twenty-nine of their number and a thirtieth which dropped out on the ice and which we could not retrieve.

That was it: a fair stalk to set the pulses racing and heart pounding so loudly that one imagined the birds would surely hear it echoing through the bottom boards. It had come at the end of a long, lean spell and was fair reward in one of the toughest sorts of shooting that exists. Now was the time to relax, to gaze for the first time into each other's faces and see mirrored there our own elation and sense of consummation. It was a time to slap a pocket and find smoking tackle, to carefully fill and light a pipe, to glance sideways through the smoke at a neat line of wildfowl ranged in proper punter's fashion, in a row under the gunnel; those glances were as much gloating as to confirm that the whole thing had not been a dream. It was a time to stretch the legs and ease cramps, to restore circulation to frozen fingers, to sit casually on the deck of the punt and gaze round at the lightening sky and to appreciate for the first time that it was beginning to snow.

Then it was back downstream, down current and downwind, no longer lying flat, but sitting up boldly to catch the wind, racing along, dodging the ice, a skimming swallow compared with the sinister creeping snake of the outward voyage. We came to rest in the shallows where the drove ran down into the water, clambered out and stamped up and down. We made all shipshape, loaded the birds into the old pick-up truck and hid the punt, securely tied under the hawthorn bush which overhung the dyke.

Down into the lonely fen, past sword-blade dykes laid neatly across the broadcloth of the landscape, past the ice-bound fields we drove to Will's snug little cottage which lay on the 'waterland' of the marsh edge. We hung the birds – two teal, twenty-one wigeon and six mallard – from the cross beam, and went in to bacon and eggs, the smell of which, with onions on its breath, had come wafting from the kitchen window across the snowy yard.

We dragged off our long boots, leaving them deflated and collapsed in the porch, hung various layers of outer garments on the nails and shuffled in to see Will's white-haired, matronly wife. Sitting round the kitchen table we re-lived every moment of the stalk which, like a symphony, had been a thing of gradual build up, of variations of pace with a whiff of tragedy but, underlying it all, intimations of an approaching climax which, when it came, was every bit as explosive as the last moments of the 1812 Overture.

Eheu; that was all of thirty-odd years ago. Will and his wife have gone to their long home; that great gun, hero of many an adventure, ended up as a down pipe for an outhouse roof, quite ruined, full of red rust, wasted and denied the dignified pasture of life in a museum to which its age and experience so richly entitled it. The punt has gone to fuel a bonfire and the other few bits and pieces of his fowler's life passed on to joyless descendants or were snapped up by predatory dealers.

Will was one of the last true fenmen, a man who wrested a living from a harsh and bleak countryside. In the summer, at the time of the August thunderstorms, it was eels, caught in nets stretched across the leams, lodes, cuts, dykes and rivers of his watery parish. When they outlawed that, he used hives or grigs, those graceful worm-baited baskets which filled with fat eels at the time of their summer migration. He made them himself, of course, cutting the whippy osiers as thick as a pencil, peeling the bark, splitting each rod into three and polishing off the pith. For each of these operations he used tools he had made from the things around him, a piece of a cut-throat razor blade set in a block of willow or two fragments of cart axle bound together with twine. It took a dire emergency to tempt Will into a shop.

His handiwork was pure art, shapely things of real beauty that also conformed to the ideal concept of design, since they were perfect for the job for which they were intended. The finished osier strap was as pliable as cord and he could weave it at incredible speed, seated on an upturned apple box and surrounded by a steadily growing carpet of peeled bark and stubby offcuts. He dropped the grigs in the water to soak them, baited and left them, checking them twice daily at the busy time, removing the whittled stopper and shaking out his catch into a bucket. The eels were kept alive-o in a large submerged box pierced with holes and called a trunk, big enough to allow the passage of fresh water (if fen water may be said ever to be fresh) but too small to allow the eels to escape. When he had collected a hundredweight or so, 'the man' came with his van and took them to market.

When he was not doing that he was shepherding bullocks on the river washes, knee-deep in waving grasses, the skies full of whinnying snipe, the wild thyme scenting the warm air. In spring he caught peewits in nets and sent them 'up Lunnon' to the great poultry markets at Leadenhall Street. He was not averse to knocking down a pheasant or brace of partridges with his double-hammer 12-bore, preferring to shoot the birds sitting if he could creep near enough. The flying shot was for the gentry and a cartridge was a precious thing, not to be expended on the empty air. In his youth he had been given two cartridges by his father and told, 'Goo yew on boy: git yourself your dinner.' He had two chances and if he should miss he went hungry. Such an upbringing makes for a deadly shot and a skilled fieldcraftsman. Those who failed that tough apprenticeship either went to the wall or sought out more predictable pay packets in the town.

He could shoe a horse, plough a furrow, snare a rabbit, make a boat, drink a gallon of beer and re-load old cartridge cases with a skill to which the modern, suburban self-sufficiency freak will for ever be a stranger. In his fierce, dark eyes and hooked beak of a nose one could see his Viking

forebears who long ago had come stealing up the meandering rivers in their longships, weaving a course through the miles of waving reeds and dank fogs, seeking a spot of dry land big enough to make a settlement. They it was who learned the tricks of eel-grig making and living off any land in which they found themselves, and these arts Will and his kind had inherited.

Puntgunning has all but died out. It is such a demanding game, full of risks as well as excitement, demanding of time, calling for guns and gear which have not been made for a century, so it is little wonder that it is now left to a small handful of enthusiasts. They shoot precious little, but preserve a dying art and experience first hand the intense thrill of the stalk, risking their lives on crawling tideways, at the mercy of sudden fogs, gales, quicksands and mechanical disasters. Deerstalking is child's play compared to it, pheasant shooting a pastime for drawing-room sybarites.

The history of puntgunning is littered with larger-than-life characters from the Duke of Wellington's Colonel Peter Hawker to Mr James Robertson Justice the actor, both dilettantes and sportsmen and not obliged to do it for a living, but curious characters none the less. Being such a giant sport, the mishaps tend also to be of an extravagant nature. Harry and Ken were two punters operating off the Lincolnshire marshes, both hard men, their blood three parts Stockholm tar and the hairs on their head rope yarn. Harry of the rosy cheeks and deceptively academic horn-rim spectacles, wore a donkey jacket appropriated from a well-known building and construction firm. It had a round, yellow sun between the shoulder blades and it was said in the village that when Harry went onto the marsh the geese began to flight: they saw his jacket and thought it was dawn.

Ken was long and lean, not an ounce of fat on him, craggy of feature, laconic of speech but with a twinkle of perpetual amusement in his grey eyes. We sat in Ken's front room watching the telly through the snowstorm on the screen which was a fact of viewing life in those days of chancy reception. The programme was a rock-climbing saga, the first ascent of The Old Man of Hoy, and the commentator extolled the virtues of the nylon climbing ropes, so thin but virtually unbreakable and 100 per cent rot-proof. The breeching rope on the punt gun was thick enough, but hard on the hands, especially when it was full of ice or sand and fingers were numb. Each spring the rope was tied onto the back of the lorry and tested to make sure that no hidden rot had set in. Sudden inspiration: why not use climbing rope? Cheap, light, strong and rot-proof – it was the perfect solution.

The man in the Outdoor Shop was surprised at an order for 5yd of rope, but he cut them off a length and they hurried home to remove the old rope and replace it with the new one. There were a great lot of wigeon in, blown in by the gales, and the time was right for a heavy shot. Ken pushed them up under a pale dawn to a solid 3 acres of wigeon packed onto a mud bank which was gradually vanishing under a flooding tide. The critical moment arrived, the flock lifted, and Harry 'pulled'.

It was a fair shot and Ken set to work to bag the runners but Harry was clutching a bloody nose and mouth, spitting teeth and favouring an eye already monstrously black. The strength of the new rope lay partly in its elasticity and the gun had whipped back under the recoil of 20oz of No 1 shot and caught Harry a glancing blow in the face. Had the butt struck him fair and square it would surely have killed him. So much for technology! You cannot put new wine into old bottles.

The following morning they were out again, the old rope back in place and the new one thrown down in the barn. Harry, his toothless gums firmly clenched, his ill-mended spectacles glaring from a swollen face which was, in turn, red, blue and yellow, was back at the gun. Once more they found a nice pack of birds right for stalking; once more Ken worked up to them with a skill learned in thirty years of punting.

'I could tell he was nervous,' Ken was to say later. 'He kept pulling back the gun to make sure there was no slack; he did not want a repetition of yesterday.' The dawn was cold; Harry's fingers were encased in thick woollen mittens and, as he was giving one extra, final heave, he caught the trigger, fired the gun prematurely and the birds fled unscathed. That made two mornings running that the air of the marsh was blue with invective, claim and counter-claim, accusation and denial. They did not care to fire the gun for less than £5 return per shot, so to mess up two chances like that. . . . They poled home in an acrimonious silence, and it was not until after breakfast that they were once more on speaking terms.

Big guns mean big bags but also big accidents. Two old fenmen, brothers who lived together in a cottage which crouched in the lee of the flood bank out of the east winds, liked a little punting and they moored their punt, the big gun loaded and ready, on the marsh side of the flood wall. Bob was working in his garden one February, forking over the peaty soil ready for potato-planting time. He stopped to ease his back, and walked the few yards to the bank, crept up and peeped over; sometimes a paddling of fowl swam in near enough for a shot.

Sure enough, there was a gaggle of Brent geese which had drifted in on the morning tide. Bob slid over the bank and like a stalking leopard glided through the thistles down to the punt. He loaded the gun

James Tidswell, a typical fen fowler with a shoveller

quickly, a handful of the coarse-grained, black powder and a 1lb scoop of shot. He pushed off and worked out to the birds which had swum out of sight behind an island of wrack. It was an easy stalk and as, with a throaty cackle of alarm they lifted, he fired.

The gun was a slipper gun with no breeching rope, the recoil being taken up by a bottom board in the punt and partly by the weight of the gunner. In his excitement, Bob had forgotten that the gun was already loaded. Two pounds of shot instead of one and a double charge resulted in a massive recoil. The blast knocked him unconscious, ripped the beam from the punt, shot the gun backwards down his body and between his legs and protruded a yard out at the stern. The punt drifted inshore and eventually Bob recovered consciousness to find his brother Jim weeping over him, believing him dead. Bob thought for a moment he was in heaven, but Jim's extravagant language of relief at seeing his eyelids flicker, brought him firmly down to earth.

He had had a merciful escape, for the gun had ripped the front of his clothing, removed both his Wellingtons as cleanly as a whistle and left him completely unscathed. A large tot of rum and half an hour in the armchair effected a complete recovery and he was back on the garden wielding his fork by lunchtime. This adventure took place in the days when Brent geese had still to be placed on the protected list and, together with wigeon, were the principal quarry of the punt shooter.

Some punters have been less lucky. A man on Lindisfarne was killed outright by a blowback, the result of a hang-fire in a cartridge which exploded just as he was unscrewing the breech. He was an inexperienced punter, but the noted Solway gunner Blackett was caught out in rough water in that treacherous estuary. He and his companion had made a heavy shot, but the punt swung broadside on to the outfall of the flooding Esk, filled and sank and both men were tragically drowned.

Down on the old fen, the big gunners had been working the fowl almost since the invention of gunpowder. Prior to that it must have been frustrating for fowlers to be surrounded by so much bounty but able to use only bows and arrows, sticks and nets to take a bird or two. There were no close seasons nor protected species in those times and the simple rule was, if you could catch it, you ate it. In summer wildfowl go into a state known as eclipse, during which they lose their flight feathers and lurk, like the Ugly Duckling, in the rushes until they became once more full-winged in the autumn. The old fen fowler would take full advantage of this phenomenon, hunting out the reed beds with rough-coated mongrel dogs, pursuing the flightless fowl from punts and knocking them down with sticks. Sometimes it was the only way to wrest a square meal from a hostile environment.

The human population was scattered whereas the fowl abounded. The whole of Lincolnshire, Cambridgeshire, the Isle of Ely, Huntingdonshire together with parts of Essex and Norfolk must have been one vast quack. When he was not wrestling with the demons of his fertile imagination, over-indulgence in laudanum and the effects of malaria, poor St Guthlac, founder in 664 of Crowland Abbey near Peterborough, recorded that the winter skies were black with the wings of uncountable ducks and geese.

At least he makes it clear that the depredations of a handful of creeping fenmen armed with staves could have had no possible effect on such a countless multitude of birds. The real enemy to wildlife populations is the erosion or removal of habitat, the drainage of a cluster of marshy fields and the planting of wheat removing the marsh birds and plants for ever; far more devastating than the keenest of the old gunners.

Much of the spirit of those times remains, in spite of mile upon mile of waving corn and shiny green sugar-beet leaves. Here and there the traveller finds a corner which the reclaimers have missed. One such place is the National Trust reserve at Wicken Fen, a place full of ghosts and atavistic figments of the ancient fens. Once the boyhood haunt of that noted fenland chronicler, the late Jimmy Wentworth Day, who immortalised it in his early writings, Wicken was drained by the 'War Ag' as part of the 'Dig for Victory' campaign in World War II. Jimmy never forgave them for what he considered a piece of gross, bureaucratic vandalism. His beloved meres, sedge beds and acres of tawny tasselled reeds which tossed lion-brown in the autumn suns, together with the birds, beasts and fishes vanished in a blitzkrieg of heavy machines, mud and fire.

In the mid 1950s the fen was re-flooded and allowed to run riot, but somehow it was never quite the same. I cycled over from school at Soham to witness the little opening ceremony. A few like-minded souls stood huddled on the flood bank, doing our best to avoid the bite of the north-easterly while Dr Eric Ennion, another noted fenman, a famous ornithologist and bird artist, said a few appropriate words prior to Peter Scott swinging the handle of the sluice. The muddy water surged through, brown and yellow, to add to the oily sheet which lay in the bottom of the new mere. Already a few tufted duck bobbed and dived on its hammered-pewter ripples.

There are still forgotten, unfarmed corners in the fens

Old fen 'slodger' scanning the flooded washes for fowl

The re-making of Wicken taught even the most experienced conservationists an important lesson. It was not enough to allow the fen to revert naturally, otherwise the jungle would creep in to the detriment of many of the old fen natives. The scrub of stunted thorn and willow which grew quickly was harbourage for crows, stoats, magpies, feral cats and a few songbirds. The old fen had been – after a fashion – managed, for the farmers dug peat, cut crude drainage channels and harvested the Norfolk reed on a three-year cycle for thatching. Drains were kept clear of silt and weeds to allow the water to flow. *Viola stagnina*, the marsh violet, would flourish only where dykes had been maintained. Bitterns and harriers required the great expanses of thatching reeds, the wildfowl needed sheets of open water, each of which could be provided by the hand of Man.

Even the rough, bony cattle and scattered flocks of sheep played their part, since they cropped the coarse pastures and created another habitat for yet another series of plants, and nesting sites for lapwings, partridges, stone curlews and godwits. The 'restored' Wicken Fen – managed by default, and kept sacred from what were held to be the depredations of Man – was a poor place and bore no resemblance to the fen it sought to represent. Today there is proper, enlightened management; reeds are cut and scrub cleared by armies of volunteers. The old Warden, Colonel Mitchell, was instrumental in organising the change and he strode round with a swagger stick, able to dig peat with the best old-timer, supervising the loading of the barges with bundles of osiers and thatching reed until they appeared from a distance to be floating mountains of rush, moving slowly and apparently at their own volition, along the sluggish waters of the lode.

Today the hen harriers swing and glide low over the reeds as they did in Hereward's day. Coots skitter and squabble on the mere; the grasshopper warbler reels his summer song and countless mallard, wigeon and pintail make the winter skies clamorous with the noise of their passing. Rare migrants drop in, unexpected and unannounced. An osprey may pause on his migration south and take a week's fishing; bearded tits have been recorded and the bittern heard. The rare and beautiful Montagu's harrier, familiar of Jimmy's boyhood, is too scarce to have made a return, but I do not doubt that, on some misty October morning, one has passed over, unnoticed and unrecorded by birdwatchers still abed.

Now the old dyke diddlers and fen slodgers in their rabbit-skin caps and moleskin waistcoats have gone from Wicken. Where grimy urchins once babbed for eels, the well-shod children of the 1980s keep carefully to the mown paths, gaze through their binoculars and tick off the various species in their bird books.

There are other places where the water is still master in this curious half-land of the fens. Heavy rain or meltwater in the East Midlands runs down to the fens, much of which are still below sea level; exceptionally high tides on the coast may hold up the outflow of this natural drainage, so to prevent flooding, each river has its own little 'wash', a strip of fallow ground on either side which runs back to a lofty flood bank.

These washes – in summer, riots of giant water dock, nettles, thistles and teazles – serve their real purpose in a wet winter. Then the overloaded river spreads across the wash only to be contained by the banks; when the pressure of water subsides, the spate water swirls out to sea through the mighty Denver Sluice, and the river returns to its normal course, leaving the wash a patchwork of shallow splashes, silty mud and a litter of freshwater mussel shells – swan mussels, we call them.

It is a bold farmer who will try to cultivate a wash, for a sudden flood in July is not unknown. In 1957 two farmers ploughed their washes; there had been no summer flood for fifteen years, so the gamble was, they decided, worth taking. One field was drilled with barley, the other with red beet. In early September there was a week of mighty rains: great drops bounced on the roads, hammered on the tin sheds in the farmyard and turned the dusty droves into muddy tracks. The system could not cope with this sudden influx; the operators of the flood gates were caught napping and up 'she' came.

Stockmen rushed out to drive their cattle off the marsh, herding them along the low banks into holding pens on the outskirts. The barley and the beetroot fields grew soggy and then a film of water slid among the stalks, rose up the stems and a scummy tide swept over the whole wash. The beet was ready for harvest and a pile of wicker potato baskets had been left handy for the work to begin. A long line of them bobbed and floated down the wash towards the sea. I took the punt and gathered a few of them, legitimate flotsam. I have one by me still.

As for the barley, mallard will fly miles for a grain, so a 10-acre field of unthreshed ears floating in a foot of water was Paradise for them. They found it and poured in in uncountable numbers from the bloodshot evening skies, unmarked by any save me, for the field was miles from civilisation. I haunted the washes almost daily and so my intelligence was bang up to date. I had an 1897-model Winchester repeater in those days, when it was still permissible to load five cartridges in such a weapon.

No decoys were necessary, and standing out up to my knees, my leaky boots squelching in wet barley, I made hay while the sun shone, bagging 17 in the first evening and ending an amazing week with exactly 102. I sold the lot to the Cambridge butcher at 6s each and paid for my cartridges for the whole season. It was tricky shooting and I had no dog with me, since he could not be expected to tread water for two hours at a time: there was not a square foot of dry land on which he could stand. This meant I had to wade about to gather the slain, while carrying that great weight of birds off at night meant a very real risk of walking into a hidden dyke and 10ft of muddy water; then there was the 2-mile hike back to the road and a further mile of precarious cycle riding.

It's an ill wind, and a gambling streak in an eager farmer gave me the best mallard shooting I have had before or since. In those days I was a keen bag-filler, still to learn the lesson that quality is better than quantity. However, I had earned this bonanza by means of countless blanks and frustrations and, in fact, looking back on the occasion with thirty years of hindsight, that flooded barley was one of the times when both quantity and quality were a well-matched pair.

Most famous of the river washes and by far the biggest are the Ouse –

or more properly called Bedford – washes which run between the New Bedford or Hundred Foot River and the Old Bedford which becomes the River Delph a third of its way down. Thirty miles long and a mile wide at its widest, this marsh is part of the main drainage system of the fens, starting at Earith in the old Isle of Ely and running, arrow straight, diagonally north east until it reaches Denver where, by means of highly technical sluices, the water flushes out into the North Sea.

Between the two man-made rivers is a strip of washland faintly reminiscent of the undrained fens, consisting in summer of miles of waving grass with fat bullocks standing in it belly deep and becoming at the height of the winter flooding an inland sea of tumbled, slatey water. The clumps of the osier beds and an occasional willow holt in which the cattle shelter, serve to break the ruler-straight skyline and add another shade of green and brown to please the eye. The wild marsh pheasants lurk in them, the piratical harriers glide overhead and just now and then, a lucky fenman who trusts his ears may hear the throaty snore of the 'bittore that bumbleth in the bog', an ancient and delightful title for the bittern.

Between the two excesses of deep flood and dry grass, the washes are a mixture of open water in large sheets or tiny flashes. The slight eminences, usually near the droves or dykes, are hairy fringes of rush

Bedford Levels in full flood, a haunt of thousands of wildfowl

around a malformed dwarfish willow, the result of a duck shooter long ago jabbing in a willow stick to make a hide. Stick a willow rod in any part of the fens and it grows. An outlying farm with a rectangle of mature willows at the foot of the garden is an unmistakeable sign of where the hen-run once stood, the poles being made out of the most easily available local wood.

The half-flooded washes are a haunt of thousands of wildfowl. The wigeon deserted the coastal marshes with the demise of their favourite grass, the *zostera marina* (zos grass to fowlers). What little of it escaped disease is gobbled up by the waxing army of Brent geese. The wigeon found sanctuary on the washes, on the open water and on the bird reserves and, within a short flight, rich feeding on the winter-sown corn in the surrounding fields. This heavy grazing did the crop no harm: it was the 'first bite' which held back the corn but allowed it to grow all the stronger in spring.

The old fenmen made part of their living from wigeon shooting, sliding out of brassy dawns in their ghost-grey gunning punts or lurking near the osiers armed with crazy, long-barrelled shotguns waiting for the flight. A wigeon was always worth half a crown and, in days when a farm labourer earned 12/- a week, a bag of duck meant the difference between comparative comfort and penury. Mallard, teal and pintail were also common, and all were grist to the fowler's mill. Rarities could turn up at any time and gargany, shelduck, ruddy shelduck, mandarin – you name it – have been recorded there. In recent years grey geese have been appearing regularly.

The most spectacular and well-known bird of the washes is the Bewick's swan. The old gunners knew the bird well and I can remember as a boy finding groups of these little swans, with their distinctive black-and-yellow bills, cooing and hooting delicately, mingled with the wigeon or gliding in family parties down the Hundred Foot River. I had to look in my bird book to identify them, but then they became frequent and familiar companions of wash expeditions. It was many years later that the birdwatchers discovered them; the Wildfowl Trust bought a reserve at Welney to harbour them and put that noted old fenman Josh Scott in charge of them. The numbers built up, and every autumn they flew in from their Siberian nesting grounds until now they come in their thousands rather than hundreds.

Each Bewick's swan has its own peculiar pattern of yellow and black on the bill, as unique as a human finger-print. Some birds have made the journey for fifteen years or more, each year bringing a little family – for they are constant and faithful spouses – to add to the grand army guzzling the potatoes and corn which the Warden provides for them.

The washes have been a breeding ground for ruffs, godwits, sooty terns, short-eared owls, snipe and many other old fen birds which all but vanished during the centuries of drainage. Now they are strictly protected and cossetted, but in the primitive days the gunners shot them down and either ate them with relish or sold them to Mr Fallon, the renowned Cambridge taxidermist. Conservation was a hard concept to sell to a starving man whose only meat ration consisted of what he shot.

Many years ago, on New Year's Eve, I was gliding in my punt between two large osier beds when I spotted a small bird perching halfway down a stem. The long tail and Zapata moustaches made identification easy; it was the rare bearded tit, another spirit of the undrained fen and not recorded there for many years. Being young and vainglorious I wondered with whom I might share my secret. With hindsight I ought, like King Midas' barber, to have whispered it into a hole in the ground. I told the best-known birdwatcher I could find: that was my second mistake. Two days later there were birdwatchers from far and near crowded on the nearest bank like a row of cormorants on a breakwater. Word had travelled through the bush telegraph and the 'twitchers' had turned out in force. I could have made a small fortune ferrying people out in my punt. I believe the bird had moved on, for nobody reported seeing it.

Why should I have felt responsible for their failure? I had fouled my own nest by attracting hordes of strangers to the very place I valued most, mainly because of its wild desolation. The only other human I was likely to meet was a marsh shepherd or another wildfowler and I had been responsible for this influx. They were soon gone like the ephemera they were, but I had learned a lesson. I saw many rare birds thereafter and confided in no-one, in the belief that a secret told is a secret no longer.

The washes will crop up several times in my tale, for I lived on their banks and spent many happy times there. Like Richard Jefferies' Bevis, I found out for myself about boats, guns, birds and the curious folk who lived 'down the fen'. The washes have been 'discovered' and human traffic in the form of bird spotters and expensive-syndicate wildfowlers have detracted somewhat from their old loneliness. The RSPB, the Wildfowl Trust, the Nature Conservancy, the Cambridgeshire and Isle of Ely Naturalists' Trust have all bought parcels of land where no shooting is permitted. Other washes have changed hands for sums far in excess of their agricultural value – they provide only summer grazing and some rough hay – but the modern, suburban sportsman who likes a shot at the duck is prepared to pay vast sums for the privilege. The mix of shooting, reserve, shooting, reserve, along the washes seems to provide a reasonable balance with both interests adequately served.

For the romantically inclined the Bedford washes remain simply places of fascination and a strange, rare beauty. Growling pack-ice under a blood-orange dawn, waving reeds, lapping water and the winter presence of 40,000 wigeon blackening the sky like autumn starlings or, in an uncountable twittering, whistling army winging over under the moon.

As well as the great washes and Wicken Fen there are other corners overlooked by the production-conscious farmer. Here and there is a spinney of mixed carr, thorn and elder where one of the last true polecats of the fen strain may be found. Like animals seeking refuge from a flood or a forest fire, it is not surprising that these victims of a mono-cultural farming system should have sought and found these dwindling sanctuaries, oases in a hostile desert. Jutting out into the North Sea like a swelling womb on the map of Britain, East Anglia is a popular staging post for migrants moving north or south in spring and autumn. It is into these wild spinneys and undrained corners that they drop to rest and pass a few days, breaking their long voyage. Sometimes they will stay and nest.

I was once out feeding the pheasants in a poplar planting and I heard a clear, bell-like ringing call. I stalked up the ride keeping in the shadow of the bushes until I could bring the binoculars to bear, caught a flash of yellow high up in the branches and realised with a start that I was looking at my first pair of golden orioles. They stayed; others came from nowhere to join them, for they are ever gregarious creatures, and they nested. Mindful of my experience with the bearded tits I kept the matter to myself but after two successful years' nesting, the keeper described their whereabouts to an eminent Cambridge University zoologist. Coincidence it may have been, but the fact remains that the nest and eggs were stolen shortly after and the birds left, never to return.

For some years I had the shooting on a remote fen farm which lay in one of the great, meandering bends of a minor Ely river. There was no telling what rare bird might appear from an otherwise normal morning. One winter it was a pair of rough-legged buzzards which roosted in the oak wood and spent their days pestering the pheasants. Then, one day, there was only one of them and a week later both had gone. Six months after, one of the farm workers called me into his cottage and showed me, in pride of place on the hall table, a beautifully stuffed rough-legged buzzard, its wings outstretched in the act of alighting. He was ingenuous in his replies to my questions. It had, he claimed, dashed itself against the wire in his hen-run in the act of attacking his fowls. It was so badly damaged it had to be destroyed. I wonder. That bird had a look even in its yellow glass eye which implied outrage. A pole-trap illegally set or a shotgun was the more likely cause of death.

The Victorian sportsman/naturalist had a clear policy on such occasions: shoot first and identify later on the way to the taxidermist. A rare bird seen was a challenge to bag it before the next chap spotted it. A flamingo once settled for a month on the Humber estuary. All the

gunners were after it, for the skin would have fetched a good price in Hull. Every rusting fowling piece, from garden guns to full-blown, 20oz punt guns, was pressed into service, but the flamingo led a charmed life. He escaped scot-free and moved north, doubtless to receive an equally hot reception from the Holy Island boys. Half the museums in the country are populated by victims of the old gunners; doubtless they made a contribution to ornithological research at the time, but their approach has long grown outdated. In Scotland it was even worse. One Charles St John shot down the last breeding pair of ospreys in the country, knowing full well at the time what he was about. Eagles, harriers and owls were shot or poisoned without a thought.

No sportsman shoots a rare bird now for, apart from anything else, most birds are protected by law. However, in the fens the old habits died hard. Fenmen are notoriously slow to change the customs of generations and they have an innate suspicion of strangers from the next parish and even more so of those from 'up Lunnon' who sought, by desk-top legislation, to change their way of life. Thus the old suspicion of the new and the unfamiliar lingers on and, sad to say, there are some old hard-bitten bank dwellers today who maintain the cavalier approach to what does and does not make a proper mark for a fowling piece.

So, the wild places remain for discovery by those with good leg muscles, an eye to the possibilities of that smudge of green and brown in the middle distance which denotes a forgotten willow holt where the hand of man has rarely set foot – as the saying goes. There will be the odd bird, colony of adders, a few frogs or a wily old cock pheasant lurking in the brown stalks of the dead stinging nettles. There will be the spring of teal catapulting up from the dyke, their paddles dripping as they rocket vertically away, almost before you can bring the gun to bear. There will be the leash of mallard caught sunning in the lee of the flood bank, neatly killed with a right and left as they top the willow poles.

It is about such places, few and remote although they have now become, around which these tales revolve. Those who describe the fens as 'gloomy', 'miserable', 'boring' and suchlike epithets have no eyes to see. The spokesman for the Cambridge boatrace crew in 1985 who bemoaned having to train on the Ouse at 'dull-as-ditchwater Ely', comparing it unfavourably with the middle Thames which he vastly preferred, was a soulless creature. Anyone may stand at the foot of a range of snow-capped mountains, caught and reddened by the evening sun and comment on their beauty. Tumbling becks and heather hills, broad valleys and vast forests all have their appeal, but it is an obvious one, there for the philistine to gawp at, drool over and take snapshots with his Instamatic. The fen landscape is an acquired taste, but its subtleties, frightening

Fenmen ploughing under a stormy sky

stillnesses, wild skies, wild men and lonely birds are there and intensely compelling for the sensitive spirit.

If one sought a more easily identifiable element of the spirit of the fens, it must be in the skyscapes. The horizon is so low that sometimes and in some places such as Prickwillow Fen or out beyond Chatteris, one can swear that one can see the curvature of the earth. That endless artist's palette of a sky is an ever-changing kaleidoscope of colours, from delicate lime greens to savage reds and purples. I was flighting duck one night on a minor river wash in a bitter January when the cold soaked through the thickest clothing and numbed nose, fingers, ears and feet with a painful anaesthetic. As the frost tightened its vice, a freak mist arose, shrouding the angry red ball of the setting sun which perched precariously on the tips of the horizon willows. Within minutes the mist became a cloudy, purple haze, the colour of blackcurrant juice mixed with cream. The hard edge of the sun blurred, spread, and ran across the west until the whole horizon was cloaked in a frozen pall of purple smog. High above it, the stars twinkled watchfully.

When the duck came it was in a short, sharp flurry out of the chilly furnace, black specks half seen at first, but then resolving themselves into solid blobs of vitality, arrowing down to race their reflections along the surface of the river. The gun barrels were so cold that bare finger-tips stuck to the metal, but I swung well in front and fired, the leading bird bouncing down along the water like a skimmed pebble. My second cartridge killed a tail-ender which towered on fluttering wings, suddenly aimless and shrunken, and then tumbled down to fall with a thump among the water docks on the far bank.

Cassius, my dog of the day, furrowed the water twice making the retrieves, two drake mallard with bottle-green heads, hot-orange paddles and chestnut breasts. I folded them up carefully lest any mud sully that gorgeous plumage and that they should not stiffen in unnatural, nightmare postures. I came off the marsh, crunching through the frozen grass, away from that frightening dusk, to the fire, laughter and comfort of untroubled men in the prosaic escapism of the village inn.

Another time we were coming home in the punt, poling steadily down the washes, full of thoughts of dry clothes and a hot meal waiting for us at home. The flood banks were thinly carpeted with snow and, as if from nowhere, a silvery mist arose. At first it curled and smoked on the water, eddying round the boles of flooded willows like something out of a mediaeval fairy tale. Then it thickened and rose to head height, covering everything with a white blanket, but leaving our heads out and above it in the still, sharp air. Disembodied willows stuck up, seeming to hang in mid-air: the roof and bedroom windows of the marsh-shepherd's cottage hovered mysteriously above the ground. Then, as swiftly as it had arisen, it faded, as though the ghosts of all the old marshmen had risen and floated past, gliding on to some spirit convention in the next parish.

In autumn it is not unknown for the jack-o'lantern or will-o'-the-wisp to scare even hard-headed marshmen out of their long boots. Albert was not as spry as once he was, having turned sixty-five, but no point, as he remarked, in growing old unless you grow crafty. Long experience told him where to be and when if the wigeon were flighting. So, one November night he was tramping determinedly along the foot of the flood bank to a small wash he knew well. It was near dark, with the bronze dregs of the sunset lingering in the west, but he knew that the moon would rise in an hour or so.

He found his favourite clump of reeds in the dark as easily as a man finds his pocket. Almost by instinct he homed in on the old spot, the downtrodden rushes and handful of red cartridge cases already flattened, discoloured and trodden into the mud showed where he had enjoyed a good flight ten days before. He leaned his brown-barrelled hammer 12-bore against a willow stub and rolled himself a cigarette, tamping down the ends with a horny thumb and removing the trailing shreds of tobacco with the aplomb of a smoker of fifty years' standing. Almost as he struck the match, the russet rim of the moon eased itself over the rim of the marsh and peeped at the reed tips, bathing them in a coppery light.

His cigarette glowed, a firefly in the dark and then the wigeon began to arrive. It was ironic that, for once, they should flight at intervals and in numbers suited to the lurking gunner, for the first six lots came in fives and sixes and from each he was able to take a measured right and left, snapping back the hammers smoothly as he mounted the gun, a trick dying out, now that the new-fangled hammerless guns are all the rage. The birds splashed down on the water, but the gentle breeze gradually drifted them almost to his feet so that he could gather them easily. This was good shooting, even for him, a good shot in a land of good shots; his heart warmed.

More birds whistled out on the flats, so he fished his call from the pocket of his threadbare jacket. He blew the fluff from the holes, gripped it in his gums and the silvery call of his favourite duck, wheeeoo, wheeeoo, floated like gossamer, tantalising and alluring but with a hint of command over the empty distances. With a sudden rush of wings another party swirled round and tumbled like falling leaves onto his splash. His first shot missed, but his second knocked out three birds: this was surely going to be his night.

A few hundred yards to his rear stood a raised, grassy mound. The vicar had told him once that it had been a small, Roman settlement. Locals tended to shun the place for several 'ghosts' had been reported. Albert treasured his reputation as a man who was 'afeered o' nothing' on two or four legs and, while the dark held no terrors for him, he had a

deep-seated respect for 'them ol' Roomans' who, centuries before, had stood where he stood now. He glanced round to take stock and the mound, now fully lit by the bronze moon, stood still and silent. He pulled his ragged scarf round his neck. 'Tales for owd women', he muttered, sounding more confident than he felt.

There was a lull in the shooting and he was thinking of rolling himself another smoke, when there he was! A Roman soldier, as sure as harvest, standing and swaying gently on his feet as clear as the picture in the history book of his brief and distant schooldays. He could even see the pale eyes glaring straight at him, make out the detail of a loose sandal strap, the stubble of beard and the rough ash wood of the spear handle. The hairs on Albert's head shot erect, his skin crawled. Then the Roman suddenly began to caper and skip about in the most un-Roman and inappropriate fashion, ballet steps, entrechats, great leaps from place to place, sudden pauses and then a crazy dash across the marsh to a new spot.

Albert's departure from the scene was less spectacular but more direct than the cavorting of the Roman. He did not pause until he reached the marsh road, his old heart and lungs hammering like a steam engine. He glanced fearfully back, the Roman had not pursued him but was still there, a distant flicker far up the marsh.

By the time he had reached the door of The Anchor he had slowed to a walk and was clearing his wits. To do as he intended and blurt out his experience to a taproom full of cronies and rival fowlers would expose him to unsympathetic jest and undermine his reputation for fearlessness.

He bit his tongue, swallowed hard, took a deep breath and walked to the bar with his dignity intact. 'The usual, Albert?'

Back on the marsh, the will-o'-the-wisp or, to the unromantic, spontaneous combustion of marsh gas which had run like wildfire over the bog, thinned, flickered once more, and died An untidy pile of twenty-six wigeon lay in the rushes on a deserted marsh, their pale breast feathers touched by the last rays of a dying moon. Albert told me this tale against himself and it encapsulates much about life in Hunter's Fen. It had the moody distances, the solitude, the wildfowl, an old gunner, the water and the wind in the reeds, but underlying it the whiff of superstition given weight by the timelessness which characterises much of life in the waterland. One could not imagine such an event taking place in Middlesex or Surrey.

Wordsworth, who felt 'a spirit in the woods' in his native Lake District, would have understood, although the spirit of the fens is a more elusive creature than the fauns of his hazel coppices and craggy fells.

Rum Old Boys and Hard Times

Fenmen are ever suspicious of strangers, fiercely parochial and have no time for 'furriners' who might live as far away as the next county. To this day there are old-timers who live in Lode who have yet to visit Cambridge 6 miles away. 'What have they got that we haven't?' they ask with a flash of asperity. If a stranger wants anything of a fenman then it is he who must do the travelling for the mountain will not go to Mahomet. It follows that in their limited world, despite its limitless horizons, even their field boundaries are matters of universal knowledge.

One night towards the end of the last war, a fen gunner was trudging home off the marsh. He had one mallard in his bag but felt that it should have been half a dozen, so he was in a black frame of mind. Then he heard the droning of a bomber, no unusual sound in this land peppered with wartime airfields, but this one was approaching uncomfortably close. He looked up: 'It was a Gerry plane, that had them black crosses on it: that came lower and lower and black smuk were a'pouring owt on it. It ploughed along the marsh, just missing the big willow, and 'druv along and lit agin the flood bank.'

The young pilot was totally disorientated, unsure of what country he was in: was he in France, Belgium, Holland or had he possibly even reached German soil? Tom ran across the wash to the stricken machine. 'The lid came off it and a head poke out: ole Jarmin he wore. "Where am I?" he say.' Tom gave the reply which only a fenman could have proffered. 'Why,' he said with an air of injured surprise, 'You're on John Hammence's ten acre, and look what you've a'done to his grass!' Of course everyone knew John Hammence's ten acre, its history, who had shot what on it and the complete family history of the owner.

Such views are not surprising when one considers the history of the region; the problems of communication in that watery wilderness were more than enough to persuade the locals that life as they knew it ended beyond the willow bed on the horizon and old views die hard. Solid land was rare, the countryside consisting of swamp, marsh and mere through which broad, sluggish rivers meandered like lazy snakes, ebbing and flowing with every turn of the tide on the coast.

Noted travellers and diarists such as Arthur Young, Dugdale and the great Lord Macaulay passed through the fens as rapidly as they could, concentrating their attentions on more congenial areas, but they found time to vilify the climate, the vista and the half-savage 'breedlings' who thinly populated the place. 'There is no element of good, the air being for the most part cloudy and full of rotten harrs, the water putrid and muddy, yea and full of loathsome vermin, the earth spongy and boggy and the fire noisome by the stink of smoky hassocks,' wrote Dugdale in 1772 and his opinions were about par for the course.

There is a great sweeping bend in the Little Ouse which, were he to return and visit it, Dugdale would have no trouble in recognising. I had the shooting on it for some years and, with its quaking bog, silky treacherous sheets of deep mud and tangled jungle of rushes it encapsulated much of what the fens must have been like in the eighteenth century. Just to walk across it was a severe effort and the mosquitoes in autumn were the big, four-engined-bomber variety which homed in on your hat and dived on each spot of exposed flesh, driving the patient wildfowler into a paroxysm of thrashing his arms in the air or scratching at visibly swelling white weals and bumps on his face, neck, hands and ankles.

However, the duck shooting was incomparable. I would go down in mid-afternoon on a windy winter's day, park in the lee of the ragged straw stacks and walk over the bank into a world different from the one of intensified, mechanised agriculture I had left. There was nothing in view which gave any indication of what century I was in; no pylon sullied the skyline, no telegraph pole broke the smooth run of the eye from east to west.

I would set the dog to work tramping and bustling in the brown tangle, hunting out the marsh pheasants which lurked there. Usually the birds were too crafty for us, always running rather than flying, and dodging back and forth in front or creeping into the thickest impenetrable dyke bottom. All my dogs have been educated on these birds, so we were able, now and then, to get a shot. With a frantic whirr of wings and a choleric chortle, a cock would burst up out of the brown with a suddenness which startled. There was a vision of red, gold and bronze feathers, an angry orange eye and white collar as the bird, jewelled like a raja, curved away to cross the river to safety. They were easy to miss, for one usually shot behind and far below them, flurried by their unexpected, electrically frenetic appearance into firing too quickly. If, on the other hand, you left things too late, the bird dropped in the river or on the far bank making in the latter case a difficult retrieve and in the former a sodden bundle of feathers – not an object to be presented proudly back home.

With a brace-and-a-half in the bag I would reach the end of the reeds and the difficult walking. Often the *Phragmites* were above head height, the ruins of last year's growth forming a knee-deep cat's cradle to trip the unwary. The shooter was obliged to struggle on, lifting his feet high at every step, keeping an ear on the progress of the dog, his barrels held high and doing his best to keep a reasonably straight line. Half an hour of that was enough to show, at first hand, why the old fenman was a reluctant traveller.

Then the scene changed: the reeds fell away, the ground became first spongy then muddy, a raft of the rotting weed of decades floating on a semi-liquid bog which grew wetter and more splashy until it became a sheet of open water of about an acre. This was where the duck would come later, especially so since I had made a habit of scattering a bucket of barley in the shallows. I would put out a few rubber decoys which bobbed and glided on the surface, reassuring black blobs for the real thing coming in later which would reasonably expect the pond to be tenanted already with some early arrivals.

I would make a hide between the river and the pond, gathering armfuls of dead rush and draping them on the stiff, dead stalks of the

water docks and lurk there, a burly but dangerous sentinel in the half-
light. Then in the gloom, from the flaming bowl of the western sky,
there would come a chatter, a staccato stuttering high above which told
of mallard beating over from the old potato fields. I gripped the gun
afresh, hissed the dog to immobility and crouched the lower, peering
with dilated pupils from under my hat brim. With a whicker and a
whoosh the birds would be over, wings set, losing height, arrowing in to
the water. Then, choosing the exact, psychological moment, I would rise
slowly and choose two careful shots.

Later in life I became quite good at this sort of shooting, but it was at
the cost of a long and painfully difficult apprenticeship. Even today I can
wake up at night and reflect with a shudder of horror, on potentially
super flights which I wasted or ruined by rank bad shooting. In my youth
I have fired almost fifty cartridges in a night at these duck and, I blush to
recall it, come home with two birds in the bag. It was inexperience, lack
of a shooting tutor, unsuitable gun and cartridge and other things, no
doubt, and there were times when I could cheerfully having abandoned
shooting and concentrated on playing rugby. With hindsight I was
'poking', failing to swing the gun properly and invariably missing
behind. I would come home depressed and sad after failures too
numerous to reflect on too closely.

Painfully slowly I got the hang of it, learning to keep calm, choose my
bird, stick to close-range shooting and swing the gun. It took me five
years of trial and error before I felt I could shoot flighted duck in the
company of another shooter and, like riding a bike, the knack once
learned was not easily lost. It was still possible to miss, but at least you

knew why and where you had missed, and there were some easier birds which you could reasonably expect to shoot every time.

The duck loved this forgotten corner of the old fen and on some nights they poured into it in almost uncountable numbers. A friend and I once shot thirty-two teal in an hour-and-a-half in a gale, and many nights I came off with a mixed bag of a dozen or more, choosing my shots and leaving while more duck were eager to come in. On one night as I was thinking of packing up, a woodcock came flickering over from the river. I swung round and fired as it vanished in the gloom behind, and I was conscious of the bird tumbling down in the jungle of rush. I put Cassius in and he crashed about searching for it but returned empty-mouthed. I was not going home without that bird. It was an hour later and in complete darkness that I heard his triumphant snort and his muffled breathing which betokened a full mouth. Was it another moorhen, for already he had caught one? All was well for he had the 'cock, wing tipped only, but safely held in that black velvet bag he called a mouth. It was the only woodcock I saw there in many years.

I was in my hide on one autumn evening when a marsh harrier came and hung in the upcurrents directly above my upturned face. Her fierce head turned this way and that, great eyes gazing down at this strange,

moonlike object in the rushes below, her canopy, buzzard-like wings catching the wind. Short-eared owls often did likewise and peered down at me, curious and unafraid, no more than six feet above my hat. On another evening a great shoal of rudd had swum up the narrow channel which linked my pond with the river. They kissed the surface as they cruised round, taking in the mosquito larvae as they hung stationary in the surface film, until it seemed that the whole pond was dimpled with the dorsal fins and questing snouts of roving fish. I never saw them again.

The savage mosquitoes were difficult to escape from, however. Modern insect repellants are meat and drink to them, seeming to attract rather than repel them. The only one which seems to have any effect is the old backwoodsman's secret recipe imported from the USA and known as Jungle Formula. I believe that it is now available commercially from a few places. The only alternative is to puff dense clouds of shag tobacco at them, for they do not care to face such acrid stuff, but too much of this gives the smoker a headache and a sore throat, not to mention the strain on his pocket.

It is cold comfort to reflect that things were much worse before the fens were drained, when the unmapped miles of stagnant pools and turgid meres were a mosquito paradise. The autumn skies of those times were blackened by incalculable swarms of the creatures which could, like locusts in Africa, blot out the evening sun with their numbers. The marshman and his family would swathe their heads in muslin when they went out but fevers and disease caused by poisonous bites were rife and they alone were a cause of infant mortality and much sickness and debilitation in adults.

The other horror of autumn and early winter was the fog, not the effete mists of today, but dense, yellow, swirling miasmas which began far out on the bottomless quaking bog and banks of rotting rushes, thickened and congealed and came creeping and swirling up from there to envelop the turf hovels on the slightly higher ground. Huddled round a peat fire and wrapping up as warmly as they could, the marshman's family tried to keep the insidious chill from invading their bodies. An eel skin dried and worn as a bootlace or necklace was held to be a powerful protection but despite its magic, most fenmen were riddled with rheumatics and aching joints. Worst of all was to succumb to the ague, a feverish state brought on by mosquito bites but exacerbated by the fogs, and not unlike malaria. The sufferer tossed and turned in an agony of freezing cold one moment and burning heat the next, tormented by hallucinations and bedevilled by trembling and fits of violent, uncontrollable shaking.

I have mentioned St Guthlac and his founding of Crowland Abbey in 664. He was a Saxon, a man of noble blood and strong principle who

Fen gunners, punts and guns on Cowbit wash near Peterborough

determined to become a hermit. He found his way through the dark and noisome fens, heavy with the wings of wildfowl, clouded by winter fog and snow, stinking in summer with marsh gas, and inhabited by a wild, amphibious race of savages, fishers and fowlers, robbers and murderers who paddled from reedy isle to quaking reed beds in tiny coracles made of skin stretched taut over frames of willow: their skins were painted blue with woad. There was a woad mill at Parson's Drove until well into the twentieth century.

Dugdale the diarist records poor Guthlac's experiences on his first night alone on his island. Troops of unclean spirits invaded his cell, arriving from the sky and from the earth:

> In their looks they were cruel, and of form terrible, having great heads, long necks, lean faces, pale countenances, ill-favoured beards, rough ears, wrinkled foreheads, fierce eyes, stinking mouths, teeth like horses, spitting fire out of their throats, crooked jaws, broad lips, loud voices, burnt hair, great cheeks, high breasts, rugged thighs, bunched knees, bended legs, swollen ankles, preposterous feet, open mouths and hoarse cries who, with such mighty shrieks were heard to roar, that they filled almost the whole distance from heaven with their bellowing noises; and by and by rushing into the house, first bound the holy man, then drew him out of his cell, and cast him over, head and ears into the dirty fen; and having so done, carried him through the most rough and troublesome parts thereof, drawing him amongst brambles and briars for the leaving of his limbs.

The troubled Guthlac was probably suffering the hallucinations of high fever, seeing the visions of a man stricken and wracked with ague and every sort of malarial disease that could attack his wretched frame. It may even be that, like many fenmen throughout the centuries, he had drugged himself with poppy-laced tea, that deadly opiate which has been the root cause of lunacy and death in many a fenland parish within living memory.

Despite his troubles, St Guthlac founded his abbey, a labour of missionary work and evangelical zeal which might fairly be set beside any expedition into darkest Africa or the 'Cannibal Isles'. For all their troubles, the fenmen built mighty churches with sweeping arches, flying buttresses and spires and towers as high as any in the land. It may be that their flat lands and humble existences caused them to build high, reaching up as high as they could, speaking to God with their buildings when they felt they could reach Him in no other way.

In a land with no local stone, they imported it, one stone at a time, on board barges pulled by horses along the winding rivers to the highest point in the village. Sutton in the Isle of Ely is a case in point of a church so built, begun in the early fourteenth century and completed several lifetimes later. With infinite labour they brought in Barnack rag, a grainy stone quarried near Peterborough, dragged it from the barge up the hill with horses, levered it, swung it on block and tackle and set it carefully in place. When completed the church stood like a dream from the Middle Ages, its grey finger pointing heavenwards, and a cluster of houses and hovels at its foot. The whole village population four times over would have fitted in the church with room to spare, so the building was an act of faith, a religious statement as much as a place of worship.

More famous is St Etheldreda's cathedral at Ely, built of the same stone, and a focal point for miles around, a beacon picked out by a winter sun to guide home a lonely fowler, a place of cloistered calm, full of the echoes of ancient monks intoning their plainsong.

Simply travelling from A to B remained a difficulty for centuries. I read somewhere that the old fowlers took out gentlemen gunners or students from the University (by no means the same thing), and had with them a lad carrying a long pole. The idea was that when you came upon a dyke too wide to leap and too deep to wade, you took turns with the pole and vaulted nimbly across with all the effortless grace of a Daley Thompson in waders.

I had the shooting on a remote patch of undrained fen seamed with dykes with both the shortcomings I have mentioned. Arming myself with a long pole and a short boy to carry it, I would tramp along like the snipe shooters in the old etchings with the lad following faithfully,

marking my footsteps every bit as well as King Wenceslas' page boy. We reached the first obstacle: the boy held the pole; I made a cache of my gun, hat, bag and other removables on the bank, retired 15yd and swept in on the pole with a lumbering run.

It is not as easy as it looks. My initial impetus was enough to raise me to the vertical and there, for an awful second, I hovered, defying who knows what laws of nature in that pregnant moment. The pole slowly settled, not towards the far bank but sideways along the length of the dyke into which I plunged with a depth-charge eruption of water. I hauled myself out, muddy and draped with pond weed and in a decidedly black frame of mind, like Mr Toad when the washerwoman threw him in the river. The boy had the wisdom to keep a straight face and fussed round me solicitously.

That was the end of the experiment and the pole was returned to its rightful place in the punt. No doubt the Victorian shooters were lean, hungry and agile and had had a great deal of practice at dyke vaulting. I was not, I realised, made of the stuff of persistence, so thereafter I crossed by the longer but safer route or sought out a rickety plank bridge, although they too were often less safe than they looked. I wondered afterwards how the guns and gear were passed over; probably they were lobbed over by the last man but one to use the pole. By holding the gun vertically, stock down on the first three fingers of the left hand, it is possible to throw a gun considerable distances with safety, always provided a safe pair of hands is waiting. When thrown properly it lands vertically as lightly as a feather. I have used this trick often, sometimes with even my own gun.

The other question about pole vaulting is how the last one, the boy, managed to cross. Being lightweight and nimble he could probably manage unaided, and nobody minded if a fen lad suffered a soaking; he was probably in the water as much as out of it in his daily life. However, I would make a strong plea for changing the Olympic pole vault back from a competition for height – quite useless and impractical – and making it one of length, which it was in the first place. Were shooters to be taught this skill at an early age it would serve them well when they journey to watery places for their sport. I, alas, am now too burly and aged to learn.

The Cambridgeshire fens were a favourite haunt of students from Cambridge University in the days when a steady application to one's studies and throwing rotten eggs at visiting speakers were not the only prerequisites of the student's life. The young men would mount expeditions out to what were still backward places within a dozen miles of the town. They would make their base in the local inn and pass the time drinking ale, philosophising, wildfowling, pike fishing, and indulging in bouts of fisticuffs with the bargees. It was their boast that they could reach their particular outpost whatever the weather. In summer, if the road was of good enough quality, they travelled through the fens on horseback or in a dog cart.

In winter when the floods seeped up and rendered the dirt tracks impassable they took to boats, rowing or sailing down the Cam and following the winding path of one of its sluggish tributaries until the wattle and daub, mounted by reed thatch or the scent of peat smoke over the osiers showed that they were nearing 'home'. If it froze, they took to skates and, in a merry Pickwickian throng with shining eyes, rosy cheeks and flying scarves, they glided, hissed and crackled along those same waterways in far less time than the journey took on horseback.

In 1851 just such a party of students formed a society at Upware in the fens. They were a 'Sporting Republic' based on that reed-thatched whitewashed inn, 'The Five Miles from Anywhere. No Hurry'. Alas, it stands no more, having burned down in the 1950s. The inn stood with its feet almost in the waters of the Cam, surrounded by great shock-headed willows, the old ferryboat creaking back and forth on its iron chains taking an angler, farm labourer or housewife home to some desolate cottage stranded amid an island of willows on the flat, black fields.

There the bright blades of Cambridge met to roister. Their wild oats sown, many of them went on to distinguished careers. Samuel Butler the author, Wolstenholme the mathematician and Fellow of Christ's, Rev Edmund George Harvey the composer of Gregorian chants, Sir Archibald Lewin Smith, Master of the Rolls and oar in the Cambridge boat 1857–8 and many another shining light of the age could boast of being a 'Republican'. The official musician was a mad, Irish labourer, Paddy Carey who would shin up the chimney of the pumping engine and, sitting on top balancing precariously in the fen wind, fiddle away with his violin tucked under his chin by the pressure of his right heel.

Sporting records are scant but interesting, not least for the catholic nature of the bag. Protected species and close seasons were concepts still unborn and some of the victims of those rough and ready days would cause a modern ornithologist to wince:

'Fell in with a flock of rare linnets and shot about 50; lunched; adjourned to the Fen and killed four owls.'

'Two members of the Cambridge University Naturalists Society arrived at Upware this day. Shot Brambling finches and saw a male hen harrier at Reach [25 Feb 1853].'

'Fine day, came down in early dawn – when Aurora was just peeping o'er the borders of the renowned fen of Wicken. After a great deal of trouble we killed 9½ couple of snipe and water-rails and a remarkable pied variety of the stockdove [2 Apr 1853].'

'Fen full of snipe and very wet, 4 guns – 14 couple (snipe). 6 wild duck, 3 quails, 1 partridge, 1 hare, 3 rabbits and several other little feathered monsters [9 Nov 1853].'

'We had an excellent day's sport, we killed 13 couple of snipe [15 Oct 1853].'

'Came for a day's snipe shooting but went home with but 2 couple, found fen very dry, ditto sportsmen; returned to Cambridge after a capital lunch [16 Feb 1856].'

'Fishing very good, April 1855. Caught (including an eight pounder) 38lbs weight of pike.'

Quail were once common in the fen country, but today you would have to walk many a mile before you flushed one, but, after a period of absence, hen harriers may once more be seen on Reach Fen. In fact, I return from the fen today in order to write these lines having seen two hen harriers, a male and a female, in almost the very place where the 'Republicans' saw theirs 130 years ago.

So the Republic at Upware flourished briefly and harmlessly enough but its existence showed that the fens were attractive to sportsmen, lepidopterists, 'bug-hunters' of all sorts and naturalists in general. It also reminds us who are used to clearly defined field boundaries and a strict law of trespass, that until a comparatively short time ago – the 1930s – the fens were virtually free shooting. Provided the visitor kept clear of the partridges on the scattered manors on the higher ground, he was free to wander at will. Only rarely would a local turn nasty, such as the occasion when a 'Republican' out shooting '. . . found a surly specimen of humanity in the shape of 20 stone of a fen farmer in a wossel [mangold] field. The fat party turning up savage, we beat an orderly retreat accordingly.'

For a time in the 1850s, Upware, like Reach next door, had a 'King' in the muscular shape of Richard Ramsey Fielder, MA, in his red waistcoat, cord breeches and with a 6-gallon jug of punch from which he was inseparable and from which he would ladle generous helpings for his aquatic friends. He loved most of all to fight the bargees who voyaged up and down the fen waterways, a rough, unlettered, piratical crew who wore moleskin waistcoats and round caps made of otter skin or red, woollen nightcaps with tassels hanging down. They were a tough crew, but 'His Majesty of Upware' was a match for most of them. Usually they fought for a gallon of ale but equally often, when beds were at a premium in the overcrowded Five Miles, a crew would come ashore and fight for a bed. Historian, poet, fighter and all-round extrovert, 'The King of Upware' eventually 'foreswore sack and lived cleanly', retiring to boring respectability in Folkestone. As 'King' he was never succeeded.

Reach, 2 miles up the fen road from Upware, was granted a charter to hold an annual fair on the green in May. This was once a bustling, rollicking affair with horse traders, wild men coming in from the fens, sale of produce, hiring of labourers for the coming season and country craftsmen selling their wares. Now it is a cheapjack business of gaudy roundabouts and tatty little commercial enterprises where diddicoys part children from their pocket money and peddle plastic rubbish made in Taiwan.

Reach had a 'King' in the 1970s by the name of Len Warren who went to the highest court to prove his title and declare the parish an independent state. His failure did not deter him but made him, if anything, even more determined to assert his title. He would stand at the bar of The Dyke's End discoursing of Romans, Danes, Saxons and suchlike ancient invaders and Reach parishioners; he had his own theory as to the precise whereabouts of King John's crown jewels lost in the Wash and was found one day digging an enormous hole near the lode bank, for in King John's day the fen would have been covered by the sea. His calculations must have been awry or he had not dug sufficiently for he failed to find the treasure. Len was a harmless, engaging and cheerful man, a proper successor to the traditions of the Upware Republicans, of Richard Fielder and the eccentrics of which, to this day, the fenland has more than its share.

In the apex of the triangle where Reach Lode and Burwell Lode meet is a watery patch surrounded by willows of about thirty acres in extent. Now it is owned by the National Trust and has been made into a wildfowl reserve, but in the days of the Upware Republic and before it was the site of one of the most remote houses in the fens, Pout Hall: the spot is still called Pout Hall Corner. Pout Hall was a substantial wattle-and-daub building thatched with reed, its upstairs dormer windows peeping over the bank at the water: they must have seen some strange craft pass in their time, for the building dated back to Roman times.

Its remoteness made it a safe house for criminals on the run from the law, for the police went flat-footed in such a watery land, and it was a bold constable who would pursue a fen villain out into the trackless wastes. Pout Hall was reached only by water or by secret footpaths through reeds 7ft tall. The Crawley gang used the place as a hideout in the late eighteenth and early nineteenth centuries. They stole sheep, robbed farms, brewed their own beer and went on nightly forays, flaying the sheep at Pout Hall and boating the meat to a wharf at the bottom of North Street in Burwell and hiding it in a house cellar. At harvest time they stole corn, threshed it and hid it in the same place. Local folk went in fear for their lives of these Mafiosi.

Police Sergeant Plant and two constables surprised the gang one night with a boatload of plunder. They resisted arrest, of course, but Plant was a desperate man when roused. He broke one man's arm with his truncheon, laid out several others stunned and bleeding and captured the ringleaders. Some escaped to be seen no more whereas the prisoners were transported or sent to jail.

The Badcocks were a rough, tough Burwell family who lived rough, sleeping out in the fen in summer like otters. Old man Badcock was the proud owner of a rusty fowling piece of great age and dubious safety. Halfway up the long, Damascus barrel was a hole, 'big enough for a wawsp to crawl threw'. He felt that this hole made the gun shoot

(right) *A patchwork quilt of fields marked by willows*

harder: each time he fired a squirt of smoke came from it, more than enough to give a gunsmith or safety expert a nervous breakdown. He said of it, 'That's a reg'lar rent-day gun: that'll shute a bailiff round a corner before he sees you.'

A hundred years ago, when a fen village held its annual fair or 'feast', it was a point of honour for a gang of men from the next village to come over and break it up. Men would stand up and fight with bare fists for sixteen rounds or hack at each other's shins until the combatants had to be carried home on turf barrows. It was a poor sort of market day in Ely when Fore Hill was not crowded from end to end with knots of brawling men, 'bleeding like a pig on pig-killing day'. Those were what the old-timers referred to with genuine nostalgia as 'gay days'.

'Gay' they may or may not have been, but these rough old boys – tall, rawboned men with very black hair, sallow or swarthy skinned, rough manners, gruff speech, tenacious, cunning and lawless to a degree – who wrested a precarious living from the things around them retained a soft spot for the 'grads'. These were 'toffs' who seemed prepared to take them on their own terms, live for short periods as they did and pursue their activities with genuine rather than patronising enthusiasm. A real compliment and mark of acceptance was to have your leg pulled by a local. When boasting of the innumerable flocks of wildfowl seen once in the fens one old gunner told a group of admiring strangers, 'I poked my gun up the chimney one night and pulled her orf: I went to open the back door and couldn't shift it.' 'Snow?' enquired an innocent. 'Soot?' asked a wag. 'No, blarst it, dead geese; they were so thick in the sky in those days.'

I once heard another ancient holding forth to an admiring throng of town gunners who clustered round him in the tap room of The Dyke's End. They hung on his every word, swallowed his yarns, digested them and came back for more, keeping him well plied with ale the while. 'Shooting?' he said, with a knowing wink, 'You chaps today ain't seen nothing. When I wore a young 'un I had a single-barrel muzzle loader that stood in the shed: lor, the ducks and geese I've shot with that. Anyway, I looked out the winder one day and there was a covey of eleven patrigs [partridges] standing at the foot of the bank on the mud left where the tide had gorn back. I got hold of the gun and charged her up good with a double charge of powder. Then I saw where I'd left my shot belt back in the cottage: I dussn't come out the shed dew they old buds [birds] would'a seen me and cleared orf. On the shelf I had a big bag o'

(left) *The last wind pump at Wicken Fen*

When it froze they approached the fowl on sledges. Charlie Scholes in about 1890

tintacks left over from when the missus had the new carpet. For want of anything better I got a double handful of 'em, poured 'em down the barrel and tamped 'em well down with half a sheet of the *News of the World*.

'Ever so slowly I eased open the winder and poke the barrel threw. I drawed back the hammer, waited until the buds had drawed up together into a heap, like, and let rip. Blarst, that old gun give me a clink o' the skull, a bloody nose and knocked me arse over tip in the corner. Blue smuk hung everywhere but that were a good gun – it never burst at all. I saw I had several patrigs down, flapping about on the mud.

'Nearby on the water's edge were the remains of some rotten old boats and bits and pieces piled up there for burning. I ran out the shed to grab the birds when, would you believe it, those tintacks had done no more than nail four of 'em to the blade of an old, broken oar what lay nearby. As I drew near, those four birds began to flap their wings, the oar lifted up with 'em and together they flew orf across the Hundred Foot and over the high bank the other side, so I ended up losing the lot: never got one.'

The old man shook his head sadly as though the memory of this outrageous tall story was more than a man could bear, and called for another pint. The youngsters clustered even closer to hear another remarkable episode from his amazing life.

The reality of fen shooting is far less spectacular, more prosaic but still of a rare quality not to be found in hillier regions in the comfortable shires. I took the gun one mid-winter day for at last there was some water on the washes. The up-country water had seeped, soaked and trickled down to its lowest level, ie the Isle of Ely and 'they' had opened the sluice gates. High tides had held back the water and so the wigeon had a paradise of shallow flashes and sweet grass in which to disport. David rowed Kenzie the dog and me across a river serrated with foam-flecked, leaden ripples. Kenzie was suspicious of the boat and needed much coaxing before embarking on his first-ever maritime adventure. At last we got him in and he stood trembling on rigid, splayed legs, eyeing the receding bank with a wistful gaze. I had him firmly by the scruff for, although I had committed us both to the arms of Providence, he looked ready to leap out of them at any moment. Had he done so, the frail cockleshell would surely have capsized.

The wobbly journey saved a 3-mile tramp, and we scrambled out gratefully on the far side, tied the painter to a tree and walked straight onto the marsh. Great sheets of water gleamed dully but we were able to hide dryshod on a reedy strip which stood a few inches above the water level. We draped scraps of netting round a stunted willow which had 'struck' where some old fowler had built a hide.

Dawn was already breaking in a midnight-blue sky, the eggshell sun perched like Humpty Dumpty on the distant flood bank. Great lines of Bewick swans flew over hooting and yelping, their white undersides touched with delicate pink where the sun caught them. Then it was wigeon, high and in uncountable numbers in flocks, lines, bunches and multitudes, stretching almost out of sight in both directions coming in wave after wave, twittering, whistling and growling. Every single one of them had the red sun on its pale breast and glowed flamingo pink for a few seconds as it passed overhead.

After this incredible opening pageant, the birds might trickle back during the morning and, with the wind in their beaks, they might be lower. I turned about face and rebuilt my hide, draping armfuls of bleached, dry rushes on my bush for the materials of most shooting coats and hide nets are too dark for wash wildfowling. After this improvement the birds came nearer instead of veering off to right or left as they approached. A few began to trickle over me and I hit a hen mallard which went planing down on the far side of the field behind. Kenzie had taken his eye off it, and while he crossed the dyke all right, leaping high in a graceful, powerful arc to land drypawed on the far side, he would not go out quite far enough. In the end I had to walk round the long way to put him on the line. He caught the scent almost immediately and quartered up to a clump of reeds, plunged in and brought me a fine mallard, a drake not a duck as I had thought. We plodded back, and I counted myself lucky that I had not been called upon to cross one of the plank bridges installed by the marsh shepherds.

These are flimsy, 9in-wide death traps across 10ft apparently bottomless dykes. Quite often the plank has a slight sideways cant for the unwary: today every surface was skimmed with a thin layer of ice. Boats, mud and rough weather hold no terrors for me, but those deadly planks I refuse to cross unless there is no possible alternative.

Back in position again I heard the distant baying of greylags and shortly after, a ragged skein of them came beating up the marsh. I pressed myself flat into the frosty rushes but the birds passed safely over the deep water up the Delph, far away from the dangers they knew from experience were likely to be lurking in the willows. Then more duck came and I dropped a fine drake pintail and a teal; later I took a right and left from a bunch of a dozen wigeon which approached unexpectedly from my right.

At midday the traffic slowed and we had a score of fowl between us including snipe, teal, mallard, wigeon and pintail which weighed agreeably heavy in the bag as we squelched off. On a good, or even a mediocre day, fen shooting is so outstandingly good that there is no need to exaggerate or spin yarns about partridges being nailed to rotten oars!

We managed safely to negotiate the river, topped the far bank and found ourselves back in the land of houses, roads and ordered black fields, such a contrast to the untamed desolation we had so recently left. Crossing that river can be a risky business, and it is best done in one of the heavy, square-ended flat-bottomed punts such as are used to ferry the River Board labourers and osier cutters to and from work. Other wildfowlers frequently travel in a more hazardous way and at dawn on a winter's day it is possible to see quite a flotilla of little craft from tiny pram dinghies to rowing boats and things which resemble fibre-glass bath tubs. The river is swift, deep and wide and in cold spells great sheets of pack ice can drift down upon you in the dark. Some of those crazy craft dice with disaster, broadside on to the current, the oars manned by a breed of suburban fowlers more at home on the cross-Channel ferry than a cockleshell on a dangerous river.

There have been no fatalities – yet – but there have been narrow squeaks and several chilly immersions. There was once available a type of miniature lifejacket no larger than a packet of cigarettes which, when you squeezed it and burst the magic capsule, inflated into a fat sausage which could keep a grown man afloat long enough for him to scramble to the bank. For some reason they fell from fashion which is, I think, a pity, since such a handy little device might easily save a life one cold morning. Several guns have fallen or been dropped overboard, including some very valuable ones. Oddly enough, only rarely is one recovered. Police frogmen and enthusiasts with underwater metal detectors have been called in, but the gun is either buried so deeply in the silt or washed yards downstream so that it cannot be found. Now and then a dragline will pull out the rusting remains of a weapon, a silent witness to a sad event some years before.

The best working punts for transporting human freight and heavy loads could be made by any fenman with a claim to the name. Will Kent could knock one into shape from a pile of apparently useless lumber such as most farmyards can provide. He would choose two matching planks about fourteen feet long and a foot wide: these would be the sides. They were nailed together to ensure that they matched and each end sawn and planed to shape. They were then prised apart and cross joists about four feet long nailed onto a series of sunken joints along the bottom. Onto this skeleton was fixed the bottom, a combination of what planks and odd bits of wood were available, soaked and bent round the curves and nailed in place with mighty nails. Not for the fenland boatbuilder the copper nails and expensive brass screws of the Burnham yachtsman.

When the bottom was covered with a patchwork of wood the punt was turned over and thwarts nailed across at suitable intervals. The finished article was coated thoroughly inside and out with a mixture of tar and pitch, melted in an old bucket on a fire in the yard. When this had impregnated every joint and seam the punt was dragged to the nearest dyke and dropped in. The water would penetrate and seep in here and there but the wood would swell until 'she' became water-tight. Even so, there was usually an inch of muddy water in the bottom of a fen punt, but 'that didn't sinnify', and had no effect on the serviceability of the vessel. Heavy rain or more serious leaks could be dealt with by means of an old tin used as a baler.

A willow pole cut from the nearest withy bed provided a free means of propulsion: it mattered not a jot if you lost or broke it for another could be cut in a few seconds. The principle which Will applied to his boat building was to decide how strong the boat ought to be and then to quadruple it. The result of this simple philosophy was that a punt which had cost you nothing but time to make might, if re-tarred each season, last a lifetime. Broken planks could be replaced easily and barring accidents such as being caught and crushed in the ice or becoming entangled in the lock gates there was little risk to the punt. Any legitimate traveller might borrow it to cross the river, but courtesy demanded that after his journey he left the punt on the same side of the water as he found it.

I remember Will making such a punt from a pile of wood which appeared to have no use except possibly for kindling. He wanted the boat to ferry his coal from the road bridge, along the drain and to his little cottage which nestled in a clump of pollarded willows out in the green and black of the fen. That boat was still in use twenty years later, long after Will's death, and for all I know, it is in use still. I made a similar punt at the same time, constructing it in the empty, cavernous dining room in the old vicarage. I cheated by buying most of the wood and I used brass screws rather than the Brobdingnagian nails favoured by the true fenland boatbuilder. The job was by no means as easy as Will made it look, but I was extremely proud of the *Mallard* when she bobbed on the flooded wash for the first time. She leaked rather more than somewhat, for my woodworking skills were not of the highest order. Also I had mixed too much pitch with the tar and it tended to crack and fall out of the joints when the punt was manhandled over dry ground.

However, the *Mallard* (a pretentious name, perhaps, but also an

expression of optimism) opened a new world. No longer did I plod along the banks gazing out over sheets of floodwater but now countless delights and adventures lay before me. Many a voyage we made together, exploring flooded holts, collecting all sorts of useful and fascinating flotsam, shooting wildfowl and catching slab-sided bream in the rivers. More important, I learned to handle an awkward, heavy boat and there were several useful lessons to be learned by trial and error. For example, the place in the punt you stood for maximum efficiency and ease of poling was critical: too far for'ard (as we old mariners call the front part), meant hard work while too far back made it difficult to maintain a steady course. The right point was about two-thirds of the way back. Manipulation of the pole was an art in itself for it was used to steer as well as to propel. In the hands of a waterman of sixty years' experience, the heaviest most lifeless punt became a gliding swan, sliding effortlessly over the green water while the punter seemed hardly to raise a sweat.

In time these skills came by dint of many blisters and some unremitting hard work. A boy's first boat is always a notable acquisition and an experience which stays with him all his life. The *Mallard* was no exception, more than qualified to take its place alongside Richard Jefferies' raft, the sailing dinghies of Arthur Ransome's Swallows and Amazons and Gerald Durrell's amazingly named *Bootle Bumtrinket* which he describes in *My Family and Other Animals*. Sad to say the *Mallard* missed her necessary annual overhauls when the time came for me to leave home. I left her chained in a reedy dyke far along the green distances of the marsh, but fen water and mud together with exposure to blistering frosts and broiling suns caused a rapid deterioration. She began to rot, a clumsy bullock trod on it, grass grew in its bottom and slowly, like some ancient Viking ship abandoned on the mud, she began to settle into the peat. Her ignominious *coup de grâce* was when a travelling man removed some vital parts of her for firewood. Well soaked in tar it must have made a merry blaze. When eventually I went to salvage as much of her as I could, there was scarcely a piece of her to be found, just a rotting wooden skeleton outlined in the rushes which already had almost engulfed her.

She was gone for good, the first of many boats I have owned, but the adventures and memories she gave me will never be lost.

·Fen Tigers·

Jim is one of the almost extinct race of true fenmen, one of that savage breed tempered by hard times into a toughness and instinct for self-preservation which meant the difference between starvation and survival in the cruel and hostile wastelands of the old fen. Such men are becoming rarer because, like their eel pouts (the burbot) and the swallow-tail butterflies, they need a specific environment in which to survive. Destroy that environment and the men who depended on it for their sport and their livelihood will vanish as surely as the bittern has all but done already. You might not think Jim a fen tiger to see him today as he sits on the corduroy-polished settle in the stone-flagged bar of the Eel and Becket, for he looks a frail old man whom a breeze might blow away and anything but tigerish. Remember, though, that he is over ninety years old despite being not sure of his precise age, and in his day he was reckoned a mighty man down on the fen where he lived.

Even when I was a boy Jim had seemed old, his face seamed as a pippin, but catch him in the right mood, puffing a cloud of shag tobacco at the yellow, raftered ceiling, stand him a pint and his watery eyes go back in memory to the first decade of the century and the wild, piratical crew who were his friends, now all dead and gone, back to the peat whence they sprang. They were roaring boys, the pith and soul of the fens and as different from the average farm labourer as chalk is from cheese. These men could not or would not work for any other man for a wage, so fiercely independent were they.

The first village policeman they had at Wicken they murdered. The poor man's name was Peacock and he was not short on courage for he lay in wait for a gang of rabbit poachers one night after closing time. In the ensuing fracas they rolled, punched and wrestled and Peacock was struck on the head with a spade. They took his body on one of the open-sided turf barrows and threw it into the white heat of the lime kiln where it was burned to ashes by morning. All that was found of him was his brass badge of office and his truncheon. The two brothers who had done the deed made their escape from the retribution, which they decided was sure to follow, by crossing the river on the ferry and placing as much space between themselves and the village as they could.

The ferryman was later to recall that their huge, hairy hands were still covered with blood. 'We bin pig-killing,' said one of them laconically, and the ferryman thought it wise not to pursue his questions. The two fled to America, working their passage, found anonymity there and were never to return to the fen, never to be brought to justice. Their old mother remained in the village and on her deathbed she produced a crumpled letter with an American stamp, postmarked two years before and asked that it be read to her before she died – she not having 'the book larnin''. She had not dared to reveal the letter in case she gave away the hiding place of her sons. The letter was from the fugitives and it told that both were well, so the old lady died happy although the secret was revealed.

All this happened before Jim's time, but he and his bosom pal and fellow reprobate Bob had several encounters with the law. They crept up to the Hall one dark night to raid the hen-run. Jim went in first and presently there came a squawk and a flutter and out he came muttering, 'I've got the old, brown cock, Bob.' 'And I've got you, boy!' said the policeman who had been lying in wait in the bushes. They wrestled around, but the policeman was, after a long struggle, bested. Bob sat astride him and drew his knife and held it at the policeman's throat. 'Shall I do him, Jim?' he gasped. The policeman, mindful of the fate of his predecessor, begged for his life and swore that he would not report them if they let him go. They did so, but he went for reinforcements, ambushed the two men outside the pub and arrested them. Bob was sent to prison, but Jim, whose wrists were bigger than his hands, slipped his handcuffs and escaped. He hid out in the fen where no lawman dare pursue him, until the heat died down.

Jim dug turf on the wild wastes of Burwell and Swaffham Fens. They cut the sword-sharp harvest of sedge amid the jungles of Swaffham Fen, scything acre upon acre of the surrounding 'litter fens' where cream-yellow seas of meadowsweet melted into an ocean of many-coloured grasses that undulated in the autumn sun.

They netted the fen dykes and shining lodes, splashing the fish into the nets with 'spreads', the fenland equivalent of the Norfolk quant with which they poled the tarred, black turf barges up the lodes. It was illegal, of course, but the law ran on heavy legs in that wet wilderness and fen people had been doing it since the times of Hereward. In the Saxon tradition they darted basking pike and speared eels with glaives, both beaten out by blacksmith Bill Sargent on the ringing anvil in his smithy. The best blades were made from old carriage springs because they had the whippiness and tensile strength. I have a glaive at home: I found it in the black mud dragged out of the river by a dredger. Fix it to a 10ft pole and you have a weapon which only a strong man could wield for hour upon hour.

In the final year of the Great War, Jim speared a 3½lb roach in 9ft of water where Reach and Burwell Lodes meet; it was no mean feat of hand and eye and no mean fish either. 'Bout that time, I saw a pike in Reach Lode as long as this table and black as a bit of old bog oak. That must've weighed a hundredweight. They reckoned that when it got up to Reach village it had to swim backwards to the river before it could find room to turn round in.' Jim gave the ghost of a wink. 'I darted a pike that weighed 9lb in Wicken Lode and soon after that, a seven pounder. He looked a bit fat like, and when I cut him open, so he should have been. He'd swallowed a 4½lb pike – more than half his own weight!'

'One morning I was out early when the water was as clear as glass down at Shrubb's Wharf and I saw an eel lying at the bottom of the lode

Plover netter sets his trammels. The practice is now outlawed but was once lucrative

as thick as my arm and as long as this bench. I darted him quick – Lord, he did wriggle and fight. I hulled him in the punt and he scuffled all round the bottom boards and got covered black as a chimney sweep in turf dust. He was opening and shutting his old mouth, hissing and snapping like a dog – damn near scairt me. He weighed 7½lb and that's a rare gurt eel, even for the fens – very near a record, I reckon.'

In the winter the lads took down their long-barrelled bank rails and stalked the drains, lodes, cuts and rivers of their native wilderness, and fired into paddlings; not for them the wasteful and risky flying shot for 'thim's for gintlemen and fools – and we weren't none o' them.' No species was safe: they shot otters for their skins, the last of the few wild polecats of the true, fen strain and any rare bird from a bittern to a bearded tit which crossed their path which could be sold for a few shillings to Fallon the Cambridge taxidermist. I have a Montagu's harrier stuffed by him at about this time, and who knows which of these 'rum owd boys' shot it down.

In 1910, Jim's dog ran a polecat down a rabbit hole. Jim who was 'afeared of nothing' put his arm down to pull it out, 'and my heart, didn't it bite! I got blood poisoning from that and was laid up for eight weeks.'

Another regular source of winter income was the University students who came down in their sheepskin flying jackets and battered shooting brakes with cartridge belts and their fathers' guns. The locals took out these latter-day Upware Republicans snipe shooting, puntgunning and drinking the local brew.

In spring Jim was out after the plover (of which more later), which flocked to the drowned water meadows. He paid a small rent for some washes and, by an ingenious arrangement of miniature drainage channels and some low, turf walls, he was able to hold back some of the receding floodwater and create a plover's paradise. Jim would lurk 50yd away in his sacking hide, blowing his whistle until, with a weep and a wail, a small squad of peewits would come loping over the bank. They saw his decoys, some stuffed ones and a live bird tethered to a patent flapping device, set their wings and dropped in to the silver glint of the shallow water. They settled their plumes but, the next moment, the giant clap net whipped over them and they bounced and struggled in its furls.

Now all these great doings are just memories but Jim, with the uncanny power of recall often found in the very old, can speak of those times as though they were last week.

The catching of plovers was a profitable occupation practised throughout the fen country. Not only green plover were taken, but also dunlin, knots, ruffs, reeves, redshank, godwits, golden plover and

Plover netter, whistle in mouth and hands on the cords, watches for approaching peewits

occasionally curlew. Once, a whole flock of nine spotted redshanks – sometimes known as dusky sandpipers – was caught and these were bought alive by Stevenson, the author of *Birds of Norfolk*, who wanted them for his collection. Several birds were sent to Regent's Park Zoo and to other collections, but mostly they were sold dead to the gourmet market served by Leadenhall Street in London.

As the fen drainage improved, the netter found it necessary to artificially flood his own little patch. The netter cut a 'slacker' or miniature sluice through which he could flood about 10 acres of washland to a depth of 4in or so. In the middle of that artificial flash, the fowler built a small island of turves, about 36ft long and 5ft wide. On this island he spread his net which was stained brown to blend with the ground: the meshes were 1½in for green plover, but up to 3in for bigger quarry.

The netter kept alive a small team of decoy birds, the victims of earlier catches. These were kept in pens until required, but often they grew extremely tame, following the fowler like lap dogs and picking up worms which he exposed when he dug in the garden. When in action, one of the live birds was fastened to a raffia mesh plate on a long metal arm which swung above the ground by means of an iron rod. The captive bird was fixed by a straw passed through the crooks of its knees and through the raffia. A pull on the long string would tilt the metal arm, the bird would fall off balance, flapping its wings, displaying its white waistcoat and wailing with that liquid, weeping call. This was an attractive lure to distant birds which responded to the call and the movement and flocked in to join the feast.

Other decoys consisted of a squad of stuffed birds known as 'stales' carefully placed head to wind in realistic postures so that the illusion of a contented, feeding flock was complete. The fowler used a plover whistle made of the brass ends of two cartridge cases hammered one into the other with the percussion caps removed. When gripped in the lips and blown this call sounded very like the sweetly swooping whistle of a peewit. The same call, blown in a different way, made an equally effective wigeon lure, an old dodge still in widespread use today among the coastal gunners.

The net was attached to a pole and rolled up carefully, a well-disguised stripe of brown on the muddy peat. The tethered end of the pole had a fragment of steel carriage spring attached to give it a little extra whip and speed when it was pulled. A rope, which could be as long as two hundred paces, ran back to the fowler's hide – a clump of willows or some carefully draped sacking, for plovers are sharp-eyed birds. A netter would expect to devote a whole day, possibly a week at a time, to the job so he usually made sure he had a comfortable seat available.

The plover would respond to the water, the whistling and the decoys and trickle in to the little island with its deadly reception. A plover does not care to land in water of uncertain depth. When sufficient birds have landed to make a pull worthwhile, the fowler would brace his feet and give a mighty haul on the rope. The pole would slip from its retaining peg and, hurried on by the spring at the other end, whip over through 180°, taking the net with it. A wise man set his net to throw downwind to give it a little more speed. Also, birds take off upwind and were more likely to meet the net as they rose. After a good pull, the fenman would hurry up to the net and remove the birds, breaking their necks deftly, but taking care not to damage or muddy their plumage and thus lower their market value. The netter would then re-set his toils and retire to his hide to await the next pull.

It was possible to make heavy bags in suitable conditions, some fen fowlers such as Ernie James of Welney catching thousands in a lifetime at the game. His best-ever week at netting produced the following: Monday, 100; Tuesday, 120; Wednesday, 150; Thursday, 117; Friday, 240; Saturday, 97. He gave them a rest on the Sabbath. Ernie also shot plover with his punt gun and in 1943 he killed sixty-eight of them with three shots from his big gun.

Another of the old fenmen of Welney was Josh Scott, the man who later became Warden of the Wildfowl Trust Reserve on the Bedford washes. He too had been a plover netter in the old tradition and had worked out how best to load a standard, fenman's bone-shaking bicycle with the maximum number of peewits while still being able to ride it. This was necessary for taking the birds to catch the London train. His money would be sent religiously by return of post, and that in the early 1930s. While 6d each remained the going rate, the lowest he received was 3d, the most was half a crown. When a farm-labourer's wages were about 12/6 a week, a successful plover netter was a comparatively prosperous man.

Nowadays the practice is outlawed, and the peewits are allowed to swoop, weep and wail on their club-shaped wings, unmolested over the lonely levels. In spite of it, their numbers seem to be currently in decline. As usual the reason is the erosion of their habitat.

The fenman was not averse to setting nets for other creatures, notably hares. Hares were and still are surrounded by much mystery: they were said to be the familiars of witches, sleep with their eyes open, be male and female at the same time, be the personification of the moon and other curiosities. Down on Haddenham Fen there lived in an orchard an old hare which the farmer was determined to bag. 'Puss' escaped his snares, nets and ambushes with equal ease. It was noted that she always left the orchard by a certain gap in the hedge and, heeding the old tales, the farmer loaded his gun with a silver button off his waistcoat and lay in wait by the gap while a posse of farm labourers drove the orchard towards him. Sure enough, the hare came loping past within easy range; the farmer fired and the hare expired with a series of unearthly screams. At that self-same moment, an old woman, long suspected of witchcraft, died in a fire in her cottage nearby. Such tales went the rounds and gave weight to the old legends.

A hare was a good feed for a hungry man and his family, and while not by nature a creature of the marshes, she was not uncommon on the higher ground among the scrawny cattle, sheep and the crops which struggled there for existence. In the old days, a man caught with a hare in his pocket was liable to instant eviction or even deportation, so it took great courage and an even greater deviousness to bag one. A popular method was to hang a scrap of netting from the top of a gate so that it trailed on

(right) *Sluices control the water level*

the ground below. Hares usually left a field by the line of least resistance, often nipping under the bottom bar of the gate when pursued. After the net was set, the poacher would range the field with dogs, leaving an accomplice concealed by the gate; for obvious reasons the operation generally took place at night. The started hare rushed to the gate, pushed underneath, caught the net and pulled it down over herself. In windy weather the net would have been held onto the top rail by a row of small pebbles. The accomplice would grab the hare, break her neck, slip her into his poacher's pocket, wrap the net like a scarf round his neck, whistle up the dogs and his friend and make his way home, to all appearances a couple of innocents walking their mongrels of an evening.

The other way was to set a wire snare in a likely run or crossing point in a dyke, a spot easily identified by the worn ground on either side. They could be snared on the plank bridges where they crossed the shining leams and old Charlie Barrett, coming home with his pike dart over his shoulder, spotted one lying in its form in the rushes. Quick as a flash he transfixed her in the opportunist style of one who lives off the land. 'Lor, she did holler,' he said.

A man dyking or hedge cutting might set a snare or two when he arrived at work and check them when he went home at night. He was alone and even if the farmer came to check his progress, the boss was unlikely to spot the grubby brown scrap of deadly wire on its peg, blending, as it did, perfectly with the surrounding grass. Poor Charlie Bradley set a snare for a hare in the hedge at the bottom of his garden and ran from it a long cord across his vegetable patch to his bedroom window so that, in the event of his making a catch, he could haul his victim up and away before the keeper arrived. It was an ingenious ploy but, sadly for Charlie, the keeper had already seen the snare and lay in wait to catch a poacher *in flagrante.*

Sure enough, a hare was caught late that night – or so Charlie thought at the time, for he heard the piteous squeals and felt a violent pulling on the line, the end of which he had attached to his big toe. He heaved away but to no effect: 'The old devil's got caught up in the elderberry bush, I'll be bound,' he told his missus so, barefoot and in his nightshirt, he tiptoed across the snow only to find, instead of a 6lb hare, a 15-stone keeper and his equally burly assistant. They caught poor Charlie and marched him, barefoot as he was, across four fields to the village lock-up.

It was not unknown for malicious neighbours to inform on a poacher, and once old Jenkins, the village schoolmaster, told the keeper that

(above left) *Mute, Whooper and Bewick's swans gather at Welney wash*
(below left) *Fen lode; once a busy highway, now a forgotten backwater*

young James Smith was often bringing game meat to school for his
lunch; an old woman informed the authorities that pheasant feathers
blew in from a neighbour's garden, or that her cat was bringing rabbit
bones from his ashpit. Unscrupulous keepers were not averse to placing
an already-dead hare in a snare they found and then hiding nearby to
catch the poacher red-handed. 'Darkie' was informed by the postman
that, 'I seed old Jackson a'hiding in the dyke as I came past: maybe you've
got a sneer set thereabouts.' Darkie approached the place and, knowing
full well that the keeper was lurking nearby sauntered past his snare,
hands in pockets and whistling a jaunty air. He did this on and off for the
whole day, returning at hourly intervals, leaving the keeper in an agony
of frustration, discomfort in his cramped ambush and thwarted rage
because, of course, he did not touch the snare. He told the keeper later, 'I
seed you a'peepin' out from that old elderberry bush: what was you doin',
birds' nesting?' Jackson's reply is not recorded.

Charlie Crisp was a fowler, skater, philosopher and beer drinker from
down Upware way. He was out one dark morning pushing through the
reeds in his undecked gunning punt; with a sibilant whisper man and
boat were on open water. The stone white of his open shout (punt)
blended with the silvery haze and the weak dawn glow. Charlie felt
invisible, protected by an enviable fairy-tale cloak of darkness; he was but
two miles from a busy village, but as much alone as though he were in
the middle of a desert. He pushed with an easy rhythm, sending the
slender bow slicing the leaden ripples.

Charlie was a well-built man but his face was lean, his nose hooked and his eyes sharp with that long sightedness endemic to fen people used to gazing over great, flat distances. He could see the green wall of the marsh on one side, and a vast emptiness of water and rush on the other. His local marsh had not changed that much since the Dutch drainers came all those years before.

His converted flintlock gun – 8ft long, crudely stocked, menacing of muzzle – jutted aggressively over the prow, aiming always at where the punt was pointing. The crude lock and conversion to percussion had been made by the blacksmith in the village: misfires were not uncommon since a foul touch hole, an improperly seated cap or a splash of water were sufficient to cause the gun to hang-fire or not to fire at all. As if the risks of failure and the odds against him were not already sufficient. To approach a large pack of the wariest fowl that fly, over open water and in bitter weather is a matter of much luck and no little skill. A swooping blackback, hawk or plane, a distant shore gunner, a wary outlier, or an incautious movement by the punter were enough to scare the birds. The cramps, agonising 'hot-aches' of returning circulation and the sheer drudgery of working a punt to fowl had all helped to thin the ranks of the punt gunners. Charlie could recollect the time when there were nine punts and big guns in his village alone.

Charlie had been at the game a long time and came from a hard school, but today he had not the need to go a'punting. The bad old days were long past and his arduous apprenticeship had prepared him for nothing worse than a comfortable old age with a houseful of lusty breadwinners bringing a prosperity undreamed of in his youth. Now he took out his old punt and gun only to recapture the old thrills and to prove to the youngsters that the old man still knew a thing or two.

Ahead he heard mallard stridently saluting the dawn; his lean unshaven face cracked in a toothless grin for he knew just where they would be sheltering after a week of unremitting easterlies. Sure enough, there in the lee of the distant, flooded osiers was a cluster of black specks, a party of about seventy mallard and teal, just behind a fringe of brown rushes which marked the line of a submerged boundary dyke. The mist was clearing, and the busy black dots grouped and re-grouped in their secluded corner. There was no time to waste.

Charlie gave two more long, strong heaves on his pole and stowed it silently on the bottom boards. He unshipped a pair of short, weighted sprits, checked their safety cords, heaved back the mighty hammer of the gun and with a rheumatic grunt, lay down. Being an old hand, he believed in making himself as comfortable as possible so he had prepared himself a nest of sacks on which he could lie without giving his joints too

much cause for complaint. Hands, then wrists felt the bite of the cold water as he groped for the bottom with his poles. He corrected his course, and steadily, almost imperceptibly, he slid out of the brassy image of the rising sun and set to his birds.

A faint breeze had arisen with the sun and he heard the ripples murmuring round his boat; he peeped a beady eye along the gun barrel — still a good hundred yards to go before he reached the friendly fringe of reed which he had marked down as his firing point. He pushed on, his face pressed into the sacking, his breathing short and shallow, his heart pounding so that he felt the birds must surely hear it reverberating through the bottom boards. Now the reeds were but a cricket pitch away and his movements became even more delicate and cautious. He knew that as soon as his prow cut into the rushes, the birds would be up and away for mallard are notoriously hard to approach, being far more suspicious than wigeon.

There was a silken rustle as the first strand of rush caressed his prow. Charlie seized the lanyard, lined up his gun and snatched as the fowl sprang vertically, paddles dripping, 75yd away. The cap cracked – all was silent. It was a hang-fire. Charlie's heart sank with disappointment, but even as the lump came into his throat, his big gun, with the characteristic perversity of the flintlock, suddenly went off with a mammoth roar, spout of orange flame and belch of grey smoke. The echoes rolled along the distant bank and through the osiers and set the lonely gulls complaining. Two birds from the now-distant, departing flock, one on each extreme edge, closed their wings and fell in plumes of spray a good twenty yards apart. Poling quickly to the place the old man picked up the two birds, both drakes and both stone dead. Had he made a proper shot he could have killed a score. After his initial disappointment had passed, his true fenland philosophy asserted itself and he was able to smile his crooked, wry smile. After all, it might have been worse.

That was fen gunning, but a misfire in modern times could be accepted simply as bad luck, whereas one eighty years ago was a much more serious matter and would probably have meant empty mouths at home. Charlie had been a great local champion in his time, a skater so well known that 'furriners' came from far and near to challenge him. One of his tricks was to take his mighty single barrel, muzzle-loading 8-bore with him and, when in full flight, skimming over the crackling ice, throw up this monstrous weapon and bring down a passing gull or plover.

Recreation in the fens in the hard days was rare and amusements tended to be of a primitive and earthy nature. The nailing up of a Sutton man inside the pig sty he happened to be mending at the time was considered a rare jest and the memory had to last for many years; as humour went, it was about par for the course. The only time the fenman could escape a life of unremitting toil, homespun, damp, mosquitoes, smoky tallow candles was when 'that fruz' and the dykes, rivers and flooded washes were covered with ice.

Then the plodding fenman abandoned his long boots, stilts and mud patterns and became a flying swallow, a dragonfly, confined to the larval mud for so long and then darting and shimmering in the winter sunlight for his hour of glory. However, by no means did it freeze every winter and imagine the frustration of the amateur champion of 1881 who had to wait to defend his title until 1887 before the ice would bear once more.

Early skates called patterns were made of bone, but the superior Dutch steel skates quickly became popular. It was said that they arrived after the old fenmen ambushed the Dutch drainers and stole their skates which were so much faster than home-whittled mutton bones. These *schaats* were quickly copied by village blacksmiths and, at first, were used purely as an efficient means of travelling from A to B, but *schaats* had enjoyed a brief moment of glory when, on Dutch feet, they had been responsible for the defeat of a Spanish army caught on the ice in 1572. Catsholme in the fens is but a corruption of 'Schaatsholme', the place of the Dutch skatemaker.

James II had popularised skating by trying a few rounds on St James's Park lake, while Goethe coined for it the phrase, 'poetry in motion'. Informal racing in the fens took place in the eighteenth century, but in the early 1820s a series of hard winters saw prize matches for as much as £20 on the ice at Wisbech, Crowland and the yet-undrained Whittlesea Mere. The men from Mepal, Wimblingdon, Thorney, Chatteris and other marsh villages flocked in to show their paces on a there-and-back course round a post or a barrel placed on the ice.

A century later the railways ran cheap excursions to skating matches so that folk in their thousands could flock in to see giants like the legendary Smarts (prefixed 'Turkey', 'Fish', and 'The Other'), 'Gutta Percha' See, the Tebbutts, Walter Housden and the Welney men who bestrode the skating world for so long. Races were reported in *The Times* and the fen skaters could beat all-comers from home and abroad until the arrival of

Skaters still flock to the frozen washes, but not in the numbers of ninety years ago

the great Norwegian Hagan, who could practice at home for most of the year. The local champions were amateur, unable to lose days from work or to afford to travel far, out of season, in search of ice. Their special style of flailing arms and swinging stride distinguished them from the scorned 'rink-men'.

In athletics the 4-minute mile was for long the ultimate target, but in skating the 3-minute mile was the Holy Grail. Several claimed to have broken the magic barrier, but subsequent checks invariably revealed that the course had been inaccurately measured so that, to this day, there is doubt as to whether anyone actually achieved the feat on natural ice.

Ladies also took part, hampered as they must have been by their long, heavy skirts. Prizes for ladies' races were more practical then mere money and varied from a feather boa to a joint of beef. Susan Legge, daughter of an old champion, Chafer Legge, was leading the field and well on the way to winning a leg of lamb when she was perturbed to feel her drawers slowly coming down – the elastic responsible for their safety had failed. Old Chafer realised that the prize was in jeopardy: 'Kick 'em orf, gal,' he bellowed from the crowd. 'Kick 'em orf, but keep a gooin'. You never wore none until you went into service!'

Ernie James, the Welney fowler, was also a skater and, with the amazing powers of recall given to many countrymen, can describe how in 1929 he ran third in the Amateur Championship at Lingay Fen, being beaten by Scott of Welney and Pearson of Mepal who won it. He clocked 5 minutes 5 seconds for the mile. Two days later he raced once more against Pearson over a mile and a half but this time they made a dead heat of it. In the same year he ran second in the Swavesey Cup and also won a big race open to all comers from the whole country. He enjoyed five or six good seasons but then a gun accident left him with a stiff leg, and ended his career on the ice.

In time, the fenmen were eclipsed by the continentals and the rink-men: new skates, new styles and new rules had taken over and engulfed fen skating in its pure and old-fashioned form. Welney, home of champions, reverted to a quiet hamlet and the old skaters were left with only their memories of the great days and the roaring crowds, while in the dusty outer darkness of the shed, a pair of fen runners hung rusting.

What great days they must have been! Young bloods from Ely once raced and beat the Royal Train from Ely to Littleport; there were ox roasts on the ice, hot-potato sellers, skate 'fixers' offering their services at a penny a time, blazing tar barrels on the ice at night, cups, prizes, bets, champions made and broken, the babble of four thousand spectators on Cowbit Wash and the tough, rough characters in otter-skin caps who, on their ringing steel, could fly over the ice, urged on by the crowd.

Down on the fen, fowling at night under a frosty moon and pin-prick stars, one need have no fear of such friendly and cheerful ghosts. Modern fen skating has been hit by mild winters, a lack of flood water and a shortage of protagonists. A few family groups slither and slide with fearful caution in the old places, but they are thin shadows of the great days.

A minor spin-off of the skating was the development of that little-known branch of fowling practised from the ice sledge. The ice sledge carried a great punt gun behind a screen of reeds tied on with string; mounted on four marrow bones it was used for decimating parties of fowl which sat about disconsolately on the ice. The gunner knelt or lay on the hind part of the sledge and pushed himself along with two iron-shod sprits. When the gun was fired, the sledge often shot backwards for yards over the ice. The gun was a special model, far lighter than the full-blown punt gun. It was usually percussion, about 7ft long, of 1in bore and slightly belled at the muzzle, weighing in at about 100lb. It was bound in brass and had a hole through the stock for the rope which passed round the front of the sledge and took the recoil. Ernie James had such an outfit and they were often used on Cowbit Wash near Peterborough.

On one particular evening I was out after geese on a Lincolnshire fen. Mine must have been the last vehicle to traverse the marsh road, for great, swirling snowflakes soon closed in and blotted out cottage, field and gnarled willow in an all-pervading white. The goose grounds were bleak and cold with snow-girt fields bisected by ragged willows which leaned permanently backwards after decades of blistering nor'-easters. The dykes looked black and icicles hung from the rushes. The geese had been driven down the coast from Scottish mosses to our slightly more open marshes; they sat out in roadside fields during the day, black and large against the snow, standing or sitting like dumpy teapots and scraping half-heartedly at the frozen grass. Even the Brent had come inland it was so cold, a rare thing for them to do in those days although now it is commonplace.

It was that most bitter hour before the dawn, and Jim the Keeper and I crouched in some broken ground by a dyke at a point where two lines of stunted willows crossed. The four fields round our hide had been heavily grazed and the birds had been undisturbed. We shivered down to the toes of our boots and blew on numbed hands as dawn spread its kaleidoscope over the sea wall; we could even hear the sea, sighing like silk, melting great patches of snow as the tide crept over the muds.

There was a burst of distant goose music and then a muddy thumbprint on the oil-painting of the dawn spread and resolved itself into a skein of pink-footed geese, but they went down on the next farm; we saw them through the half light bank, swirl round and come tumbling down onto a distant corn drill. The great clamour of their cries was silenced and only a spasmodic 'wink-wink' floated down to us intermittently over the snowy distances to remind us of their presence.

Then there were geese all around us, so many that I did not know in which direction to look. A small skein of greylags came over our very hide, so low that we could see orange paddles tucked in and the cold sun kissing the tiny black speckles on their breast feathers. They swung round, cupped their wings, lowered their paddles and with an audible whooshing of air they settled lightly in our field, furled their plumes and began to stalk about and pluck at the frozen tufts.

I did shoot one pink with the 8-bore, an exultantly heady experience and a good shot at a hard bird, but on this special morning it would not do to dwell on the shooting, for the whole experience was so stirring as to be above the simple making of a bag. I could have killed a score without much trouble, but I had done enough fowling by then to be content with little or nothing in the bag. A dead goose here is much the same as a dead goose anywhere else, but how often could I see sights like those of that morning? After one or two early shots, as if by mutual arrangement, for no word was spoken, we both settled down to watch the pageant which unfolded before us.

More geese came, pinks and greys with even a small skein of barnacles in their demure nurses' uniforms: they are very rare on our marsh, but the bitter cold must have moved them from their northern haunts. Birds were pouring in more like flocks of greedy pigeon than wary geese. At one point, they were landing in all four fields simultaneously and there we were, crouched in the very heart of that activity, the cold forgotten, and no one there to see it but us. It was bewildering and humbling to be under the shadow of those great wings with that stupendous symphony of goose music full blast in our ears. All this was set against a snowy moonscape of flat fields fading to a misty distance and a bloodshot eastern sky reflected dully on the oily mud of the tideline.

When they are on the ground, geese tend to lose some of the magic which they possess when airborne, but they remain a wondrous sight, especially in such large numbers. We lay still and peeped at them like a couple of old foxes through the reeds, a prey to mixed emotions which every true fowler will know.

The fields continued to fill with geese, each new skein giving and receiving clamorous welcome to and from those gaggles on the ground. By mid-morning there was barely room for any more, and late arrivals were obliged to drop into the less-desirable fields beyond. We were lying in the heart of the greatest concourse of geese I had ever seen, thousands strong and we were part of the scenery. True, we had our one goose in the bag and honour was satisfied, but how much better to have witnessed

such a great pageant than to have a row of dead geese lying on the blood-speckled snow of empty fields.

Our last desire now was to disturb this huge army, for to do so would send them elsewhere on a thunder of wings and somehow spoil it all. We wanted to be whisked away in continued invisibility and leave the geese feeding peacefully. Even a morning already full of so much magic could not produce the right spell so we stalked back to the drove along the frozen dyke, backs bent painfully, heads well down and Drake the dog creeping along in the rear. I had only to straighten my back and peep through the frozen grass to see geese within thirty yards. At one very low place a family party of greylags was standing glumly on the ice ahead of us; no chance of not disturbing them but they rose without panic with an 'ank ank', but flew no more than a hundred yards out into the field and a safer place.

At last we were there, safely behind the willows, well out of the way and we could straighten aching backs and look back, taking the broad view of a scene of which we had so recently been an integral part or perhaps we were unwarranted intruders. The four white fields were thickly speckled with an uneven pattern of black blobs which were geese, feeding, sitting down, walking about or quarrelling with hissing snake necks with some unpopular member of the party who strayed too close. It was a sight I would have ploughed through many a snow drift to see, and it was due only to the fact that we had four-wheel drive at our disposal that we made it back to the inn in time for lunch.

I have often wondered what the old skater-gunners would have made of it all, but I fear I know the answer. They could not afford the luxury of an emotional response and would have fired and fired until the black powder smoke hung heavy on the air, for such a golden opportunity was not to be passed over. Restraint in shooting is a mark of the true sportsman, but it is also the mark of one with a full belly and children with shoes to wear. The fenmen were professionals, culling a tiny part of a shootable surplus from a teeming wildfowl population, and for a so-called gunner to travel many miles, incur considerable expense and suffer a degree of physical hardship just in order to take a shot or two and then not to fire, would have seemed crass, irresponsible and inexplicable. Did the old-timers have a spark of romance in them and the power to feel a force around them greater than themselves or had lives of grinding poverty, hardship and constant worry as to the source of the next meal snuffed it all out of them? The evidence suggests that such views are of the current age and the old market gunners were unsoftened by them, while those who followed the more imaginative line could not survive. Nothing brutalises as much as penury.

The most famous gunner of them all, the late MacKenzie Thorpe, 'Kenzie the Wild Goose Man'

I suppose that the first of the real fenmen I met was the late Will Kent. As a young and impressionable savage I was captivated by the old, out-of-print sagas of shooting and life in the wild fens, but I was still to have any first-hand experience of the real thing. It could not have been timed more perfectly that I should have been reading James Wentworth Day's book, *The Modern Fowler*, with its yarns of great guns, punts, heavy shots at fowl and the extraordinary company of marsh men who pursued the clanging battalions of Brent on the Essex estuaries.

Such was the magic touch of the author that my head was a-buzz with pictures of these stirring scenes: how could a lad whose only armament consisted of an air-gun ever aspire to such shooting? I cycled slowly down to the marsh, leaned my cycle on the parapet of the bridge over the Hundred Foot River and gazed wistfully up the marsh towards the setting sun which streaked and stained the water with a mirror of its own lurid beauty. Even as I looked, a speck appeared, growing larger by the minute. The shape was familiar, for had I not been gazing at pictures of the same thing not an hour before? It was a man standing in a long, grey punt, not the square-ended punt of perch fishermen and students on the Cam, but a grey one, pointed fore and aft, drawing only an inch or so of water. On the foredeck was what appeared to be a mighty pipe which, I realised with a thrill, could only be one of those punt guns.

Man and punt slid nearer, effortless heave and push with no wobbles or unseemly splashing, until it glided up onto a grassy spit and grounded. The man disembarked, stretched, and ruined some of the magic by urinating by a willow bush, but undeterred I rushed up to make sure of this living legend before it melted in the gloaming. Having approached near enough to look into the punt I feasted my eyes on the ropes, tackle, sprits, boxes and mostly on a line of fourteen wigeon neatly ranked beneath the combing. Having so eagerly rushed to seek out this meeting, when I finally stood face to face with the lean, hawk-faced, clear-eyed man in his patched rubber waders and grubby white smock, I was tongue-tied, able to think of no appropriate opening line for a conversation.

I must eventually have stammered a halting phrase or so, and once he had recognised my honest enthusiasm and the host of questions I was still to ask him, he unbent and we became firm friends. He was one of the famous Welney family of Kents, publicans, skaters, fowlers and eel catchers to a man. Many an outing we had in the punt together thereafter and, being such an eager pupil, I absorbed all the old man's stories and tips and came back, insatiable, for more. We would sit in dead silence waiting for the moon to rise and the wigeon to flight; an hour might pass without the exchange of a word and then Will would break the silence. 'I remember once, in the hard winter of '42 . . .' and another gentle, inconsequential story would be told, slowly and carefully with no attempt to sensationalise.

'Back in '49 I took out a student duck shooting. He was a nice chap, but he kept on writing down what I said in a notebook. Told me he was interested in local speech, or something. Came eleven o'clock and I pulled out my old turnip watch and said, "Time I was off arter my dockey".' 'Dockey' is the fen word for lunch, a meal usually eaten mid-morning. Elsewhere in the country it is, variously, 'bite', 'bait', 'snap' or 'elevenses'.

'The grad whipped out his pad and said, "Dockey, that's an interesting word: how do you spell it?"' Will was a man of many skills, but 'book-larnin'' was not among them, for he had a deep suspicion of the written word. 'Don't rightly know, but I reckon that's got a "K" in it,' he said.

That was how it was, little stories of floods, otters, encounters with wild men from the next village, skeins of geese, skating matches, great eels and adventures in the punt. I had not met him before as he had only recently taken a giant step for a fenman and migrated not one but two villages up the marsh so our gain was Welney's loss. 'One night young Peter and me were working up to a pack of wigeon on these washes. There was a clump of docks sticking up out of the water on the far side of them, a dark smudge on the water. Peter was just about to pull and send a pound of shot threw 'em when they jumped early and we lost the chance.

'Then I raised my head, and what do you think I saw? There was old Bailey Winters laying to 'em in a punt and gun as big as ourn. That clump of docks was him, not more than a hundred yards away and if we'd both got twenty yards closer to the ducks, we would have let drive together. I reckon it was the mercy of God that there weren't two or three dead men on the water that night.'

Then he would tell of the night Peter fell overboard in 11ft of icy water, buoyed up only by the air trapped in his flying jacket. He dropped his gun and cartridges, but luckily he hung on to the rum flask. Will once killed 160 wigeon with 6 shots one bitter day on the Mepal Wash when the wind cut like a razor, the sleet was icy needle-points and the fowl swept back and forth over the leaden water in great curtains of wings. The biggest shot of his life was in the Twenties when he killed 53 peewits at one discharge and followed it not long after with 48 wigeon at one shot. He has had 8 pinkfeet at a shot and, as for rare birds, his bag over half a century has included bittern, smew, marsh harriers, mergansers and black duck driven in from the sea.

Bill Whitehand from Southery is another of these tough old birds. In his youth, every man in Southery was a poacher; it was a way of life in times of depressed agriculture and a badly drained fen all round. Wild marsh pheasants were common, the rivers were full of fish, partridges chirruped in the thistly meadows while the wild places were the last stronghold of the true fen polecats, otters and adders. The fen round his home is not the usual black fields clinically bisected by rows of poplars for much of it has been wrested from Nature within living memory.

Bill points out one sandy little field, now sprouting lusty winter barley. 'See that,' he says, pointing to it. 'I cleared that patch. It used to be all scrub and marsh and was a grand place for duck shooting years ago.' On the far dyke stands a sturdy concrete bunker of the sort commonly seen in remote places in East Anglia. Did the War Ministry expect tanks through the marshes, or a U-boat up the River Lark? 'Odd place for a pill-box, Bill,' I remarked. Bill snorted: that was no pill-box

Removing ice from the punt launch. Clothing in 1895 offered poor protection from the cold but a hut, massively built of concrete and used exclusively for duck shooting, 'in the old days'. The materials to build it were brought in laboriously by horse and cart in the same year as the first Battle of Ypres.

There is a low doorway and two square portholes on the corners through which to shoot. There was room for only the shortest of gun-barrel swings, but no-one minded, for the shooting was bag-filling on the French principle of *hutte* shooting in which a large-bore gun was fired into the thick of a paddling of duck on the marsh in front. The key patches would be liberally baited with unthreshed ears of barley to concentrate the birds in the right place.

I clambered in: here was where the shelf for cartridges had been, here a bench seat along the back wall, both quite rotted away over the passing years and now only the marks to show where they had been. I crept up and peeped through one of the gun ports and tried to imagine the picture seventy years ago when the mallard and wigeon poured in to the corn-fed marsh; in my mind's ear I heard the clanging reverberations of the great guns bouncing round the concrete walls: no ear-muff protection for shooters in those days. In my mind's nose I smelled the acrid reek of the black powder smoke hanging heavy and sulphurous in the November air. My eye could see the leather-booted old fenmen in their long coats, standing where I stood now, gazing out sharp eyed and stubble chinned into the gloom, their long brown gun barrels poking menacingly out into the sunset; rows of fowl hanging on the iron hooks which now jut out, rusting and redundant, from the wall.

There were other reminders of the wild old days: tangled spinneys and holts, remnants of the half-drained fen; fastnesses of thorn, elder and dogwood; and the ancient, giant ferns – of the sort sometimes found fossilised in coal – which once cloaked the drier parts of the primeval marshland, but now are rare. The fields are small by modern fen standards and they run down to water on two sides, one a winding little river with its own obligatory wash, as good a place for duck flighting as I have seen, and I was right, for Bill spoke of bags of forty flighted duck to two guns in an evening.

If the place has the 'feel' of duck about it, I have never seen a water which said 'pike' so loudly and who knows what jewel-eyed monsters lurked by the lily pads, for the water is hardly ever fished. Adders lay in the carr on the drier side of the bank and two roe deer had moved in to the old, impenetrable wood and made themselves a nuisance by overturning and raiding the pheasant feed hoppers. A long-eared owl stood tall and slim, pretending to be invisible as we peered up into the prickly heart of a hawthorn. In the wood over the boundary were the silted ponds and rotted pipes of the old decoy. A man once shot five

Plover netters in the hide preparing for a 'pull'

flying teal with one shot from a .410 in there and picked every bird.

It is a forgotten part of the country, redolent with old memories and curious people. Up the road lived just such a one, now an old man but in his day a magician with the netting needle, and an insatiable consumer of those coarse fish deemed inedible by the most hard-bitten fenman. He kept his small personal possessions and movables such as netting needle, purse, matches and knife not in his pockets, but in his bulbous cloth cap on his head. It was a matter of great local ribaldry to see him tapping at his pockets in growing frustration, looking for the tobacco pouch which was resting squarely on his head within full view of everyone save himself.

Out in the fen was a small, whitewashed cottage, built at the same time as the pill-box entirely out of the proceeds of selling coarse fish stranded in field dykes by a receding flood. An enterprising man and his family capitalised on this manna, hauled the fish out in nets and loaded them by the stone, the hundredweight and then the ton into potato sacks. When the bonanza was over they had made over £200 from the operation, no mean sum for a poor dyke-diddler in 1915. The son went to France to do his bit, expecting never to return, leaving the money with his mother, instructing her to build a cottage. This she did, and when the lad returned safely, having to his surprise survived the carnage, there was an unseemly dispute over the ownership of the property. Was it the boy's who had left the money behind, or was it the mother and sister's to whom he had, in a quixotic moment, handed it? The echoes of the feud still sound in that fen, but the cottage stands today, there for all to see.

Coarse fish were a highly saleable commodity in those days of shortages. There were no farm sprays to pollute the water, no pestiferous rows of match anglers week after week disturbing the quiet reaches, and little dredging was undertaken. Bill was in no doubt about the fish populations of his youth: 'Blarst, boy; yew could walk across the river on their backs, so thick they lay.' Surely they are bony and tasteless, I protested. Bill regarded me balefully: 'Don't yew believe it, boy!'

The system was that all the men from a few adjoining cottages went as a team to net the river and carry back the catch, heaping up the tench, bream, roach, rudd, pike and carp in the 'washus'. The assembled womenfolk would top, tail and gut the fish and throw them into the clothes copper and boil them vigorously. Next, the fish were boned, the flesh flaked and packed into 4-gallon earthenware jars, mixed with herbs and spices and the top sealed with melted mutton fat. It would keep for months like this and when eventually the jar was broached and the contents eaten they 'tasted as good as any salmon you've ever ate'. I suppose it did if you were hungry enough.

As for the game poaching, the system was so well organised and the practice so widespread that the villagers made a special arrangement with the baker to borrow his horse-drawn delivery van once a week in order to take the booty to the London train. This was the only venture on which the villagers combined; for the rest of the time they were at daggers drawn, competing for the best poaching ground and resorting to desperate measures to keep a jump ahead of the opposition. One dressed as a policeman and walked the field as a deterrent to later arrivals; another wild family dug a channel from the river to flood a farmer's fields so that they could establish a good place for plover netting. The Southery poacher-fishers of the early part of the century were, without a doubt, 'rum owd boys'.

It was early morning. Two figures, one lean and angular, the other short and stocky with fifty years of age between them, were creeping along the foot of the Hundred Foot River bank. The old one was Will Kent and he carried a long, muzzle-loading 4-bore over his shoulder. Onto the stock had been nailed a patch of leather to protect the face of the gunner from the recoil of this fearful piece. I walked in the steps of the old master; we were off to try for a shot at the wigeon.

We paused: Will cocked his head like an old dog. A distant whistle showed that a party of wigeon had landed to spend the night on the river half a mile ahead, the other side of our bank. We crept along, doing our best to judge the exact place, pausing regularly to listen. Our movements became stealthy and panther-like until Will judged we were at the foot of the bank directly in line with the fowl.

I was to shoot. A cap was pressed home firmly on the nipple and, clutching the monstrous weapon, I began to creep up the steep angle of the flood bank. I bellied through bleached grass, past teazles, ignored nettle stings, brought down showers of water-dock seeds which fell down my neck until at last, I was ready to peep over the rim. Like a poaching fox, slowly I raised my head. The water was leaden grey, but as my eyes grew accustomed to the play of the light I could make out a cluster of black blobs which opened and closed, forming and re-forming. My instructions were to wait until a sufficiency of birds 'drawed into a heap' and then fire into the middle of them.

I cocked the heavy hammer and squinted down the barrel past the monstrous blob of metal which did service as a foresight. I had deep-seated fears of what the recoil would do to me; the gun might even blow up. There came a gusty whisper from the rushes below: 'Goo on, boy; give 'em one!' I aimed at the thickest of the birds, closed my eyes, gritted my teeth and pulled.

Memories of what happened next are confused. There was a drum-splitting boom, a hot orange flash of flame and a squirt of Roman-candle sparks. I was conscious of a force on my shoulder like a giant but not un-gentle hand which slid me firmly back down through the prickles almost to the foot of the bank. Will and I scrambled back up and gazed at the water: three wigeon lay dead, soon retrieved by old Bess. They were my first wigeon, my first shot with a duck gun, my first taste of the thrill of fowling. Who cared that the duck were sitting? Nothing could detract from my fierce, wild triumph or the magic of that moment.

That was how things were.

Time and Tide

The geese had gone over high from Monk's Creek that morning. Jim had seen them pass in five ragged, clamouring skeins, each 300 birds strong. Far into the distance they went, their music fading with the black specks which whiffled down to pluck at the frozen grass on the water meadows 10 miles inland. Jim had been cutting cabbages, a mind- and finger-numbing task. However, a hard life on his smallholding, nestled in the lee of the marsh wall as if crouching down out of the winter gales which lanced in uninterrupted from the Arctic, had inured him both to bitter weather and the tedium and unremitting grind of his working life.

He bent to his task during the short, January day, cutting the football-sized January Kings and cramming them into the crates. His action had in it the steady rhythm of the true farmworker, but now and then he paused to blow on his fingers or to whet his long knife. For half an hour he stopped for his dockey, his bite of bread and cheese. Those geese were in his head, honking and crying; tonight they would return, beating out to the saltings to roost. The marsh was still fairly open, but it had taken him a hefty clout to break the ice on the bullocks' water trough that morning. The clods under his feet were an iron-hard jumble of crazy paving, rather more easy walking than they would be in the March rains. Then he felt snow, tickling and flicking on his coat and on the crisp, green cabbage leaves at his feet. He cocked a knowing eye at the heavy, oily-yellow clouds to the east; there was snow there, lots of it and the sea breeze would fill in and send him a blizzard by nightfall. It would mean those geese battling into its teeth, bemused and disorientated in the swirling flakes. The old man had suffered a lean season, but this just might be his chance to redress the balance.

His mind made up, a decision taken, he cut the last two cabbages and stuffed them into the crate; he collected his dockey bag and pedalled back to his cottage. He found his oilskin and 'ballyhava' on a nail behind the kitchen door and took his BSA Magnum and a belt of cartridges from the kitchen cupboard. He did not forget his compass. He had taken one ever since, old hand that he was, he had lost his way in a sudden sea fog; he still shivered as he recollected that hour of blind panic before, by pure chance, he had stumbled on the sea wall and safety with a rapidly making tide kissing his heels.

He cycled down the marsh lane and hid his rusty machine on the landward side of the great bank. Whistling old Brent to heel, he set off over the saltings, brushing through the white-rimed heads of the *Spartina*. The snow and wind were in his face and he screwed up his eyes as he marched out, following the serpentine meanderings of the creek as it slithered seawards. Now and then he crossed it, feeling out the soft mud with his stick, walking more easily over the hard shell bottom and floundering up the other side. He was not as young as he was. He paused to check his bearings. He had known this marsh, man and boy, for half a century, but the thickening snowflakes covered his friendly landmarks with an all-pervading, soft whiteness.

He reached the edge of the green. Somewhere out there the geese would come. A mile away the tide was turning; oily, scummy froth was creeping over the muds, melting the fresh snow, filling the hollows, gurgling in the crab holes. Despite the cold, Jim was sweating and gasping from his walk. He sought out a hiding place and, between snow flurries in fading light, he found a few tall tufts of *Spartina* near a little hollow which would serve as well as anywhere.

Neither he nor Brent heard, much less saw, the first skein until it was on top of them. One moment nothing, and then nine great shapes hung overhead, battling the wind. Jim threw up his gun, blotted out the leader, fired and swung smoothly to the next in line. Easy birds are often easy to miss, but Jim was an old hand and did not make mistakes like

that. Two black forms, suddenly shapeless and aimless, smacked into the mud with a complete and exhilarating finality. It was a good start, and they settled down to wait for the next lot.

The second skein was bigger, sixty strong and they came with that bee-buzzing hum which shows that they are uncertain of their bearings. They were rather too far to the left for his liking but, while he missed with his first barrel, his second knocked down two. His eye brightened: this was going to be his lucky night. One of these birds was a runner; Jim could not see Brent in action, but he heard the squelching and splashing of pursuit and the final, triumphant plunge as a lively young gander was finally pegged.

So it continued, a flight in a thousand and in an hour, after a quick head count, he found that he had eleven pinks in a tumbled heap by his hide. If only he could bag one more, it would beat his record. Twelve geese, a round dozen on the coast with a shoulder gun on evening flight would be something for the book. Just one more goose – only one – and he would go home a happy man. True, it was almost dark, but he had his compass. Flights passed him by to left and right, but never one quite close enough to give him a shot. He peered this way and that, glaring through the snow, his pupils dilated and then he heard Brent whine. Jim glanced down with a growl, for a whining dog might drown the sound of approaching pinions. With a cold clutch at his heart, he saw that the dog was sitting in a shallow puddle of water.

The old man had outstayed his time, shot for too long and waited for that last, twelfth goose which just would not come. How could he have forgotten the old enemy, the creeping tide closing in on him when his back was turned? The first trickle of scummy water was already caressing the tail feathers of one of his dead geese. He snatched up the birds, stuffed them into his bag and through his belt: some he carried, and set off, stumbling and running for the sea wall. None knew better than he of the hideous danger which now threatened him. Brent, unconcerned, loped beside him.

His fears were well founded, for Monk's Creek was filling ahead of him, cutting off his retreat. That muddy trickle he had crossed so easily on the way out had become a 15ft-wide river, growing wider and deeper by the second, which now lay between him and safety. His breath rasping, his heart hammering, he reached a place where he knew the creek to be shallowest, balanced his load, tucked his gun through his bag strap, grasped his stick and set off gingerly into the grey water. Brent swam on ahead of him and vanished in the gloom. Jim heard him twirling the water from his coat on the far bank: how near and yet how far that comforting sound. Would that Jim could change places with him.

The old man edged forward, a short step at a time, feeling the weight of water, sensing his feet sinking beneath him. The tide was already swirling at his wader tops and he was barely a third of the way across. He gritted his teeth: it was going to mean a wetting but a wind-backed, 29ft tide could not be stood out, but it would not be the first time he had come home with a bootfull.

He took another step. The icy water filled his waders. There was hot rabbit pie waiting for him back at the cottage. He edged further forward, his foot sank into a soft pot hole, he pulled but sank deeper. Off balance, he rolled gently, almost lazily into the water, gasping as he felt its adder bite on his belly, then his chest. The gun, that great weight of birds, a waterlogged bag and flooded waders pulled him down and hampered his frenzied struggles. His gun slipped and fell away: he cared not; his stick was gone and his feeble shout was cut short as the tide covered his face. At last, his threshings became weaker and finally ceased altogether as the great ocean took him to her bosom. He floated face down, almost submerged while, from his belt, a dead goose drifted away, turning slowly like a leaf in a summer stream.

Brent grew tired of waiting: he was no Greyfriars Bobby to guard a dead master, but he set off home at a steady trot. Next morning the RAF helicopter from the base recovered the body 2 miles along the coast where the rip tide had carried it.

Back inland the snow lay thickly on crates of freshly cut cabbages. On the sea wall an old bicycle lay rusting in the long grass: it lies there still.

High tides, floods and the subsequent drownings and loss of home and possessions were constant threats. To this day the fen country lies below sea level, and a combination of certain weather conditions and high tides could once again reduce the rich farmland to the shining watery wastes of old. The last serious flood, in the mid Fifties, came when a rush of snow meltwater surged down from the Midlands into the fen waterways. An unusually high tide, backed by gale-force winds, prevented its escape so it had no recourse but to flow back, bursting the banks and spreading over the fields in a roaring, yellow tide.

In the winter of 1946–7, the choir of Ely Cathedral sang the psalm which contained the words: 'The floods are risen, O Lord. The floods have lift up their voice.' It was a black winter of deep snow on iron frost and then the old fenland tale of breached banks and the flooding of 700,000 acres of farmland and a damage bill of £20 million. Not since the fourteenth and fifteenth centuries had such floods ravaged the fens. On a dark night in March the rivers rose and spread over their washes; then the

high, grassy banks, those mighty ramparts reared and maintained for over three centuries, were toppled by foam-crested waves which poured over in raging torrents.

'She's blew!' went the cry from the anxious river watchers of the marsh hamlets and fen villages throughout the lowlands. The waters raced across the black fields, over the fen droves and, backed by wind and rain, leaped on hundreds of remote farms and cottages, threw down the doors, burst the windows, flooded the kitchens and front rooms and swirled up the narrow staircases.

Terrified families cowered in their bedrooms, black as pitch with no candle end to bring comfort and often far away from the nearest neighbour. In some places the floods rose so high and the cottages were sited so low that whole families were driven to the roof trees, to cling there — literally for their lives — in biting wind and rain.

A farmer recorded the event thus:

> The wind shrieked across the flat countryside, blowing down trees, scattering the roofs of haystacks and tossing the tiles from farm buildings. Men on the banks watched the rising flood. The wind piled it against the banks until it began to flow, slowly at first, and then in a torrent, from one embanked level to another.

No one slept on those nights of 16 and 17 March, but every able-bodied person worked at repairing the banks until they sank exhausted in their tracks. One of Bill Whitehand's contemporaries, a lad of sixteen, had worked a whole day and half a night. A mug of tea was placed in his hand, but he fell asleep as he sat and spilled it over his knees.

Cattle had been moved to higher ground, but pigs by the thousand and chickens by the five thousands were drowned. Along the sword-straight roads crept a pathetic procession of 'tumble carts', waggons,

tractors and trailers loaded down with human and other salvage, clothing, bedding, calves, babies and even sacks of seed potatoes jumbled together in a pathetic hotch-potch.

Soldiers and airmen were rushed to the scene and army amphibious vehicles called 'Ducks' were used to rescue maroons from the outlying farms. I was a little boy at the time, but my mother took me down the village, off the ridge to where the road simply ran into the water. In the distance the tops of willows and roofs of farmsteads jabbed up out of the grey waves. An army 'Duck' approached, chugging noisily, left the water like a sea monster and trundled out onto the road where we stood. Water in cascades and rivulets poured off its khaki flanks. On board was a sad huddle of humanity: the detail which sticks most clearly in the mind is the man, surrounded by his family, huddled on board. The man's face was ashen white which heightened the startling red of a gash across his cheek. He was wrapped like an Indian in a grey blanket. In one hand he carried a stout, bracket clock, in the other a baby cocooned by shawls against the cold. Had the vehicle suffered a sudden, dangerous lurch it is hard to guess which of these two most treasured possessions he would have dropped.

Despite help from Midlands fire brigades with their pumps, and even from the Dutch government who sent a tug and a pontoon crane, the

A Roman lode, now well above the roof of the cottage on the shrunken fen nearby

'Bailiff of the Marshlands', that evicter supreme, had returned with a vengeance to reclaim his own. Many of the fen cottages built on soft, spongy soil, bent, cracked and collapsed. Roofs caved in, walls fell and cottage furniture representing the life work of many a humble family was cast upon the waters. A billowing curtain tied to a clothes pole showed where a family was still to be rescued.

What flotsam there was; what a sorry catalogue of lost hopes and dreams; what children's toys, mattresses, broken chairs, leather settees, hen coops and unrecognisable debris lay for mile after mile along the high-water mark. In one parish 15,000 acres were flooded, in another 6,000. Antiquated pumping engines tried to stem the tide but, despite unremitting toil by sluice keepers and German prisoners-of-war pressed into service rebuilding banks, one by one they failed.

Next the gale blew even more savagely and roared across the cold and sodden fens; the water poured over and through the banks even more swiftly. Trees which had withstood the tempests of centuries blew down and blocked what few roads remained dry. Men could not even stand against it, and one old farmer recalled: 'We spent the night in the fen. Most of the time we were crawling about the banks on our hands and knees.' The bank 'blew' at Over with the thunder of a cannon shot and a gap 60ft wide, and the waters roared onto yet another piece of fen. They tried to build a wall along the road to save the fen, but after toiling all night, they had to give up. By midday the water poured over in a

cataract: it was estimated that the fen was carrying 70 million *tons* of water at the height of the flood. Many of the pumping stations were themselves under water.

Finally it was all over; the sun shone once more and the farmers returned to sagging barns, rusting machinery and sodden stacks. Housewives found a foot of grey slime in kitchen and parlour and houses swept bare of possessions. They set to work to rebuild, repair and scrub. For long after the traces of the flood had been removed, wallpaper flapped off walls in damp streamers, floor boards sweated in a wet film and even the cleanest houses had that damp, dank river-weed smell about them.

Ironically enough, that black winter marked the start of the recovery of fen farming. The floods had deposited a rich layer of silt on the land, enriching it to a degree. Flood relief and government funds flooded in as rapidly as had the water. Insurance claims for lost farm buildings, tractors and machinery were made with an enthusiasm and flair for invention which made company claims managers wince, but all evidence had been swept away in the tide, and who dare be seen to be doubting the word of the victim of a national disaster?

The blame for the disaster of that winter has been laid at the doors of planners and bureaucrats, men who were strangers to the fens, men not possessed of the innate 'feel' for handling water and the instinctive understanding of land drainage and flood risk which most true fenmen possess. Safe in their offices with maps and charts they arranged to deepen and widen all key waterways in the belief that this would shed surplus water into the sea at a faster rate than before. On paper it worked, but any old dyke-diddler from Reach Fen could have told them that the art was to allow water to escape a little at a time and to have a system of relief flooding, flood gates, dams and catchwater-drains as standbys for emergencies.

The planners failed in this, failed to strengthen banks, failed to take advice, failed to provide a safety valve, failed to use the wisdom the fenman had learned in 300 years of trying to keep his feet dry. As my old friend James Wentworth Day said, 'They tried to empty three kettlefuls through one spout, and the kettle burst.' For that they stand judged by history. In 1953 the situation was slightly different but again 'they' failed us; their flood-warning system proved useless and the sea returned to claim its own and two counties felt the taste of salt water unknown to them for three centuries.

My own recollections of 1947 are poignant, but scattered and unconnected. I can see, as well as the army 'Ducks' emerging from the flood, the carcase of a cow, bloated and hideous, its four legs sticking grotesquely in the air as it floated gently under a bridge. I can see a large fragment of floating strawstack drifting by, its surface a moving carpet of wriggling, squeaking brown rats which, with their sure instinct for survival, had climbed onto the nearest floating object when the waters trickled into their holes. I see a mighty log of willow floating near the bank, its whole surface covered with the coruscating shards of countless beetles which winked and glittered, black, blue and silver in the watery sunlight as they sat on each other's backs, layer upon layer, on their impromptu raft.

Father opened the church and made it available to flood victims who piled in like any army of refugees the world over and heaped their sodden possessions in the pews. He insisted that animals be left outside. Ladies from the village lucky enough to live round the church on the high, greensand ridge above the flooding, made gallons of tea and vats of steaming soup and comforted wailing children. Father arranged for a hastily gathered team of bellringers to ring a peal to let the people know that there was a welcome for them in the church and to keep up their spirits.

Our giant Wellingtonia blew down. It was the tallest tree for miles around and, when it fell, its topmost fronds just brushed the dining-room windows so close did it come to the house. Our elms and limes were decimated; no more would spring rooks build shaggy nests in the swaying branches, nor the bees hum under their leafy canopies in summer. Snow lay well over wellington-boot depth and seemed to last for months. The memories of an eight-year-old are as selective as they are poignant.

The 1953 flood was serious, but it was merely the latest of a long line of floods which have been an integral part of life in the flat lands for three centuries. In the seventeenth century the thought occurred to a group of entrepreneurs, under the leadership of the Duke of Bedford, that the fens dry would be a good deal more profitable than the fens covered with random sheets of water which ebbed and flowed with the seasons and which provided at best a precarious living by fish, reed and fowl for a scattered tribe of primitive fenmen.

No less a personage than King James I was behind the idea of draining the fens, and declared: '. . . for the honour of his Kingdom he would not any longer suffer these counties to be abandoned to the will of the waters, nor to let them lie waste and unprofitable; and that if no one else would undertake their drainage, he himself would be their undertaker.' It was his Chief Justice Popham, still immortalised by the watercourse which bears his name, who persuaded the gentlemen 'adventurers' to venture their capital in the project and the first chapter in the modern history of fen drainage was written. It was only a partially successful venture, remembered only by local names such as Adventurers' Fen and Adventurers' Farm, for no Englishman possessed the skills or experience for such a colossal undertaking.

James cast his eye overseas to Holland, where they knew a great deal about drainage. In the province of Zeeland, in the town of Maartensdijk, lived Cornelius Vermuyden, a drainer with an established reputation. He was brought over to drain Canvey Island, Dagenham Marshes, the Royal Park at Windsor, Hatfield Chase in Yorkshire and, his most notable effort, the Anxholme marshes in Yorkshire. This marsh was later deliberately re-flooded by retreating Cavalier troops during the Civil War and in a few short hours the work of years was undone. The locals evicted the foreign drainers, levelled their houses, burned their crops and pulled down their fences, a combination of xenophobia and resentment. When the Dutch showed resistance 'the rioters stood by with loaded guns, and swore they would stay until the whole levels were drowned again and the foreigners forced to swim away like ducks.'

In 1630 Vermuyden was promised 95,000 acres of reclaimed land when he had drained the fens. There was wrangling between him and the Duke of Bedford, intrigues, double-dealing at court and lost fortunes, a tangled web of such complication that it deserves a book to itself, but Charles I sent Hayward the surveyor to survey the Great Level. He covered rather less than half a million acres, an amazing feat when one considers that most of the work had to be done by boat or in long boots through stinking swamps full of every conceivable fever and ague, and populated by a half-savage race of dark-haired, sallow-skinned, under-sized fenmen, most of whom were bitterly hostile to the very thought of drainage.

Vermuyden's plan was to dig straight drainage channels, fed by a network of smaller dykes, and controlled at the ends by a series of sluices. The problem was that much of the fens lay below sea level so there was no natural fall in the ground with the result that the sluggish rivers filled with silt, the flow ceased and the floods returned. Vermuyden was lampooned by his contemporaries, such as Sketchly, who remarked drily: 'Vermuyden began badly, progressed ignorantly and finished disastrously . . . the object Vermuyden had in view was to show how much better he could drain the land than nature could, by doing all in his power to abstract the wealth of water from *her* works and pour it into his own.' This was an allusion to the Dutchman's use of man-made channels in preference to the existing rivers.

Late in the seventeenth century the expensive drains began to fail and the age of the windmill was ushered in. These crude devices, with their black sails, scooped the water on paddles from one level to another, creating an artificial fall which was to keep the water moving for a few more decades. Early in the eighteenth century windmills were a common sight, for no less than 700 of them were working at the peak of their usefulness. As the land shrank still further, supplementary mills were needed to move the water up to the existing mill so that, in the end, tiers of mills worked the water inefficiently into the main outfalls.

The old millmen were great characters who knew to an inch the rise and fall of the flood waters over mile after mile of misty fen. They lived in tarred huts near their charges and, during their lengthy periods of inactivity, became mighty anglers and bird catchers. They fried their victims in butter in huge, black frying pans balanced on a crude brazier full of red glowing coals.

The mill days soon passed. The fen shrank too much for them to counter and they became woefully inefficient and moved little water, while in the many periods of gale, flat calm or frost they could not operate. Some of the early ones worked only if the wind blew from a certain direction. It is still possible to find the vestiges of one of these old buildings, the brick footings standing in the nettles at the head of a dyke, or a tarred skeleton of boards tumbled down in the water docks in a lonely corner. At Wicken Fen they have re-built one of the old drainage mills so that the uncomprehending may go and gaze at it. It still works, and will go clanking and rattling round, slopping a few pails of water from one dyke to another per revolution of the sails.

When the windmills failed to cope the waters once more took over the land and 'The Bailiff' indiscriminately threw the settlers out of their homes. The age of steam was dawning and the efficient beam pumping engine pumped water at a rate undreamed of by the old millmen. The outfalls were deepened and kept clear and the major step had been taken. Vermuyden's two Bedford rivers were embanked and improved and to this day remain as the boundaries of the Bedford washes. Steam pumps replaced the perpetual clack-clacking of the windmills with a regular, ground-shaking thump-thump, a lumpish lullaby as you lay abed in your cottage; each thump spewed a hundred gallons from one level to another. The eventual conversion of these pumps to diesel power put the seal on the story of fen drainage.

It had been a long and complicated tale of two steps forward and one back, of individual efforts by monks, farmers, adventurers, imported entrepreneurs and others, often working independently of each other to drain their own little patches which inevitably re-flooded after a few years. It was a tale of lost fortunes, of Vermuyden returning to Holland a ruined and broken man, of strange laws such as the one imposed by the medieval Commissioners' Court of Sewers. The penalty for those who broke the banks or neglected their own particular stretch was to be

Pumping engine at Upware, one of the many perpetually in action to hold back the waters

arrested, bound hand and foot and staked down in the gap in the bank and buried alive, thus forming a part of his neighbours' flood defences. No one made that mistake twice.

Through the story runs the recurring theme of local resistance to drainage. The old fenmen could not grasp that the fens dry and farmed would be worth a thousand times more than the fens flooded. They could appreciate only the fact that with the departure of the waters, the fish, wildfowl, reeds and turf on which they depended for their livelihood would be gone also. Accordingly the locals gave the drainers a hard time and harrassed them cruelly, murdering them, throwing their bodies in their own dykes and blowing up their sluices with gunpowder. The drainers, however, left their indelible mark on posterity, their industry, labour and faith in a daunting project ensuring their immortality. Local place names and words, such as New Zeeland and decoy, and the quaint, distinctively shaped gable ends of the old houses in some fen-village high streets, also show where they have been.

Discounting the machinations of the 'rough old boys' of Southery and elsewhere who deliberately flooded fields for their own ends, it was possible for odd fields still to become inundated. A small dyke system neglected for a year or two too many and a thunderstorm at the wrong time could still send the water creeping up the wheat stalks and cost a man his harvest. It is an ill wind, and I have a happy memory of just such a field which flooded in the wet September of 1969. The farmer was careless with his dykes: they were choked with silt and vegetation and the grey-bearded Norfolk reeds — the roots of which go down deeper than a man with a spade can dig in a long day — had crept out and colonised several yards into the wheat on three sides of the field.

I had seen clouds of mallard over it like gnats dancing on an autumn evening. I was out tramping my own bit of shooting, a brace-and-a-half of grey partridge and a hare causing my bag strap to bite into my shoulder. In the distance the cluster of specks said 'duck' as clearly as a human voice. I took a bee-line cross-country onto unfamiliar ground, leaping dykes, skirting fields of green sugar beet and yellow barley, past clusters of tarred and tatty farm sheds. The black specks were closer now, easily identifiable as mallard, and the staccato stuttering chatter came to me on the evening breeze.

I reached the field, a poor crop of wheat, badly laid by the wind and half flooded owing to a build-up of water in the blocked dyke at the top end. It seemed as if every mallard in Christendom had found the place and flocked in for the feast. How could I find the owner? A combine was working three fields away and I plodded on, asked the driver and he gave me the name of a farmer two villages away. Many miles of walking and cycling later, I ran him to ground as he stood contemplating a herd of pigs, grunting and squealing, belly-deep in straw in his yard. 'Any chance of a shot at the ducks? They're really caning the wheat on your fifteen acre in the fen.' He gave me a shrewd glance, weighing-up the stranger: was there a pound in it for him? Visibly he relaxed and grunted his assent; after all, it was I who was doing him the favour.

The next morning I was there with a friend, three retrievers and plenty of cartridges. We crept into position and were startled to the soles of our boots by the roar of wings as an uncountable pack of mallard, black against the blacker bowl of the night sky, sprang and flew off. We stood for a moment, breath held. Somewhere a mallard quacked and an owl shrieked; some small creature of the night rustled minutely in the grass. The dew had soaked us from the waist down as we pushed through the hogweed and cow parsley.

On we crept, Sam taking one side of the field, me the other, draping a scrap of netting and lurking like two old herons in a stand of Norfolk reed a few paces from the field boundary. The stars paled and a red slash across the east showed that dawn was near. There was a stillness, characteristic of those few magic moments when it seems as if the weather is brooding about what it will give us today. The mallard started to come, high up in the pale-grey bowl of the sky, a distant chatter, sharp whicker of wings and a small party of seven, arrow sharp and starkly etched, came purposefully onward. I crouched behind the feathered heads of the *Phragmites*, waited until they banked low overhead, and fired two careful shots.

Two shapes, one moment so direct and purposeful, became flat and aimless and plummetted down into the wheat. My dog of the day, a black labrador named Cassius, an extrovert and ruffian by nature, still in his first full season, went galumphing out through the stalks and brought me in succession two mallard, one of them already showing his early drake's feathers, both with bright-orange paddles, eyes demurely closed in death, plumage beaded wetly with dew from the field.

That pack of seven was the first of countless flights, for they came in echelons, arrow formations, vees, long strings and tight clusters. Sam shot from across the field and I saw a bird fall. Then it was my turn again and I knocked down another, then another, for this was the chance of a lifetime and, young butchers that we were, we showed no restraint.

Gun barrels grew hot, duck tumbled down, hitting the top layer of flattened corn, breaking through and the corn stalks closing behind them. Now it was full daylight with a bright sun beating down. The dew and with it the scent had evaporated: it was going to be a hot day. For all his great strength, even Cassius was beginning to flag; he went out to retrieve less eagerly and took more time to find each bird. At one point I had five birds down, only carelessly marked by me and the dog began to fail. Sam came over with a similar story, for his two labradors, gentle maiden ladies both, had thrown in the towel and could not raise the energy or enthusiasm for another single trip out into that cornfield.

That was it: even we insatiable bag-fillers demurred at shooting birds which we had no hope of retrieving. With more duck still eager to land, we tramped about the field searching for lost birds, finding a few, but losing many in that impenetrable tangle of stalks. The dogs were no help: completely exhausted, they lay on the muddy, trampled straw of our hides, tongues lolling almost to their chests, panting like tank engines. We completed the pickup and found that we had exactly eighty-nine ducks which it took us three journeys to carry out of the muddy field and to the little grey van waiting in the stackyard. Two humans, three dogs and that huge weight of dead birds put us flat on the springs, and several times we 'bottomed' on the bumpy track back to civilisation.

Pricks of conscience began to assail us. Had we shot too many? By today's standards of course we had, and neither of us would consider taking such a bag again, even in the unlikely event of the opportunity arising. What could we do with such a mountain of the slain? The weather was warm and already the blow flies buzzed ominously: the whole adventure would be soured if the birds were allowed to go to waste.

It was all right in the end and, two telephone calls later, the grey van drove slowly into Cambridge and we sold the lot at 3/9d each, to Mr Sennitt of the famous Cambridge poulterers. The money paid for our cartridges for that season and the next.

Mr Sennitt employed as head plucker a wizened, gnarled old man of indeterminate age. His time for a mallard, he informed us proudly, was an amazing two minutes. It took me quarter of an hour, which I thought was pretty quick and I expect that after another sixty years' practice I might be able to improve on it, but whether I could ever break the two-minute barrier is doubtful. I wonder how many fowl that old man had plucked in his feathery cellar, day in, day out over the first half of the twentieth century.

Floods brought strange birds which, sensing somehow that conditions were favourable, came sailing in under the moon and were there next morning to surprise and delight us. Short-eared owls always seemed to know when the river washes were due to flood: one day there was no sign of them, the next it was common to see seven of them at once, wheeling and banking on mothy wings, and then, on the third day, the waters arrived. The owls migrated from Scandinavia and, while not aquatic birds, they had learned that a flood drove all the rats, mice, voles and insects onto the banks and that the resulting concentration of food creatures was a feast not to be missed. How did those 'woodcock owls' as they were known, owing to their custom of migrating with the woodcock during the first November full moon, know that the floods had come?

I was shooting along the flood wall during one wet winter and the dog was busy examining a forest of brown rushes in case one of our scuttling little marsh pheasants had taken refuge within. There came a flip of wings and a small, brown, speckled heron flew up and away over the Hundred Foot bank. I had plenty of time to identify a bittern, the first (and last) I

had seen on those river washes. Mindful of my early experience with bearded tits and birdwatchers, I told no one. There was no way of predicting what might appear next: it could be an osprey or a snow bunting, for I have seen both attracted to seasonal and unseasonal floodwater.

One year it was geese, rare for us in those days and only in recent times becoming more frequent visitors. Even more unusual was that they should be whitefronts. I was crouching by a flooded wash, trying to blend with a half-rotten oak gate post festooned with rusty barbed wire in which had gathered the floating grass and rubbish of a hundred floods, giving it a hairy coat. I was waiting for wigeon, a burly, dangerous sentinel, looming there in the half light, when I heard a distant laughing cry, a sound to stir the pulses; it grew louder, a gabbling, yelping, gossiping murmur, coming and going on the breeze.

Suddenly I saw them, a skein of about forty on set wings topping the low bank and making as if to settle on Peter Hammence's wash where an open sheet of water gleamed dully. Then they were racing their reflections along the surface but, at the last moment, they changed their minds, beat their wings and came to my wash. The next moment they were about my ears. My old BSA magnum spoke twice. One goose collapsed dead in the air and smacked down onto the exposed wet mud. The other set its wings, separated from the rest of the skein which had gone shouting off into the gloom whence they sprung, and glided off and out of sight. Such a bird is invariably mortally wounded and will fall dead within half a mile. At first we could not find it. My very first dog, Ajax, and I quartered every yard of the marsh, slipping into unseen dykes and stumbling in reed tangles but no luck. Then I could see it, a white blur on the mud, lying beyond the wide dyke. It was only my second goose and I did not care for Ajax to retrieve it. He was growing rather hard-mouthed in his dotage, and I did not wish to have my beautiful bird flattened between his crocodile jaws. So, I was obliged to walk three-quarters of a mile to the bank, over the plank bridge and return on the other side – a mile-and-a-half tramp in the dark, to pick up a bird which lay thirty yards away.

The head of that goose, stuffed and mounted on his shield, gazes down on me as I write. That boot-button-black eye holds a faintly censorial glint, but his presence there reminds me of a memorable evening, of a stroke of luck and the power of unexpected flooding to draw strange and exciting birds, 'ghosts' of the old fen returning with the waters.

Shelduck and even the sea-going scaup appear from nowhere and I have seen goosander and smew on the Bedford Levels in a hard winter. Established pools – those with high, old reed walls and clean-cut margins – are completely sheltered on a windy day. The water is either deep and clear brown, or flowing and strewn with young reed, loosestrife or sallows. They are perfect resting ponds for mallard, teal and pintail. Shovelers drop in during spring evenings and, for a lucky fenman, a pair of delicate little garganey might spring on whirring, clockwork wings and delight him on an otherwise normal summer morning.

Shallow, more temporary waters with their less-defined margins were the haunt of other birds. At the deeper end there was often a clump of giant reed mace, usually mis-named bulrushes by townsmen. The fat, brown pokers of their seed heads broke the monotony of the skyline and made perching places for reed buntings. In the 1939 floods the noted ornithologist, and friend of my boyhood, Dr Eric Ennion recorded a wave of black terns passing through his beloved Adventurers' Fen. With sloe-black foreparts, white undersides and pale, smoke-grey wings and tails, their flight is altogether delicate and full of Dresden-porcelain grace. They hawk daintily for insects over the stagnant pools, competing with swifts and bats for the dragonflies, moths and sedges which dance and whirl in the eddies above the surface.

One autumn evening saw me alone out on the fen armed with nothing more formidable than a Norfolk pole, one of the sturdy, long spades developed in that county. With it I was clearing a choked drainage dyke to allow some water to freshen the little corner where the snipe loved to foregather when the marsh proper was hard frozen. I was surrounded by birds. Swallows skimmed and audibly 'snipped' at midges; a pair of moorhens bickered and a gnome-like water rail crept through the tangle of rush at the foot of the bank. A grey heron flapped slowly overhead. The cut-throat reed blades were a charm of birdsong: sedge warbler, reed bunting and once I thought I caught a snatch of the sewing-machine song of the grasshopper warbler, the 'reeler bird' of the old marshmen.

I worked quietly, almost a part of the landscape, the birds trilling and flirting their tails within feet of me. Then there was a black speck on the horizon which wafted on, slow and wavering: no darting swallow or soaring skylark this, but a black speck different from the others, one which exuded latent menace. The other birds had seen it before me; it was their reaction which caused me to glance up, sensing a change in their untroubled carolling. Reed buntings dropped down the stems like stones; the moorhens forgot their difference of opinion and faded into the shadows; suddenly the sky was bereft of swallows; the whole scene was empty and silent.

The speck was a speck no more but a great bird which beat, beat and glided on ragged wings, drifting, hanging like a shallow vee. It was a hen harrier, a male in full, mature plumage of lavender grey, white and startling black tips to his wings. His very shape, his great head and fierce eyes turning this way and that, his trailing talons and his whole aura were a threat: he wore his cloud of fear like a cloak. He flew almost directly over my head, peering from side to side, a true buccaneer, a reiver, a savage throwback to the old fen which knew King John; perhaps a descendant of the harrier which flew over King Canute as, born on a litter, he crossed the ice of Soham Mere in order to 'hear the monks of Ely sing right merrily'.

Possibly I romanticised, but at the time that was how it felt. He passed by and faded to become a speck once more. Then, it seemed, the sun came out; nature which had been holding its breath relaxed, and the humble birds returned to the sky and played once more in the rushes. The black cloud had passed by, but the ancient, atavistic fear of the raptor had preceded and followed him by.

In 1957 there was a flash flood in mid-summer. Usually our floods are affairs of the winter months, when we are physically and mentally prepared to capitalise on or to suffer their arrival. A record rainfall of 3in in 48 hours caught the sluice keepers napping and the Bedford Levels were flooded. It was strange to see full-leafed willows jutting from blue water and fresh green grass swamped on the margins while a benign sun shone.

I took out the punt and poled along a flooded drove where, only three days before, slab-sided bullocks had chewed the cud. Summer flotsam is a different matter again from what you find bobbing about in winter. I collected several useful logs, half a gate, several buckets as good as new, and a telescopic gaff lost by an angler. More tragic was the dismal row of partridge, pheasant, mallard and peewit eggs which bobbed along the high-water mark. They must have been on the point of hatch (or addled) to have floated for, as anyone knows, a good egg sinks like a stone. There were also pathetic little scraps of down which had been newly hatched ducks, overtaken by the waters as surely as the fen cottager in the Black Winter of '47. Carrion crows and black-backed gulls had, with the opportunism of their kind, discovered this bounty and stalked, keen-eyed, along the tide-line.

Vermuyden's Old Bedford River at Sutton

Nature would recover from this setback and re-build her stocks easily enough. I approached the old willow spinney, in summer a haven for wash cattle to shelter from sun and wind and escape the flies. These gnarled veterans were used to having their feet in water as the series of white tide marks round their trunks testified: each ring marked the high-water point of successive winter floods, like the marks they chisel on dock walls and inscribe with the date to record some or other monumental tide. My trees must have been surprised to receive an unseasonal soaking.

On the edge of the holt a giant log lay, half-submerged, saturated, black and heavy. On it, in the exact centre, squatted a rabbit, its eyes bulging and whiskers quivering with fear as I approached. Two more pushes and I was up to him and his impromptu Noah's Ark. I leaned out to grab him, intending to transport him to terra firma, but he gave a great leap, landed with a belly flop and set off at a rapid dog paddle — or should it be rabbit paddle? — for safety. He passed some willow fronds trailing in the water and seized them in his teeth on the principle that even a drowning rabbit will grasp a straw.

He was quickly exhausted and I was able to draw alongside and lift this saturated, dripping lump of fur in and onto the bottom boards. It sat quite still, water forming in a pool round its feet. I poled 30yd across the swollen river and grounded on the safety of the grassy bank. I lifted out my passenger and put him on the ground. He sat still for a moment, taking in his stroke of good fortune, then he twirled himself into a shower of silver spray like a mop, and scuttled over the flood bank and away in a blur of flying feet, white scut and damp fur.

He was one of the lucky ones, for who can guess at how many creatures perished? The troubles were not over, for the water receded leaving a scummy film of mud on every leaf and every blade of grass, and the once-green meadows grey and stinking. It was death for cattle to eat such stuff, for it 'balled' in their stomachs and blocked their digestive systems. The farmers would have to wait a good month and several heavy rains before the vegetation would be fit to eat.

Worst of all, the silt-laden water flowing back into the rivers stifled and killed the irises, flags, water lilies and mare's tail which oxygenated the water and supported the animal life. All the fish died. I stood on the Old Bedford River bridge and looked south-west along Vermuyden's old digging. The setting sun glinted and shone on a silver carpet along the shelf at the foot of the bank: it was a sheet of dead coarse fish stretching as far as the eye could see (and the nose smell) into the distance towards Earith.

Once more I launched the punt and poled, like Charon, up the oily, black water. Fish of undreamed-of weight and quantity had perished. A great pike of at least 25lb floated belly up against the reeds. Whole shoals of dustbin-lid bream lay where they had suffocated; golden tench gasped their lives away; roach, rudd and even the rare burbot or eel pout had succumbed. The only fish with a vestige of life were the hardy carp which lay, just alive, with their snouts buried in the bankside weeds. The other survivors were eels; distressed and oxygen starved though they were, they had the strength to wriggle away as the punt rippled the water close by. One of those eels was a 'masterful gurt 'un' and was as thick as my punt pole and a cloth yard long.

Those were the floods – a web of change, development, drownings, drainage and adventures. Times of strange beasts and rare fowl, but the old fenmen in their eelskin garters and moleskin weskitts had learned to live with them. Who can tell when the waters will once more 'rise from their appointed place'?

'Thim Old Roomans'.

I stood on the green bank of Swaffham Lode, gazing out across the fens which lay on either side, lush and green on a May morning. At my side stood George Darby, fenman of note and a slodger of the old school who knew most of what was worth knowing about the flat lands. With an expansive wave of his arm he indicated the placid green waters of the lode. 'Know who dug them?' he demanded truculently. I thought I knew the answer but not wishing to spoil his moment of triumph, I professed ignorance, but could it possibly have been the MacAlpine Brothers? He fixed me with his good eye and taking a prodigious pinch of snuff from a dented silver tin, he timed his answer to perfection: 'Roomans – that's who, boy. Dew yew set down here and have forty winks on a summer's night, thim old Roomans will hev ye – sure as harvest.' He winked his own wink and knowingly tapped the lid of his snuff box.

His words rang faint bells: were not they almost identical to those used by old Albert describing his encounter with the will-o'-the-wisp? 'Thim old Roomans' were an important factor in local legend, often spoken of as though they had been a travelling caravanserai of gypsies who had passed through the area six or possibly seven years ago.

Most local historians, even those with 'the book larnin' ', seem to agree that it was indeed the Romans who dug the lodes, centuries before Cornelius Vermuyden crossed the Channel. The Romans penetrated the watery wastes of the fens with the thoroughness which they applied to all their undertakings. Other invaders, as often as not, sidestepped the trackless wastes partly because they held nothing worth conquering but mostly because of the problems of transport, communication, food and the attentions of the local residents who pestered and harried like some of their own stinging mosquitoes. Here and there a Saxon arch, a lonely abbey or symmetrical mounds in green turf show where an adventurer braver than the rest, took his ship up river and settled on the first patch of dry land he found. No African missionary could have found the surroundings or the natives more hostile.

The Romans found some moderately prosperous villages – Reach with its ancient traditions, Burwell, Swaffham Bulbeck and Lode – and dug a canal from each one to join the Cam a few miles away so that goods might be ferried from the heart of the wilderness, up to the river and thence to the sea. One may only guess at the heavy labour which went into that first digging, with baskets of earth carried on the heads of the ditch diggers. The result was to open those villages to the outside world and those canals, or lodes, became humming arteries of commerce: barges laden with turf, coals, thatching reeds, fowl, sheep and human freight plied back and forth in endless strings. This traffic continued until the coming of the railways and was only finally killed off by the roads.

Those once-bustling villages, each served so kindly by its own lode, reverted to peaceful dreaming in the quiet, green heart of Cambridgeshire, their great days gone. Only a half-covered staithe, a wharf accidentally exposed during a routine excavation, the preserved skeleton of an ancient barge dredged from the mud or an iron ring for tying up boats unearthed in a cottage garden remind us of how things once must have been.

The lodes too are now quiet with green, hairy, overgrown banks and a leaning willow or scrub thorn to catch the eye. Nothing breaks the placid surface save the 'plop' of an angler's float, a scurrying moorhen or a squad of mallard on an autumn evening. The paths trodden by countless thousands of rough-shod feet and hooves over the centuries, now see only a well-heeled hiker, a booted farm labourer or a wildfowler. It is hard to imagine that a place that is the epitome of greenness, peace and neglected calm was once a bustle of travellers and merchants.

Great fish live in those lodes, the shallow silted water being ideal for shoals of bream and eels large enough to make the angler gasp in disbelief. On a sunny May morning when the pike are spawning it is possible to see, with the aid of Polaroid glasses, every twenty yards or so a great hen fish accompanied by her diminutive consort. The fishing is difficult, since the shallow, clear water and steep banks make it almost impossible for a fisherman to keep himself and his tackle unseen; so the monsters are permitted to grow fat in peace.

When the Romans dug that first spit of mud in the dim attic of history, they created a river which flowed on a level with the surrounding marsh. As the following decades became centuries, the banks were built up and reinforced to prevent leaks and the surrounding fen shrank as does a sponge when the water is removed from it. The fine, black soil blew in the gales of late spring, filling the sky with black clouds, penetrating the most tightly sealed window and even working its way behind the glass and through the frames of pictures. With each 'blow' the fenland shrank further and the lode bank had to be built higher.

Today the lodes run high above the land around them. Near Upware pumping station, where Burwell and Wicken Lodes run into the Cam, stands a cottage. The pitch of its roof is on an exact level with the waters of the lode which creep past a few yards away. It surely calls for an untroubled disposition to live thus and lie in bed during a screaming February gale, high tides and heavy rain and recall that, at the foot of your garden, is water piled up as high as your house held only by a bank of green turves.

It is not to be wondered at that an area of such strange history, land won painfully and dearly bought from Nature, full of mists and wild imaginings, should be thickly populated with ghosts. The fenman tends not to be an imaginative chap, but the faintest suspicion of the supernatural will reduce him to a bundle of quivering nerves. Albert was not the only one to be scared of the will-o'-the-wisp whose corpse candle danced his deathly dance. Even if he had identified the flickering light for what it was, he would have been just as scared, for the sight of jack-o'-lantern meant that you would be a dead man within the week.

Sometimes a haunted fenman stood his ground. Tom Robinson once saw the corpse light dancing towards him over a quaking bog, beckoning him to follow and be sucked down in the mire to an awful death. Unlike the rest, he stood firm, upped with his double-barrelled, muzzle-loading 8-bore and 'gie the owd bugger one, right amidships'. When the flash and pall of smoke which hung heavy in the autumn mist had faded, Tom saw 'a hoppity little old man running for me with a lanthorn', and decided that discretion was the better part of valour, so turned tail and ran.

Sometimes a trigger-happy fenman could cause more serious damage. 'Admiral' George Phyppes, so-called because of his distinguished bearing and mane of snowy white hair and beard (for he had never seen the sea),

was once hiding in a hole down on Wicken Fen waiting for the mallard to flight in from the stubbles for their nightly wash and brush-up. He lit his pipe and a whiff of blue tobacco smoke drifted up from his white head as it protruded, apparently trunkless, from the mud.

Quarter of a mile away, Josh Harrison was creeping along in his punt, searching in vain for a paddling of those same mallard when he saw the indistinct white blur over on the mud by the rushes. 'I thought it was an old swan set there for the night,' he remarked later. He lay down, cocked the punt gun and began, with infinite care, to stalk the bird. Oblivious of his impending doom, the 'Admiral' gazed round, waiting for the flight; of the punt he saw no sign, for the stealthy approach, and its design and colour were all to that very end. Josh reached what he felt to be a satisfactory range, and, gratified that the bird was still there, 'drawed back' and 'gi' it one'.

There was a shriek of anguish from the swan. The Admiral had had a miraculous escape, one moment day-dreaming in his hole about nothing in particular, the next enveloped in a cloud of BB shot, buzzing like hornets and hissing like red-hot needles into the mud around his shoulders. By a curious coincidence, two pellets removed each of his ear lobes sweetly as a surgeon's knife; another cut his scalp to the bone while a fourth – the unkindest and most undignified cut of all – sliced off the tip of his nose.

'The old davil wore a'bleeding like a pig,' recalled Josh later, 'while as for language . . .' He rolled his eyes heavenward, his own vocabulary unable to do justice to the blistering wrath of the old man. The Admiral wore his scars with distinction, eventually even reconciling himself to the appearance of his nose: he informed visitors that he had won them in the trenches at Ypres, a ruse which won him many a free pint.

The oldest chroniclers have sensed the haunted feel of much of the fen country, a sensation felt more strongly in pre-drainage days. 'Old Bushman' of the *Field*, wrote as follows in the mid-nineteenth century, at a time when the Upware Republic was at its most roisterous:

Vast must have been the extent of fen land when Ethelwold was king and the monastery at Crowland, (whose ruins still form a bold memento of the days that are past), was founded. Many are the traditions of genii and kelpies inhabiting the fens at that time and the benighted traveller has trembled in his lonely journey over the dark, dank fen, as the sullen boom of the bittern shook the night air, or the deep, solemn note of the curfew bell from the distant abbey of Crowland borne upon the night breeze across the dreary flat, fell upon his startled ear. Benumbed with cold, his senses bewildered with fear, how many a one has sunk in hopeless despair upon that damp, cold bed, from which few have ever risen again alive; or misled by the treacherous flickering light of the 'will-o'-the-wisp' dancing 'in murky night o'er fen and lake', has wandered out of his track, and, floundering on through bog and mire, has found a grave in the dark pool and the last despairing shriek of the dying man sinking below the surface was carried on the night breeze over the dreary marshes, where there was no one to hear it.

Many of our ghosts must be those of such poor travellers lost in the trackless waste or caught in a sudden fog and pulled down to a ghastly death in some turgid swamp. Jem and Bob were reed cutting one day, swinging their glinting scythes like the old hands they were, when Jem gave a sudden cry: 'Bob, come here; here's a chap drownded in the dyke.' Bob came up and there below the surface was a pale, moon face, eyes staring and open, the body fading to featureless black, vague of outline, the head swathed in a cowl-like rag. Jem was for taking to his heels, but Bob was made of tougher material. 'Well, let's get the poor owd chap out, anyway,' he said and, taking his scythe, hooked the point in the dead man's cloak. At that moment they both realised that the eyes were looking at them, full of knowledge and life while the corpse began slowly to drift of its own volition to the surface.

That was it: they both turned and ran as fast as they could in marsh boots. A posse was got up from the tap room of the Dyker's Arms and fortified with brandy, went to investigate the phenomenon but of the mysterious body they found not a sign. For all that, neither Jem nor Bob could be persuaded, for all the eels in the Hundred Foot, to venture onto that stretch of marsh again, lest 'that owd monk' should rear from his watery hole and drag them down.

A rather more formidable spirit was that of the spectral hound of Spinney Bank, known to history as Black Shuck. A giant, black hound is part of the folklore of many parts of the country beside the fens. His origins probably lie deep in the legends of the Norse invaders and may be an offspring of the fabled Hound of Thor. To see Black Shuck was death within the week, so it was wise to keep away from Spinney Bank after dark, just in case you caught a glimpse of him. To old fen folk for whom the nights held nameless fears and in whose benighted brains strange monsters stalked, such a ghost was real indeed and there are attested cases of those who were frightened to death by him. Jem and Bob with their 'monk' in the dyke may have seen a reflection of the moon or even of their own pale and startled faces in that placid water. The explanation would be quickly accepted by modern, supermarket man, but try telling such a tale to Bob and Jem!

A fen lass was courting a young man from the next village and, as anyone knows, those in love are 'afeered o' nothin' '. After her nightly assignations she was in the habit of taking a short cut home along the

Spinney Bank, Black Shuck territory. One night, just as the moon rose silver and pale over the distant marsh willows, she 'heerd a snufflin' ahint her, looked round, and there were a gurt, owd black dawg with one red eye as big as this bike lamp, in the middle of his head. She hoisted har skirts, lit out a holler to raise the dead, and set off a'runnin' like a redshank toward home.' Thus, Charlie Smith as he told me the tale one day when we sat together in a tarry punt, fishing for pike.

No matter how fast the girl ran, and she was fleet of foot and flew like the wind, the great dog kept at her heels, loping along, unhurried, snuffling the ground, his red eye glinting sombrely. She shrieked again and ran even harder until she saw the leaning post which marked the end of the bank. At that moment, Black Shuck stopped, lifted his great head, and uttered a blood-chilling howl which had in it all the sorrows of the world, an echo of Hades and a breath of the charnel house.

Ashen-faced, incoherent and sobbing, she fell into her mother's arms, took to her bed and rose from it not again for, 'she wore dead within the sennight, and she weren't the first to go that way, neither.'

I often shot duck on the rivers round which Black Shuck held sway. One particular evening stays in the mind, for it was especially suited to a suspect imagination. Then too there was a full moon, a coppery red one, known to countrymen as a harvest moon. It hung in the east, tinting the wisps of clouds with a bronze glow. The rusty sabres of the reeds clashed gently in a fitful breeze, but it soon died and left the fen silent. Mallard were flighting up river, the whistle of their wings and guttural quacks audible from far away in the still conditions. I had shot seven, the stabs of orange flame from my barrels and crack of the explosion rolling along the low bank setting the peewits complaining from the water meadow. Each bird had been fetched from the river by the mighty Cassius and with a heavy bag and the flight over, it was time to plod back to the old van parked beneath the willows in the lee of the bank.

I reached the bank and began to follow the line of the ancient bargees' track, the moon bathing the solitude and desolation of the marsh in a soft glow. Then Cassius, walking at my side, glanced back and gave a low growl. He feared nothing on two or four legs, but the thick mane of hair on his neck bristled and stood almost vertical. He was looking at something behind us, something which I could not see. He wrinkled his lip and snarled again. I felt my own scalp begin to prickle, for everything seemed to have gone very quiet: no moorhen clucked, no duck wing broke the silence and no breeze rattled the dry sedge. Then I was mindful of the old legend and I hurried along the bank, not exactly running, but a bit sharpish nonetheless.

It seemed that, after all, supermarket man was not immune to the ancient, atavistic fears for the terrible hound of the fen had, I sensed, been close to me that night. If I felt a twinge of fear, then how much more susceptible to such fancies was that poor girl who died a century before. I left the marsh and hurried to The Swan to seek out the comfort of their blazing logs, and the laughter of untroubled men.

Demon worship is never far away, even invading that troubled outpost of Christianity, Crowland Abbey. In AD 869 the monks dabbled in pagan rites and practised black masses even in front of the high altar while their gentle but weak Abbot closed his ears and eyes to what was going on and prayed in his cell. On Christmas Eve in that year, the wicked monks succeeded in calling up Lucifer himself in a clap of thunder which struck dead Brother Jerome, scorching the hair round his tonsure as though by electricity. The Devil claimed Crowland for his own, as it had been before St Guthlac wrested it from him, and predicted that within twelve months not one stone of the abbey would be left standing on another.

Some months later, Brother Cornelius on watch from the high tower saw a speck and then another, then a cluster approaching over the waters, advancing over the mere and up the silver stripe of the river. Soon the glint of armour was seen and wild cries floated over the water to the trembling monks. The great bell tolled the alarm, but the savage

Shock-headed willows of great age guard many dykes and mark field boundaries

Vikings landed, cut down the Abbot at the altar, and sought out and butchered the cowering monks. Then a thin trickle of smoke leaked through a chancel window and a crackle of flames rattled dryly along the cloister until with a roar, fire burst from every corner and the main tower came crashing down. The invaders loaded the booty onto the hawk-billed ships and chanting fierce paeans of victory sailed away from those blackened ruins. The curse and the prophecy had been fulfilled.

Lady Godiva and Earl Leofric's favourite son was to become a famous rebel and a bright legend in the fens in general and the Isle of Ely in particular. He made his reputation in France and Scotland before retreating to the fenny wastes to harry the Normans by firing the reeds to smoke them out, luring them into bottomless swamps, striking when least expected and vanishing into the reeds whence he had come. The Normans built wooden causeways over the marsh, but they sank under the weight of mailed soldiers and horses. For years after, the fenmen were dragging the remains of armed knights out of the mire.

The tales of Hereward's feats are as legion as those of Robin Hood. He was a symbol of resistance and refusal to bow to the tyrant, who caught the imagination of his contemporaries and successive generations so that, to this day, visitors travel to see the remains of his castle at Bourne.

When the Norman laid siege to Ely, gazing across the marsh at the high tower from the nearest high point at Stuntney, not all the residents were opposed to him. Some monks decided to strike a bargain with William and one of them sneaked out at night, crossed the bog and promised to lead the invaders across the marsh in return for which he would be made Abbot of Ely. So it was done. The Normans wrapped their weapons in sacking and followed the traitor across quaking bog, stepping from tussock to tussock along the winding track that was known only to a few locals.

Hereward was away in Lincolnshire at the time, and Ely fell with but a token resistance. The false monk came whining to William for the promised reward. William called for the Abbot's throne and set the wretched man upon it, placed the ring on his finger, the crozier in his hand, the cope round his shoulders and the mitre on his head. With due solemnity he declared the man Abbot of Ely. In his next breath he commanded that the new Abbot be taken out and hanged, because such was the proper treatment for a traitor. An invading ruler who combined a sense of justice, pragmatism and a sense of humour was sure of success. The Norman Conquest alone peopled the fens with enough unhappy ghosts to give the lonely marshes, and even the wide fields, a sense of brooding forboding, especially when autumn fogs roll in from the beds of the old meres.

Not all the spirits would be malevolent. A friendly ghost would be that of Bricstan of Chatteris, a true man of God but with enemies such as the evil Malard. Falsely accused in the reign of Henry I he was imprisoned in the most wretched conditions and his wife tortured. He was visited in his foul cell by St Etheldreda, her sister Saxburga and St Benedict, whereat his fetters fell off. On the orders of Queen Matilda who heard of the miracle, Bricstan was released, became a monk at St Etheldreda's Abbey at Ely and the remains of his fetters hung on the wall as holy relics. The rascally Malard was charged with heresy and burned at the stake.

Sometimes I wonder if it was his ghost who saved a fowler from certain drowning on the tidal marsh at Holbeach in Lincolnshire. Two men had gone out in fog to flight the geese, one staying close to the sea wall, the other opting to go far out on the mud where he felt he would have a better chance. Tom set off into the fog, leaving Tony with his pipe in the safety of the creek. The geese flighted, but neither man had a shot, for the skeins were to left or right of them. Tony waited for Tom to return and began to grow anxious for a big tide was due and the fog grew no thinner.

Eventually, to his relief, the shadowy bulk of his friend loomed up through the murk. Tom reported that he had been lost and, completely disorientated, had set off in completely the wrong direction, actually walking towards the making tide instead of away from it. It could have been a fatal error but luckily he met another fowler, a parson whose dog collar flashed white at the throat of his oilskin. After some remonstrance, Tom was at last persuaded that he was walking in the wrong direction if he wished ever to see the sea wall and his friends again.

The two walked off together, saw where the worried Tony stood on the bank, and hurried towards him. 'I wouldn't have got off if it hadn't have been for my mate, the parson here,' said Tom, turning to indicate his saviour. 'What mate?' said Tony, peering this way and that. There was no one to be seen: the mysterious cleric had vanished completely and, when the two men cast about them, they saw not two but only one set of footprints leading in from the muds. Often I reflect that it may well have been the good Bricstan, a man full of kindnesses and generous deeds, who in modern clerical dress and not his monk's habit, had guided Tom to safety that night.

Tom could count himself fortunate that he had not met the infamous Simon Greenleaf, squire of Nut Hall at Quadring on that night out there alone on the muds. Greenleaf was a rich man but he was addicted to black magic. He planned to replace the pitcher of holy water used by the parson for christenings with a hell brew he had concocted which would destroy the soul of any infant baptised in it. He was found by the villagers next morning, sprawled over a tomb, his own pitcher smashed over his head, a mark of fire on his breast, his face besmirched with his hell brew and on it a look of such terror as to make the strongest onlooker blanch.

Sometimes an old fen fowler had the opportunity to better himself but, then as now, he found that a new prosperity was his undoing. Just such a one was John Leaford of Oxlode who lived in a rough mud hut at the foot of the bank; it was a poor place with rough mud walls, a little horn window pane and a dank smoky interior. There he lived in the same style as many of his neighbours, racked with ague, tortured with endemic coughs, weakened by poisonous fogs and a damp climate. His face was pallid as he crouched over his fire of cowdung in his dark hut, an old cloak round his shoulders, chewing opium as an antidote to his perpetual rheumatism.

When the weather was fine he worked at clearing dykes and doing his share of building up and strengthening the flood banks. When the winter floods spread over the land, he took to his punt and big gun and plied the fowler's craft. However, a series of mild winters and kindly summers caused his crops to prosper. He bought a field, sowed again and it seemed that every grain bore fruit. He believed that the floods, the old enemy, were beaten and tamed at last.

John Leaford grew rich and built himself a handsome red-brick house with real glass in the windows. He bought cattle, hired teams of labourers and waxed fat, illiterate and unlearned though he was. No longer did he bother to maintain the banks, but put his large team of workers to tilling his new fields. He was not a popular man, but proud and overbearing, wearing his new-found wealth badly and known in Oxlode as 'the rich fool'.

Then came a bad winter with days and nights of torrential rain and a gale from the south. The neglected banks sprang a thousand leaks and in vain did John Leaford summon his workforce to repair the damage. Too late, for the bank burst and the farm and most of the parish was submerged. As far as the eye could see lay open water with flotsam bobbing on the choppy surface. Gulls screamed and tossed while the new jerry-built house collapsed like a house of cards. John's old hut, however, withstood the flood and only then did he realise the extent of his folly.

He had taken the men from their legitimate work in order to advance his own fortunes and now they cursed him for it, for he had set back the reclamation of Oxlode Fen by twenty years. He went back to the old fowling life and lived once more in his battered hut. Aesop could doubtless have made a telling moral from the tale for it contains many of the original seeds of human folly. Today the great bank at Oxlode stands secure, safe and well maintained by more reliable hands than those of poor, deluded John Leaford all those years ago. Some of the locals claim that on a windy night when the river is brim full, the ghost of John Leaford may be seen, flitting from place to place along the bank, beckoning wildly to teams of invisible labourers to come with pick, shovel and bags of clay to shore up the crumbling ramparts.

Another fenland victim was an old gunner called Joseph Hempsall who lived in Soham Fen but liked the beer at The Five Miles From Anywhere, No Hurry, at Upware. His profession meant that he knew the dangerous swamps better than any man and he had no fears of tramping across the marsh every evening and back later, a few pints to the worse. The route was far quicker than the long road round, but more dangerous, for it skirted the notorious Big Bog; despite this Joseph preferred his short cut and sometimes guided other adventurers by the same way. He brought several folk safely home to Soham, crossing the dykes with his old-fashioned leaping pole and sensing his way past the treacherous outskirts of Big Bog.

On one Christmas Eve a sudden fog arose, so thick that even the old gunner could see barely a yard in front of him. The regulars at The Five Miles tried to dissuade him from taking the short cut home, but he would have none of it. 'I be a'gooin by the way I knows,' he insisted stubbornly, and set off with his hurricane lamp: the murk swallowed him in a moment. For three days nothing was heard of Hempsall, but the dense fog had turned day into night so that no one dared seek out his lonely, fowler's cottage to see if he were safe.

The fog cleared, and one Elijah Boggers set out to visit the old man. Halfway there, Hempsall appeared, not his usual cheery self, and fell into step beside Elijah. They reached the cottage and the creature spoke in terrible tones: 'Go not in there – my body lies in Big Bog: as I am now, so one day wilt thou be. I drowned in Big Bog on the first night of the fog – go to Eaudyke for there lies my body.'

Trembling with fright, poor Elijah hunted in Big Bog and sure enough, there he found Hempsall's body up to its armpits in the swamp, plastered with slime and on its face was a look of such unspeakable horror that Elijah ran for his life, not stopping until he had reached the bar of The Five Miles. A search party set out, but Elijah could not be persuaded to join them. They hunted in vain and again the spectre of Hempsall led them to his corpse and again it spoke: 'Fear not – as I am now, so must ye all be. Recover my body from the west side of Big Bog and bury it in Wicken churchyard.' The speaker faded and vanished. The party recovered its composure, set off towards the bog and found the body just as Hempsall had described it. They dragged it out with a rope and took it back for burial.

They buried him not as he had asked in Wicken, but in his native Soham, so his ghost still haunts those desolate levels and will not lay at rest until he is re-buried in Wicken churchyard. Strange groans may be heard over those fields where now corn and sugar beet grow. Some say they are caused by the natural settling of recently reclaimed marsh, but others attribute them to the final desperate gasps and strangled cries of poor Joseph Hempsall as the Big Bog sucked him down and stopped his mouth with mud.

I was shooting marsh pheasants on that same ground. It was late autumn and the first frost of the year had tinted the willows with yellow, but the sun shone warmly enough. I had tramped hard all day, not meeting another human being, carrying my own bag, shooting what I found, leaping dykes and quartering the metallic-green sugar-beet leaves like an old setter. Partridges sprang in chirruping covies and sometimes I kicked a pheasant from a rough, hairy dyke at the end of the field.

Walking thick sugar beet is hard going, the sun was warm and the bag heavy. The sun was already swimming down in a blood-orange sea spread over the western horizon and I was far from my bicycle. Belatedly I sat down for a breather before starting the long tramp back. I drank a bottle of beer and ate a hunk of bread and cheese as I sat with my back to a gnarled and ancient willow which leaned dangerously over the green water of the dyke. I lit a pipe and watched the pageant of the setting sun as it put on a kaleidoscope especially for my benefit.

I smoked and watched the sky through my fumes, my eyes half closed, body weary and the beer soothing and relaxing in my stomach. I must have drowsed, for when I awoke my pipe was cold, the sun had gone, it was all but dark and I was shivering. I put on my coat and hunted round for my bag and gun. Just as I stretched to ease my stiffness I heard it. Deep down from the bowels of the earth it seemed to come, a deep, sighing groan like some great kraken imprisoned in a grim, subterranean cave. I froze with horror, breath pent up and there it came again, a sound to echo the first, sighing and grumbling from beneath my feet but somehow also in the air about me.

I left the scene as swiftly as had Elijah Boggers all those years before and regularly, like a waft of bitter air, that booming echo followed me until the moment I dragged my cycle from its hiding place beneath the elder bush, when the sound seemed to cease as suddenly as it had started. I have thought often since about the adventure: could it have been a lonely bittern lurking in the reeds or some great aeroplane high in the stratosphere? Was it after all the subterranean settling of land which had, a mere four generations before, been the deadly Big Bog in which, among others, the old puntgunner died? I was reluctant to espouse the theory that it was the old boy himself searching for a last resting place in Wicken churchyard, but it was, nonetheless, a disturbing experience.

In another corner of the fen lay a hidden and almost-forgotten pond. A few farm labourers knew of it and now and then a wandering entomologist or shooting man, tramping over the vast dry plain of stubble, his throat parched by the dusty silt, comes suddenly and unexpectedly on a clump of green willows. He draws nearer to the oasis and catches a glint of cool grey water between the fronds. He is tempted to take off his clothes – for there is no one there to see – and slide into the cool depths and sluice the baking dust from his face and body.

Most of our local works are connected with agriculture or with keeping at bay the Bailiff of Bedford: an unsuspected pond shows where the old dyke repairers discovered a seam of clay beneath the peat, just the stuff to hold the banks together. So they excavated a huge pit, 2 acres in extent and many feet deep, taking the spoil to reinforce the bank a mile away. The job done and the men gone, Nature moved in: dense reed colonised the margin; the pit filled with water, marsh birds dropped seeds and fish eggs, and a raft of lily pads, some notable pike, willow, thistles and water dock all established themselves and thrived, as only things on that rich soil can thrive.

It was perfect for duck, of course, not as a feeding pond for it was too deep but a day resting pond. In late autumn, when the first frosts have bitten short the leaves and the mallard are feeding on the barley stubbles, the pond is thick with duck from bank to bank. The roar of their departure is that of the night express thundering through a sleepy hamlet. Coot and moorhen scuttle and there are strange rustlings in the dry reeds.

It was not a pond for heavy bags, but a lucky fowler might come home with five or six duck and a pheasant. I ran the shooting on this estate and once was required to take a group of visiting Continental sportsmen to walk the pond, flush the duck, and have five minutes of exciting action as the birds flighted out. I sent half the party with the keeper to ring the far side, stressing how important it was that no noise should be made, far less a shot fired until the pond was completely encircled and the unsuspecting duck surrounded. My own party was to cover the near side while team A set off on its mission in the fog. My team was half deployed

A lone fen gunner can still find the remote places

Tiny settlements huddle together on the plain

when there was a distant shot: someone had fired prematurely. The duck rose with an eruption of wings, the first wave passing over the untenanted portion of bank, the second coming over my straggling group and we managed to drop seven between us, saving the operation from total disaster.

There was a severe post-mortem afterwards and the miscreant identified. The excitable Latin had, while creeping along with the others, spied a flock of starlings sitting on some straw bales. To the incredulous horror of the keeper, he had levelled his piece and fired into the thick of them, knocking out a brace, thus ruining the carefully planned stalk and the chance of a duck flush which might have produced forty birds. I was not sure whether to laugh or cry, but the last straw was when the intrepid shooter insisted that his two starlings should be retrieved from the nettles where the disgruntled keeper had thrown them, and hung on a string on the game cart with the rest of the birds. We did as he asked, but made sure that he took them home with him at the end of the day.

Hiding in the reeds, all alone on a winter's night, the pond was a different place again. The reeds rustled in an agitated way not entirely attributable to the mean little wind. There were times there when I felt my scalp prickling unaccountably, for it was a place full of old ghosts: was it Black Shuck snuffling and padding through the rushes on the far bank? Surely that was a human figure by that leaning fence post under the hawthorns. 'Hello; anyone there?' my voice echoing cold and eerie, unrecognisable as my own, across the grey ripples. There was no reply.

No doubt the fen ghosts gathered at this watering hole as did the duck and for much the same reason. It was one of the last parts of the fen which they recognised from the old days: most of the rest was now great fields, efficiently farmed, as soulless as a sack of potatoes. Little wonder that the troubled spirits and the wildfowl homed in on these last few remnants of fen with the sure instincts of animals seeking out the last eminences in time of flood.

Even when shooting over those prosaic sugar-beet fields or the boundless stubbles, I feel that the ghosts are never far away, for the fens have more than their share of them. As you tramp along with dog at heel, stand in a line of guns waiting for the first covey or plod with the beaters along some eroded, green bank, once part of an ancient drainage system, who is to say that pale-haired Saxons, dark Normans, monks, abbots, raiders, stubble-chinned Roman legionaries, merchants, Dutch dyke men, and an army of sallow-skinned fenmen – living amphibious lives like water-rats, digging ditches, cutting reeds, drying turves, herding bullocks, spearing pike and taking toll of the clamouring battalions of wildfowl – do not crowd about you?

Witches, warlocks and werewolves were once to be found in every parish and their legends linger long and die hard among the old timers who still live in the remote cottages which crouch at the foot of river banks, under a sheltering line of leaning willows, in this youngest but somehow also the oldest part of England.

Birds, Beasts and Fishes.

I was out on an early winter evening, reclining on the rushy bank of one of Vermuyden's great rivers and awaiting the mallard. The calendar showed November, but the thermometer spoke more of August, for the air was balmy and midges danced in a cloud over my hat: I kept them at bay by puffing dense clouds of tobacco smoke at them. I gazed under my hat brim at the setting sun; my gun lay over my knees, jutting out in front of me, ready for action should it be needed, but not in a manner which anticipated much serious use.

There was a flutter of tiny wings and a cock blackbird skimmed over the bank and actually settled on the muzzle of my gun. I froze into statuesque immobility and watched him. For a slow count of ten I gazed into his lustrous, black, yellow-rimmed eye and admired his trim shape and glossy black feathers, not one of them out of place. I could feel his weight, miniscule though it was, levering down the weapon. Then, with a flirt of his tail he was up and away.

This in itself was a curious and rare experience. No doubt the bird mistook the protruding barrels for a branch. Even more curious, however, was the fact that precisely the same thing happened two nights later, a mile further down the river, but this time with a robin. He and I contemplated each other for a few seconds and he too dashed off into the thicket of reeds nearby. Such a thing had never happened to me before and has not happened since: perhaps the magic and mystery of the fen was especially strong that week.

Watery country has ever been attractive to birds and, as already mentioned, the East Anglian fens, protruding into the North Sea, are a natural crossing point for migrants travelling up and down the Continent. Many learned treatises have been written about the wildlife of the fens and there cannot be a bird on the British List which has not been recorded. You can never tell what will turn up next. Only last week I discovered a sparrow hawk on the shoot. These dashing little hunters were persecuted to extinction, largely by the Edwardian keepers who believed that every hooked beak was the sign of an enemy. The little musket had taken up residence in a belt of poplars near the pheasant feeder and every day, it being winter, he took a blackbird or a yellowhammer from the flocks which gathered for the corn. I wished him well, for we had more than enough pheasants and he was welcome to the odd chick, should he stay until spring.

Kestrels are now common and nest in hollow willows or stacks of straw bales. It is hard to look anywhere across the levels and not see the tiny speck which is the windhover, hanging on the breeze and scanning the ground for the field voles which it loves. As I fed the pheasants in thick snow I began to feel like St Francis, for clouds of brother blackbirds, finches, tits, robins and sister yellow buntings dogged my footsteps, their natural fear of Man blunted by their hunger. It was only to be expected that the predators should also move in and prey on them. Once I found a blackbird freshly killed by the spar hawk, the tell-tale gash across his back showing where the talons had slashed him.

The harriers too have made a cautious return, and they too have adapted to a fen landscape of regimented fields which their ancestors would not have recognised. Sadly, the Montagu's harrier, the 'blue hawk' of the old marshmen is still very rare with possibly only half-a-dozen breeding pairs in the country, but even they pass over occasionally in the quiet, early mornings while the commuters are still abed.

The hen harrier is a good example of Nature working at her most subtle. As in most birds of prey, the female is considerably larger than the male. Early in spring, the female incubates the eggs while the small, agile male uses his speed to catch what small birds and rodents he can to feed her on the nest. Later in the year, after the eggs have hatched, the parents change roles, the male tending to and brooding the chicks and the female doing the hunting, her greater bulk enabling her to take young rabbits, moorhens and mallard to feed the growing brood. The rabbits were not available earlier in the year and nor were they needed, so

the behaviour of the two birds matches perfectly the requirements of the family with the food available and the partner best equipped to take it.

There was a roost of hen harriers alongside the wash bank at Sutton in the fen. I had often noticed harriers flying round the spot on a winter's evening, but it was a local, amateur ornithologist who established that they roosted there. I went down one dark evening to spy on them and sheltered in the lee of a massive oaken gatepost. At last light I became aware of dark shadows, not wafting in high but flitting over the bank, almost parting the long grass with their beaks, and settling quickly in the tangle of osiers and scrub on the half-flooded marsh. They arrived from all over the county, for there was one handsome male bird with two of his secondary feathers missing, a gap as sure an identification as a thumb print. His hunting ground, I happened to know, was down on Swaffham Prior Fen, 25 miles away as a harrier flies. These beautiful, savage birds, usually such lonely buccaneers, sought each other's company at roosting time and had formed their own club for crusty old gentlemen, down on that forgotten corner. The last remnants of a neglected and lost world, it pleases the fancy to reflect that it is for that reason that they forgather in the lonely winter evenings.

Every year, according to my old friend Colonel Mitchell, the former Warden of Wicken Fen, a knowledgeable pedestrian walking along Trinity Street in Cambridge, gazing at the heavens instead of watching the traffic, will see an osprey, high above, on his migration. I can well believe it, for barely a year passes without one staying in the fens for a few weeks, raiding the squire's trout pond, or seeking more homely fish from the lodes. Before the fen was drained they must have been a common sight. Only last year, while fishing on the great Huntingdon lake of Grafham Water, did I see an osprey, sailing on canopy wings over a quiet lagoon. I put the binoculars on him in time to see him plummet into the water in a burst of white spray. He missed his strike, but it was, nonetheless, a stirring sight.

Other raptors seen include a hobby which appeared as a miniature blue thunderbolt from over a wood and dashed through a party of swifts and martins which were hawking insects as they trickled off the water. He too failed to make a kill, but he was probably only sporting with them, for a hobby is the only raptor fast and agile enough to take a swift on the wing.

All the British owls may still be found in the fens. The decline in numbers of hollow trees and old barns and ever faster and faster road traffic has caused the most beautiful of them, the barn owl, to dwindle sadly. When I was a lad in the rambling country vicarage near the church, our kitchen window overlooked the vestry on top of which was a

Little owl; an unwelcome import, introduced by an early Duke of Bedford

Gothic, mullioned, false chimney. A barn owl nested in it for many years; the snoring and wheezing of the ullets, and the parents returning at 5-minute intervals with rat after rat from the stackyard, were the annual companions of boyhood. Poor Miss Russell, who lived in a great house of Dutch-drainer origin down on the fen, had barn owls actually in her own chimney. One evening she made a routine visit to the bathroom to find a rather soot-grimed barn owl glaring down at her like an old witch, from the top of the cistern.

As already mentioned, the traditional fen owl is the short-eared owl, a Scandinavian migrant who arrives before the floods. Many a time have I been waiting for duck down on the marsh and one of these mothy, soft birds has come and hovered a few feet above my head, gazing down full of curiosity at the upturned moon of my face. I knew that I was perfectly safe, but could not suppress a slight flicker of fear that the owl might swoop down and attack me. Did not that king of bird photographers Eric Hosking lose the sight of one eye to a strike by a tawny owl he was studying? I had heard also of other lonely fowlers who had had their hats carried off by owls – or so they said – so when a short-eared hovered too attentively, I waved my arms to shoo it away.

Sometimes one would nest in the litter of the Bedford Levels, one even nesting on my own little parcel of land which I considered to be a great honour. Like all owls, they could be quite aggressive in defence of nest and territory, so I did not care to venture too close. After the ullets had flown I inspected the flattened platform of reeds which had been the nest, well splashed with white mutes and peppered with regurgitated pellets. Later in the autumn, when hunting marsh pheasants in the rushes, I saw no less than seven short-eared owls hawking and wheeling over the place. I wondered if they were my own little family party.

Small birds are easily overlooked, especially by the fowler whose knowledge tends to focus on the larger, more easily identifiable species. Flocks of small, twittering birds scattering into the reeds like a handful of brown pennies shot from a gun are easily dismissed as 'finches'. Among them may be a snow bunting, rosy pastor or a bearded tit. The old marsh gunners had an eye for a rarity and would pursue them eagerly for they fetched a good price from the taxidermists. They went to the lengths of loading their big guns with dust shot and firing into the tight, feathery

(above right) *Beam pumping engine used to drain the fens; this one is at Stretham*
(below right) *A lonely fen farm under a wild sky*

balls which were family parties of bearded tits clinging together for warmth as they roosted in the reeds at night.

The fens are well endowed with game birds. Time was, in the carelessly farmed, weedy, overgrown fields of the bad old days when the European quail was common. The cock bird's cheery cry of 'wet-my-lips' ringing over the unkempt stubbles of an evening was a lullaby for many a fenland youngster. The Chatteris gunners thought little of going out with their long guns and in a short afternoon shooting seven or eight brace of plump, little quail. Today even a Chatteris man would tramp many a weary mile before he heard that rusty chirrup or saw a bevy spring like whirring, brown, electric butterflies from the sunny side of a hawthorn hedge. The quail loves not the ways of the modern, cost-effective farmer. I kept a pen of quail on my lawn for many years. They were cheery and undemanding friends who laid a great many eggs and asked little in return save a degree of protection from a life, outside their pen, which had passed on too quickly for their comprehension and left them behind. Despite being the latest of a long line of hand-reared birds, they had not forgotten the ancient instincts of their ancestors. Let the shadow of a crow or even a gull fall across the pen and the whole bevy stuck its chins on the ground and its tails in the air, trusting to its stripy camouflage to save it as the old enemy passed overhead.

The pheasant has been so often claimed to have been introduced by the Romans that it must be spurious! There is no reason why the pheasant should not have been an indigenous species, for it loves marshy country and, Romans or not, has been a native of the fen country since the earliest chronicler put quill to parchment. Even in my boyhood it was not a common bird for, rather as in Peter Hawker's eighteenth-century Hampshire, the whisper that one had been seen in the parish was enough to have every cottager reaching for a rusty fowling piece. A pheasant tends to be conspicuous in the vast open spaces of the fens and it was not too difficult to drive it into the nearest cover, walk it up and shoot it as it went clattering away.

The emergence of the reared pheasant as a sporting proposition, together with its propensity to roam far from home, populated the fens with new stocks so that today it is the commonest game bird. It thrives on the light soil, clement weather, sugar-beet fields and stubbles of the fens and is so well established, thanks to the shooting man, that its future is assured. Another matter is the remaining stocks of the old breed, birds half the size of their hand-reared cousins, inhabiting the

(left) *Snowy afternoon on the Cam*

Pheasant shooting is excellent in the fens, but once the bird was a rare sight

forests of reed, trusting to their legs rather than their wings for safety and leading even the keenest gundog on a one-sided game of catch-me-if-you-can in the thickets. Many a weary hour have I spent in pursuit of these wily escapologists, my dog of the day snorting on a red-hot scent which dodges this way and that, myself panting along behind, stung by flies and tormented by a tangle of rush, bog, dyke and fallen trees.

Just occasionally dogged persistence was rewarded and the bird would find himself in a cul-de-sac. Even then he was likely to fly out in a way which placed a bush or a forest of feather-headed reeds between him and you; but if you were lucky and knocked him down in a tumbled flurry of red, black and gold against the tawny tangle, you felt a real sense of achievement, far more so than after having shot twenty 'tame' pheasants on a covert shoot. To walk home on an autumn evening with the weight of that one bird in your bag and his long tail poking out under your arm was to feel a thrill and sense of triumph. What matter if, when you plucked him later, every feather was fixed to his body as if by Superglue or that his spurs were like scimitars or that he was about as tender, when cooked, as a fen-slodger's boot?

The strutting pheasant being tough, hardy and adaptable, has filled the gap left by the gradual demise of the grey partridge. In the first decade of the century a team of guns at Holkham in Norfolk shot two thousand of them in two days, all wild birds and no more than a reasonable cull from the six coveys which inhabited every rough-grazed field or neglected stubble. It was the bird of my own boyhood, and the warm Septembers were spent with dog and gun quartering the potato fields where fat hen, redshank and willow weed made ideal feeding and cover. Walking from ridge to ridge gave one a steady, rhythmical stride, rather like that learned by the old railway gangers who walked from sleeper to sleeper for most of their working lives.

Just when least expected, a covey of the brown birds would be up and away, scattering over the brown haulms; it was hard to pick one out as they were gone and out of range unless you were quick to aim. If you knocked one down you marked well the place it fell since, especially in dry, scentless conditions, you did not trust your well-meaning but – truth to tell – rather inadequate labrador to find it for you. If the bird was lost, I would drop a white handkerchief on a tall weed near the place and walk round it until either the dog or I made the retrieve.

I would be hard put to it now to bag a dozen grey partridge walking-up on an autumn afternoon, despite the fact that this type of shooting is falling from favour. At that time of year there are many young birds in the coveys; they are the last to rise and thus are most frequently shot.

A covey of grey partridge in the snow; they are hardy birds

Ideally it is the old birds which should be taken and they are best shown by driving. Modern farming has reduced the grey partridge to a few scattered pairs in country where once they were more common than sparrows. The less attractive French or red-legged partridge is an introduced species, but it is in every way a lesser bird than the grey, being a dilatory parent, once-only flyer and aggressive holder of a territory. To its credit, it is easy to rear and is an adaptable bird which has come to terms with most of the horrors of modern agriculture.

The grey is a staunch parent, defending its nest against marauding stoat or cat; it is a constant spouse for sometimes a cock who has lost his mate will, singlehandedly, incubate the eggs and bring a brood to maturity. A grey can be very trusting when on the nest, sometimes allowing herself to be handled without taking fright. A keeper told me a delightful tale of a grey partridge which nested in a cottage garden on his estate. The old lady who lived there regarded the bird as a family pet and had placed near the nest two fish-paste jars, one full of corn, the other of water, in case the incubating hen felt peckish. Later a series of torrential storms washed out every grey-partridge nest on the estate, but the lady had jabbed an umbrella into the ground so that her pet was protected. That was the only nest in the parish to hatch successfully that year.

It would be a sad comment on modern times if the chirrup of that most English of game birds were, because of our systematic rape of the countryside, to follow the dry rattle of that other farming casualty, the corncrake, into oblivion and the memories of old men.

I did see a corncrake, only once, when I was walking in my beloved potato fields after the partridge. A curious russet-rumped bird sprang and flew low ahead of me, just clearing the reedy fringe along the far dyke. A careful check in the bird book on my return home proved conclusively that it had been a crake. I have never seen another, and I doubt if, at the time of my sighting, there was such another in the whole of the fens. I once saw a pair of quail in much the same circumstances. I raised the gun to them, believing them to be partridges, but I realised my error before firing. As is characteristic with these birds they pitched a short way up the field, as suddenly and steeply as they had sprung. I have heard of other odd sightings and someone once brought me a dead one which I had stuffed. It is hard to say if they were descendants of the old fen quail or escaped reared birds.

I have mentioned my very few sightings of that voice of the undrained fen, the 'mire drum' or 'bull-o'-the-bog' as the old marshmen called the bittern, owing to its eerie, echoing, booming roar. At the time of Vermuyden, such a sound would have been permanently in the ears of the fen dwellers. Lacking the power to change, chancy and exclusive feeders, demanding large territories and intolerant of disturbance, they dwindled and all but vanished as the waters drained away.

Its cousin the heron is far more common, a frequent sight as it flies on canopy wings across a low fen sky. It is adept at fishing in the man-made cuts, dykes and rivers, spearing eels deftly, wrestling with them and finally managing to swallow that writhing, slimy serpent. A heron will often strike at and kill fish far too large for it to swallow, giving its victim a deft but deadly stab on the head as it cruises by. Like the bittern, the heron was once a popular bird on the table, roast 'crane' being the dish that you saved for the important occasion. Farm lads had an effective way of catching a heron. He saw one standing far off, a ragged emaciated bundle of grey feathers fishing in the drain. The bird might make a catch, that long neck becoming a darting snake, a deadly rapier as it speared a small roach.

While it was thus preoccupied, the boy would make an invisible approach, by no means easy, as the bird usually fished in a place whence

Bewick's swans apply the air-brakes

it could command an all-round view. By using every scrap of broken ground, each clump of rush and fallen willow, a lucky lad might creep within a few feet of the unsuspecting bird. Then he would leap up with a mighty bellow and a waving of his arms so that the heron, normally such a shy bird, was startled out of its wits and fell down, literally in a faint. The boy would nip out smartly and bag it before it could recover its wits.

Herons are among the first birds to nest in spring. I once did a great deal of pigeon-roost shooting in a wood which held a heronry and you could smell the accumulated guano and remnants of fish half a mile away, downwind.

This book is, sadly, not a learned treatise on the birds of the fens, but rather it seeks to capture the essence of the curious birds which live or lived once in the wild marshes. Oddities such as the water rail with its stuck-pig scream; the swift which sets no foot on a solid object for twelve continuous months; the grebes, warblers, woodpigeons, electric-blue kingfishers, swans, ruffs, dusky redshanks; the spoonbill I saw looking like a white ghost as I stalked to within yards of him in my gunning punt; the peregrine which shot like a cross-bow bolt over my head, a wanderer from more rugged, mountainous country – each is a story itself: this is not the place to tell it. The old fen gunner would have shot down any one of them, and been glad of the chance of a square meal or a few shillings for its skin. His modern counterpart may but gaze and admire, for his list of quarry species is, very properly, strictly limited.

The fens were never as rich in animal life. In ancient times great herds of red deer haunted the marshy islands. Every autumn the locals herded them into a trap or drove them into swampy ground, strolling casually among the exhausted animals, selecting the fattest and slitting their throats. Open marsh tends not to be good harbourage for any mammal which likes a dry bed at night. The amphibious otter was a notable exception, equally at home in water and on land, and with more than enough fish in the ancient meres and marshes to satisfy them all. The otter was deemed to be as much fish as flesh and could therefore be eaten with impunity on a Friday, but from my knowledge of the *Mustelidae*, it must have been pretty rank fare, even for a hungry fen tiger. Otters were probably common in the old times, and an otterskin cap was standard wear for many marshmen, valued for its warm and waterproof qualities.

The animal was persecuted by the fenmen who caught them in nets – even today otters are tragically drowned in eel bow nets – chased them with dogs or transfixed them with pike darts. When I was a lad, an otter was rumoured to have a holt in the cavernous hollow on the waterline of a giant, leaning willow. It certainly looked a likely place, and although I looked at it every time I found myself in those remote parts, I never saw

Otter; once common in the fens, now all but extinct

signs of occupation. The only otter I have seen on the fen was on a sultry autumn evening when I was tench fishing. My red, quill float had been undisturbed for an hour when I heard a soft, low whistle. A moment later a dark head arrowed across the pewter ripples, the vee of its wake spreading ever wider. Then it dived, rolling smoothly forward and down, the rudder of its tail just breaking the surface before it vanished. I saw it no more that night and have never seen one since.

The otter now is a rare creature in places where once it was common. There are many reasons for its decline: they include riparian disturbance by mostly urban weekenders, pollution from farms and factories, vandalism, and the increasing popularity of match coarse angling. He can count himself lucky indeed who catches sight of an otter or hears its liquid whistle in the gloaming. The sight of a family party of young otters playing and sliding down their muddy water chute, splashing time and again into the water, like children on a playground slide, is vouchsafed to even fewer.

The fox is a comparatively recent immigrant to the fens, its rising star matching, although unconnected with, the eclipse of the otter. When I was a lad, a fox in the fen was as unusual as a pheasant in the fen and just as much cause for comment. An earth was discovered in the cinder bank which once carried the railway line on which our beloved 'Fenland Flyer' ran twice a week with its cargo of milk churns, baskets of eggs, bushels of runner beans and cut flowers. The vixen had made a snug, dry earth, but a local keeper ambushed her one night, and that was the end of that attempt at colonisation.

Eventually the national explosion in the fox population made it inevitable that the spread would continue into the fens. The dry, soft soil made it possible to dig out a good earth with no trouble, game birds abounded and rabbits had staged a recovery from myxomatosis. Foxes moved in with a vengeance and now most fen farms hold an earth or two. The locals view them with mixed feelings. A fox represents the key element of another man's sport as well as keeping down rats and rabbits. On the debit side he is an inveterate nest robber taking a sitting hen pheasant or partridge together with its nest and doing tremendous damage in that way in May. Anyone who has suffered a nocturnal fox raid in hen run or on duck pond will know, to their cost, how a fox will kill indiscriminately, chopping a bird, allowing it to fall and turning to the next until a hundred lie dead and dying. A fox will also take new-born lambs, rob duck nests and catch songbird fledglings.

We have well-used fox earths on our shoot, and the entrance to each is a carpet of game-bird feathers, bones, rabbit skins, the feet of hares, egg shells, the remains of wings and other tragic debris. The vixen delivers her cubs in the earth, suckling them for a few days, but then she moves out and lives 'rough', bringing them food at night. She does not care to be followed when she leaves the earth. I saw once a vixen bring a rabbit to a litter of cubs. She left it for them, saw that all was well and trotted away up the field. One cub bolder than the rest set off to follow her. The youngster had gone about fifty yards when the vixen turned, glared at the wanderer and hissed like a cat. The miscreant stopped in its tracks and scuttled straight back home after this admonishment.

A vixen whose earth is disturbed by a real or even an imaginary intruder, will move the cubs that very night to one of a series of other earths which she has prepared for just such an eventuality. She carries the cubs, one at a time, by the scruff of the neck, for as much as a mile to a 'safe house'.

A fox will often show on a pheasant shoot, bolted from sugar beet, from long stubble or a spinney. In non-hunting country it is considered permissible for a shooter to take the opportunity this presents, although there are many who do not care to do so, while the old school of sportsmen place vulpicide second only to regicide in the catalogue of crimes against God and Man. A keeper will, more discreetly, set snares in well-used runs or gas the earths, simply because he cannot spare his carefully husbanded stocks of birds just to feed foxes. He does this in the knowledge that a fox removed from a territory this year will be replaced by another one next year, for Nature abhors a vacuum, and a slight over-population on the farm next door will quickly fill the gap. My own view is that a farm without a fox is a poor sort of place but I am not prepared to feed, at my expense, unlimited numbers of them. Rest assured, the fox is the new resident of the reclaimed fen, and he is here to stay.

Two even less welcome newcomers are the mink and the coypu; St Guthlac would have been familiar with neither of them. Both are escapees which have found life in the wild to their liking; both have an instinct for survival and both have become unmitigated nuisances about which it is hard to find anything good to say. Their only possible redeeming feature is that both are comparatively easy to catch in cage traps.

The coypu is a native of South America and was farmed in the UK as nutria for the fur trade. It went out of fashion and the stock escaped to live an amphibious life in the remote dykes and reed beds, emerging at night to strip whole fields of sugar beet. Apart from Man, their only population controller is a hard winter which locks away their food supply and their channels of communication beneath the ice. Their crop depredations became so severe that special trappers were employed to keep down their numbers. I celebrated the acquisition of my new 15-shot pump-action Winchester .22 rifle by shooting two of them in one of Vermuyden's rivers. I had heard it rumoured that the skins were still worth something, so I skinned them carefully, and a dirty, smelly job it was, pegging out the pelts in the sun to dry. Alas for my hopes of cartridge money; no eager purchasers rushed forward and eventually one of my skins was eaten by the dog, and in a mood of depression, I threw away the other.

Even less attractive is the mink, predator supreme, escaped from fur farms or deliberately released by Animal Liberation fanatics. The mink can swim, climb trees, explore tunnels and travel fields. Where they establish a territory no water vole swims, duck or moorhen nests, and every ground-nesting bird in the area goes in danger of its life. The mink is easily caught in a trap and one family group will hold a large territory, keeping out other mink, so at least there is little risk of a concentration of them. The mink is also a deadly killer of fish while, in a pheasant release pen, one will do as much damage as a fox.

Stoats and weasels abound; unlike the mink these fearsome little hunters are indigenous, and they kill rabbits, mice and rats as often as partridge chicks. I was once afforded a rare glimpse of Nature in the raw

Field mouse; staple diet for many predators but not encouraged by modern farming

when a weasel ran down a furrow in a ploughed field; it had a mouse in its mouth and I watched it through the binoculars. Then, with a dash of wings and flash of grey, a female kestrel swooped on the weasel, fastening needle talons across its back. For a moment, bird, weasel and mouse became airborne, but the weight was too great and the weasel dropped the mouse and twisted, struggled and bit at its assailant but, luckily for the kestrel, unable quite to reach it with its rat-trap teeth. The bird realised it had over-estimated the task and released the weasel, but the event might give food for thought to those who claim that a kestrel will never attack anything bigger than a black beetle.

Stoats are great rabbit-killers, a stoat selecting a victim, invariably the best and healthiest rabbit, and pursuing it steadily, relentlessly wearing down its victim – psychological as much as physical warfare. It may pass other rabbits during the pursuit; they may lollop out of the way, but no more, for the stoat will not change from one to another. Eventually the rabbit, which set off so confidently, gradually becomes more and more demoralised, slows its pace and finally stops, trembling with terrified, bulging eyes, waiting for the deadly bite on the neck. The old countryman knew that, if he could get to a stoat-struck rabbit within a couple of minutes of hearing the scream of the victim, he was sure of a good dinner, for he knew that the stoat chose only the best.

Sometimes the worm turns and the victim defends itself vigorously. Just as the needle teeth sink in, a rabbit suddenly dashes away into a dense bramble patch, whether by design or in blind panic it is hard to tell, but it has the desired effect of dashing off the attacker, and tumbling him in the grass. Once I saw an old buck rabbit, with a stoat

clinging to its neck, launch a mighty kick with its powerful back legs and knock the attacker several feet away into the stinging nettles and thus make his well-deserved escape.

Frogs and toads must have once been so common in the fens as to form almost a living carpet in some places. The ancient chroniclers who recorded the dense clouds of ferocious mosquitos hanging above the great meres, wrote also of the choruses of frogs, massed choirs of guttural songsters which filled the spring and summer evenings with their lovesongs. The endless miles of solitude, turgid waters and unlimited insect food must have made the old fen a frog paradise. In their turn they formed a vital link in the food chain, for herons, bitterns, duck, geese, hawks, otters, grass snakes and pike feasted on them. Nowadays you may see one frog where once you might have seen a million: the dreaded insect sprays are responsible for a decline that is little short of complete. Here and there, in an odd corner or a quiet village dew pond, a small colony survives, existing tenuously, out of reach of the pollutants and providing sufficient tadpoles to keep a few village urchins with well-stocked jam-jars.

There was once a Frog Hall in the marsh near Whittlesea Mere, doubtless a pretentious title for what was probably no more than a wattle-and-daub hut amid the reeds. This shack was inhabited by a fowler/fisherman named Norman, possibly a descendant of the Invaders of 1066. The chronicler says of Norman:

> . . . huge ungainly, maim'd, but angler strong;
> He spreads his nets alike for pike and eels,
> Makes laws at pleasure and again repeals;
> In wild seclusion hid he lives afloat,
> With sprit and gun arranged in open boat.

Fallow deer, a woodland animal once common in the marshes

Norman had let his house be known as Frog Hall probably because frogs were the commonest creatures to be found; their croaking must have sung many an earthy lullaby for him as he lay on his rush couch.

Toads, newts, lizards, grass snakes and adders have all suffered a decline in places where once they were common sights. They too have suffered from a loss of habitats and the propensity of the modern farmer to plough and sow with wheat any little marshy corner on his farm where these creatures had their foothold. The corn he grows adds to a grain mountain which nobody wants and which costs a fortune to store. Consequently a breeding colony of grass snakes has become a thing of great rarity on a fen farm.

Sometimes a grey seal will come up on the tide, working its way well into the fens along the river system. I have seen a seal several times in the New Bedford River and, on one occasion, a trigger-happy local shot and killed one with a .22 rifle.

The undrained fens were suited to every coarse fish on the list. The slow, shallow water, equable climate and teeming insect life made for such perfect conditions that many a modern angler can only lie and dream of the great fish in that almost-virgin water. I have written of the 'hard cases' of Southery who capitalised on the fish and made a living from them in times well within the memory of the village ancients. The modern angler needs must go to great lengths to make his tackle as fine as possible with nylon little thicker than a hair, hooks of microscopic size, specially prepared baits and clouds of expensive groundbait. Failure to take these steps will mean no catch, for the modern fen fish are far more sophisticated than their ancestors.

Visitors to the aptly named Three Pickerels pub which hides just off the bridge over the New Bedford River at Mepal will, if they use their eyes, see a remarkable photograph. It is of a sturgeon caught in eel nets in July 1907, measuring almost 9ft and weighing an amazing 294lb. It required four men and a woman to haul it in. To record this remarkable catch, a photographer travelled by horse and trap the 5 miles from Chatteris to take the picture of the monster, with a row of stern-looking old fen tigers standing behind it. Ancient law required all sturgeon caught in British waters to be handed immediately to the reigning monarch, but knowing fenmen I suspect that this rare fish found its way to Billingsgate with the rest of the catch or ended up on the local tables. I wonder what a fenman, used to jellied eels, duck stew and boiled mutton would have made of caviar.

Another sturgeon was caught in the Delph in 1913: this one weighed 32 stone and fell to Jim 'Fish' Smart, the famous skater. He caught his between two fyke nets set for eels and had to shoot it before they could haul it out. They caught another in August 1924 in a net set in Hemingford Mill Pool: this one weighed 185lb and measured 8ft 2in in length. It was exhibited for some days at St Ives and later at Cambridge

until the warm weather caused it to deteriorate. 'Fish' Smart had no doubts what to do with his sturgeon: he sold it to the fishmonger for a tenner which was 'a deal o' money in them days'. It is odd to think of the great king of all fish, native of the Caspian Sea, finding its way with its cold, moonstone eyes, to the inland heart of the Cambridgeshire fens.

Other oddities include flat fish which come in on the tide, sometimes as far inland as Earith where they are caught by rod-and-line anglers with ledgering tackle. Mr Skinner, for many years the Sutton carpenter and a lusty singer in the church choir, was a noted catcher of 'flatties' which he took home and ate with relish, much to the chagrin and envy of his neighbours who could not catch them. Sometimes a salmon is caught on a pike spinner and more often a sea-trout such as the big, nine-pounder caught in the Cam a few years ago. An experiment was tried whereby sea-trout fry were released upstream in the Ouse system in the hope that they would repopulate the rivers. It was only partially successful owing to the shortage of natural, gravelly breeding redds, but now and then an odd one is caught by a lucky lad dangling a worm for more humble quarry.

There are wild, brown trout in the River Lark and the emergence in recent years of new strains of hardy, quick-growing rainbow trout has seen them stocked in many a farm pond and reservoir. Sometimes they will escape into the river and only last summer I met a boy, beaming from ear to ear and clutching a two-pounder which he had caught on a maggot in one of the lodes which the 'Roomans' had dug. Rainbow trout will not breed naturally in UK waters, but there is no reason why one might not turn up anywhere. Generally speaking, however, fenland waters are too muddy and slow moving ever to hold a good head of game fish.

A real curiosity is the eel pout or burbot, always scarce but now so rare that a national angling magazine has offered a hefty prize to anyone who can produce evidence that they have caught one. A good one may weigh up to 3lb, but it has an unprepossessing appearance with a flat head, large mouth, heavy shoulders and three feelers, one on the chin and another over each eye. They eat frogs, worms, insects, crayfish and even water rats, but their own flavour is so foul that even the most hard-bitten fen tiger would think twice before eating one. The eel pout is confined to the fen-country rivers, although it is rumoured that there are a few to be found in Yorkshire.

(above right) *Entrance to the decoy pipe at Borough Fen*
(below right) *The lodes; they have seen some exotic river traffic in their time*

A far more familiar fen fish, and one with which the whole area is closely associated, is the pike. Pike are very numerous, but they tend not to grow to record size: for the monsters you must seek in the Norfolk Broads or the Scottish lochs. However, our most famous pike was the one found threshing in the liquid mud in the last remnants of the newly drained Whittlesea Mere in 1850. This was a huge pike by any standards, weighing 53½lb, but sadly it was not caught by fair angling so it could count on no record books. There is a wooden carving of it in Huntingdon inscribed, 'Such were the giants of Fenland in the olden time'.

Run-of-the-mill pike of 20lb are not uncommon, sometimes being caught in quite small drainage channels. All the big fish are hen fish, and it is not unusual to see some monsters in spring, each with the smaller cock fish in attendance, swirling and basking near the spawning beds.

One of the best rod-caught fen pike was taken on 26 February 1957, by Col Harold Atherton OBE, in Vandervell's lake near that home of the old gunners, Welney in the Isle of Ely. By the time it was weighed it had shed six or seven pounds of spawn, but even then it weighed 36½lb. It was 49in long and had a mighty girth of 33in. Had the fish been weighed in front of witnesses and before it shed its spawn, it would have constituted a British record. A curious fact which came to light later was that Col Atherton had hooked the fish the day before but it had broken his line above the float. He returned the following day, caught his float which he discovered bobbing on the ripples, and landed the fish.

Those who think I lie may go and see for themselves the monster stuffed and displayed in a handsome glass case at that noted hostelry for wildfowlers and fenmen, the Lamb and Flag in Welney High Street. Also in the case is the trace, snap tackle and roach bait (the latter not, I guess, the original) used to bag the creature.

There is something about the pike which feeds the imagination and locals each have their favourite location wherein, to their certain and unshakeable knowledge, a monster of incalculable weight is lurking. The myths are fuelled by the pike's voracity, its willingness to have a go at anything from nudists to toy yachts, from swimming dogs to fully grown mallard, and even other pike as big as itself. That dark monster – 4ft long, lurking in the shadow of the streaming weed, still save for the rhythmic movement of its great gills, the sad, liquid jewel of its stricken deer eye gazing out above the serried ranks of needle teeth and lean

(above left) *It was a lucky fenman who could find farm work in the old days*
(below left) *A fiery sunset in Black Shuck Country*

chops, cruel and pitiless, which rake back below – is the stuff of dreams and nightmares.

Let a wounded fish waver past its lie or a mallard paddle overhead and, at a speed to bewilder the eye, that lean body shoots forward, the cavernous jaws open and from them there is no escape. There is a swirl and glimpse of a wicked wolf's head, a long flash of silver and green and the victim vanishes.

Another fish synonymous with fenland is the eel, for centuries a staple diet, a valuable source of revenue (it was not unusual for rent to be paid in so many stones of eels) and basis for whole rural economies. Sometimes they grew to enormous size such as the terrible monster found, like the great pike, threshing in the last puddles of the drained mere at Whittlesea. On that occasion fenmen paddled about in the liquid mud looking for treasure lost from boats or carrying off sacks full of stranded fish. Then, in one of the deeper holes, one of them spotted a slowly writhing blue/black back, the thickness of a man's booted leg. He called his companions to him and they gazed in disbelief at this apparition, some of them claiming it to be a water monster or sea-serpent and taking some time to realise that it was, in fact, the biggest eel ever seen. One man fetched a pitchfork and stabbed the great fish, but it gave a twitch of its coils and threw him over into the mud. However, the eel, big though he was, was at a disadvantage and he was at last dragged out, battered with a thousand blows, transfixed by a hundred forks, and stretched out on the drying mud of the mere bed. It was a tragedy that this eel was never weighed, but contemporary witnesses described it as having a head as big as a dog's and teeth which bit through the heel of a gutter boot and crushed the foot of its wearer.

Eels of more modest dimensions were taken in vast numbers from the drains, rivers and cuts. There was what amounted to a local industry of osier growers, cutters, peelers and basket makers, threading at bewildering speed the pliable willow 'straps' into hives, putcheons and grigs. Cartloads of wriggling eels, all alive-o were taken to market weekly. Poor Tom Metcalf's father was taking the result of a week's work, fully six hundredweight of eels, all the way from the fen to London. The horse stopped *en route* for a drink at a roadside stream, jerked back in alarm at a moorhen which dashed away from under its nose, a wheel came off the water cart, and all Metcalf's eels went tumbling down into the stream and freedom.

Ernie James of Welney was a mighty eel man and he set nets across the dykes: each net ran into a cod-end where the catch was kept safe. There were times when the whole cod and the net was jam-packed with eels; once he had about forty stone in one go. Over one notable summer run, he and his mate caught a whole ton in a few weeks. Sometimes he set trimmers, baited hooks in the river and the line fixed onto a springy willow wand jabbed into the bank, each one about twenty yards from the next, along a great stretch of the river.

He went one morning to check them and saw one of his trimmers rushing towards him down the stream. He hooked his pole over it, drew it in and, to his surprise, an otter popped up. He had taken a big hooked eel but as soon as it saw Ernie, it wisely let go. Once he caught two 7lb eels in two days: he sold the brace for 5/-.

Another dodge was to tie a bale of hay onto a rope and lower it into the water. Eels would discover the bale, burrow in and find a refuge there. The fisherman simply hauled out the bale and there was his catch. Groundbait was sometimes considered an advantage, rabbit guts or any offal being the favourite lure. One enterprising fenman once murdered his sweetheart in a lover's quarrel. In the true spirit of his race, and not caring to let anything go to waste, he chopped up her body and used it as groundbait; according to the locals, he caught some 'masterful, gurt, owd eels' by this means, so much so that he became the envy of the parish.

As for size, there are many records of eels in the 5–6lb class, while four-pounders were commonplace. Many big ones were taken at the time the unweighed monster of Whittlesea Mere was hauled out and battered to death. Old Cole of Holme recorded that there were times when he was almost frightened at seeing a hole in the mere bed filled with large bream and eels struggling and splashing, the eels 'ravenously fixing on the large bream as if they would devour them. So immense was the quantity of fish which died in the mud that, for days, a pestilential vapour hung over the mere, so great was the destruction of the fishery.'

Bream, tench and great roach still haunt the lodes and drains, bronze, mail-clad warriors like Norman ghosts drifting through the half-light of the green water. Bream will grow to great size in conditions which suit them so well, but for such an unintelligent fish, they can be very difficult to catch. I have seen, in one of the lodes, a shoal of bream the size of dustbin lids, which ran fully fifty yards along, from bank to bank. No-one could ever catch more than one in that clear, shallow, silted waterway without scaring the remainder.

The tench is a fish of high summer, full of associations for me of early rising while the rest of the world slept, of morning mists and a dew-soaked walk to the river bank, of vapour curling like smoke from the glassy surface, of purple loosestrife and heavy-headed reeds, of the gentle plop of a float on the water and of curious bullocks clustering round to see what I was about. When the float bobbed, ducked and slid away and you felt the kick of a two-pounder and then had him in the net, you gloated over the sight of that metallic green skin and the small red jewel of its eye.

The tench slime was said to have medicinal properties, for other fish will rub themselves against a tench when they are poorly; hence his nickname of the 'doctor fish'. I slid my tench back gently into the water whence he came. His ancestor may have swum that very water when the Dutch drainers were here: they would have eaten him fried in mutton fat, so not everything has changed for the worse.

·Punts and Pack-ice·

A hundred and fifty years ago there lay at Whittlesea, 3 miles off the Great North Road near the village of Stilton, the last of the great fen meres. Various drainage operations down the centuries had left it as one of few reminders to our great-grandfathers of how the ancient fen had looked. Three thousand acres in extent in summer drought, but much greater in winter flood, it was a place of shining water, winking ripples and acre upon acre of reeds. Charles Kingsley was one of many visitors captivated by its magic, recording that:

> . . . the coot clanked and the bittern boomed . . . While high overhead hawk beyond hawk, buzzard beyond buzzard hung motionless, kite beyond kite as far as the eye could see. Far off from the mere would rise a puff of smoke from a punt . . . then down the wind came the boom of the great stanchion gun: and after that sound, another sound louder as it neared: a cry as of all the bells of Cambridge and all the hounds of Cottesmore; and overhead rushed and whirled the skein of terrified wildfowl, screaming, piping, clacking, croaking, filling the air with the hoarse rattle of their wings, while clear above all sounded the odd whistle of the curlew and the trumpet note of the great, wild swan.

This remarkable lake became a recreation ground for the well-to-do who flocked there in great sailing vessels to admire the view, eat gargantuan picnics and take on the locals at their own sports and activities. The place was also a birdwatcher's and entomologist's dream, for here the swallowtail butterfly was common, while the now-extinct large copper fluttered and danced above the margin reeds in dense throngs. The rich visitors moored their yachts and indulged in excursions round the lake, setting trimmers for pike, hauling out eels by the bushel, catching butterflies and stealing birds' eggs.

The water level fluctuated depending on the weather, so that the fenmen who lived nearby led amphibious lives. Heathcote's bailiff, Sisman, used to draw on his fen boots when he left his bed in the morning, the floor of his cottage, as well as the legs of his bedstead being covered with water for weeks together. Bricks were piled on the hearth on which to light a fire.' Mrs Moysey, an old lady of Connington, could remember when the whole countryside was drowned for weeks at a time and the water came into her cottage and floated the ground floor. Her husband had to carry the children to the bank.

Whittlesea Mere was famous for wildfowling and, at the time it was drained, could support nine professional fowlers. Every sort of duck, goose, hawk and wader frequented the mere, while the snipe shooting was superb. A Norfolk visitor once killed 123 snipe in a single day and a week later shot 106; that was in 1860, just after the mere had been drained and while the ground was still boggy. Bitterns were as common as crows and Mr Cole thought nothing of shooting seven or eight of them in a day: he once caught two in a fishing net which accidentally entangled their feet as they walked over it.

It is remarkable to reflect that this great water existed so comparatively recently in terms of human affairs. Appold's Pump had been shown at the Great Exhibition of 1851, where it created great interest. In 1850 it had been put to work to drain Whittlesea and hurry the foaming, brown torrent away to the sea at the rate of 1,652 gallons a minute, while a small group of beaver-hatted fen squires stood on Foleaster Point and watched it go, the last, dim whisper of the old fen.

The countless fish, including the giant pike and the monstrous eel described in the preceding chapter, which lay revealed were a wonder, source of income and eventually a health hazard to the locals. In time the plough came in and threw over the first shining furrow of what was to become the richest farmland in Europe, and some strange specimens they found in that peaty soil. The almost-complete skeleton of a grampus was unearthed; an antler of the long-extinct giant red deer, bones of beaver, wolf, bear, and aurochs, all excellently preserved in the peat, came to light. Some found their way into museum collections and others onto

cottage hall-stands; no doubt a great many more were left where they lay, passed over unrecognised by the ignorant or indifferent ploughboy. A farmer friend from Upware has the whole of his farm office decorated with such ancient remains, both natural and human artefacts, which the plough has exposed on his own little farm. He once found the partially fossilised jaw-bone of a Neanderthal woman.

A most interesting find in the silt on the bed of the mere was a one-piece boat, cut out of the trunk of an oak. It was of crude construction, the thwarts being fastened on with wooden pegs, but it was perfectly preserved, merely blackened by the immersion of centuries. It was 27ft long and 3½ft wide in the middle: some nuts were found lying inside it. Nearby was a silver-gilt, boat-shaped vessel elaborately embossed with a fluted lid. The experts identified it as a salt cellar or possibly an incense container. The ram's head on the lid indicated that it had come from Ramsey Abbey. Also recovered were a silver censer and a silver chandelier on which was a decoration depicting Peterborough Cathedral.

It is interesting to conjecture in what storm or other mishap or by whom these treasures were lost. Maybe some savage Viking raiders let them slip overboard in a sudden squall, or possibly a monk capsized his frail coracle and saw, with anguish, some of the Abbey plate with which he had been entrusted sinking in the grey waters of the great mere.

Today we may feel a twinge of regret that the mere has gone, and that the black terns no longer hawk for dragonflies over its silver ripples, the hawks hang in the autumn skies nor the wildfowl rise from its surface with a roar like a great tempest. At the time, however, everyone was enthusiastic about the project. Local farmers were tired of fixing mud boards to their horses' feet before they could plough, and of harvesting

poor waterlogged crops which had to be taken by boat to drier parts. The mere drained was incomparably more valuable than the mere in its original state. As usual, the 'Bailiff' had a trick up his sleeve: a local clergyman, the only man to voice his opposition to the drainage, predicted that 'Whittlesea Mere will come back down here and drown us'. In 1862 the great Marshland Sluice blew up under the pressure of an especially high tide, the salt water rushed in, banks burst and 6,000 acres were drowned.

One of the great old fowlers, now alas gathered to his fathers, was the white-haired, wizened Walter Cross who had, in his day, shot every species of bird and animal found in the fens. It was said of him that he would have shot his grandmother if he could have earned a shilling for her leathery old hide. He was also a romantic and a romancer so that it was hard to discern which of his yarns were true and which were old wives' tales. He told me one which fell firmly into the latter category and which even my youthful gullibility refused to swallow. We sat together, him very old and me very young, on the bank of the river one drowsy summer afternoon, watching our two red, fat floats which sat motionless on the green, plate-glass water. He spoke in the lazy, drawling vernacular of the fen, pausing to roll a smoke, tamping down the tobacco with a yellow, gnarled thumbnail.

'Years ago, when I were a young chap, I was gunning pretty steady on these here old marshes. One February that came very cold, it blew, fruz and snew: the whole marsh was froze over. Lord, there was thousands of

ducks come in on the gale, the marsh was black with 'em, thicker than hairs on a cat's belly. Every day it blew more and more, and more snow came and there was ice an inch thick on this here very river where we're now a-fishing. All the ducks sat out on the ice in a huge, great, black flock. One night it thawed on top for about an hour so's water lay on the ice, but then that fruz again and went harder than ever, and all them duck still sat out there, nowhere to go and all the feeding grounds hard froze.

'Dad and me decided to try for a shot at 'em. We fixed the ice runners on the bottom of the punt and loaded the big gun with her full twenty ounces of BB shot. We poled down the open channel, dodging ice floes the size of my kitchen table; get caught between two o' them and we'd a had it sure: they'd have laid us out instead of the bag next morning, I reckon. The other boys said we was mad to go out, but Dad, he weren't scared o' nawthin'.

'We got to the ice, slid the punt out and started pushing towards the birds half a mile away. I had the short pole with a spike on the end to dig into the ice and get a grip. I got on all right, but that was hard work, and I began to sweat I can tell you, never mind the cold. We got nearer and nearer to those ducks and I could see Dad getting the big gun cocked. About seventy yards is about right to get your pattern at its best and we were only ninety yards off 'em now. I could see the birds' heads was up and thought they would be up and off in a moment.

'We got to seventy yards and Dad began to get anxious: he wanted the birds up, just on the wing as he fired but the old sods wouldn't move, just sat there looking at us. Dad said to bang on the ice to put 'em up, as we were now getting too close for a heavy shot. I banged my hardest but no good, they still didn't move a muscle. I pushed on and now we were right up to 'em: they'd obviously seen us and I could see that Dad had sat up in the punt.

'Dew know what had happened? Them ducks stood there in that thaw, the water fruz again and fruz their feet to the ice! They couldn't move a muscle, but every one on 'em was stuck fast to the ice and its wings fixed to its body just swivelling their heads round. When he realised what had happened, Dad turned to me and said, "Boy, take the punt, leave me here, goo you home and git the scythe from the shed." And dew know what we did? We scythed them ducks off at the knees, just like cutting corn, it was, and we loaded 'em into sacks and ferried 'em back to the bank. We filled twenty-three sacks with birds. I don't rightly recollect exactly how many we got, but we had to borrow old George's horse and cart to git 'em home.'

He met with an unblinking stare my look of disbelief. Could that possibly be true? It sounded just feasible and was certainly the sort of thing which *might* have happened in those curious old days. It was two or three years before I realised that he had been pulling my leg, but the fact did not detract from a good story.

Far more likely was the tale of the nice young man who came down to the marsh for a fortnight's duck shooting. He was not short of money, while as for wildfowling what was he not going to show those poor old local boys about shooting? He put up in the pub, unpacked his monogrammed hair brushes and his London gun and went downstairs to join the locals in the choking mixture of shag and slops which constituted the atmosphere in the bar. 'What'll it be, sir?' said Bert Haddock the landlord, trawling in the regulars in his all-encompassing glance. The visitor capitulated, as many a stronger man had done before him: 'Er, what'll these gentlemen have?' he asked in a voice which had barely broken.

'Best respex to you, sir.' 'Hope they flies your way, sir.' 'I can see you're a proper wildfowler, sir. I dessay you can larn us poor old chaps a thing or two afore you're done with us.' Thus welcomed and his visions of huge bags of duck and geese well fuelled, the lad went to bed to dream of great flights of fowl, all of which came his way.

Before the end of the week he had bought a second-hand punt, its leaky seams stuffed with putty the night before, and to go with it, a tenth-hand muzzle-loading punt gun which had done years of honourable service as a fence post before being resuscitated, painted and oiled. He paid Jim 5/- an hour to guide him and Charlie the same amount to accompany him as dog man. Everyone was happy.

Eventually the visitor decided his apprenticeship was over, and he took to the marsh on his own. That was his biggest of many mistakes for out there, alone with the moon and the wailing peewits, he was undone. Henry came along, 'a-sprittin in me little owd punt when I sees a black patch on the water, just like a gang o' wigeon. I sets to 'em with my big gun loaded with half a pound of shot as big as asprins. Seventy yards, sixty – now, me beauties, I thinks, I'll hev ye. And I pulls. I got the biggest bag of me life: that were a *man*, that young stranger. Seems like he couldn't rightly manage the punt; got athort the Old Bedford River in flood and was driftin' sideways and, being an ammiture, his backside was a-stickin' up. Git him? That I did. Reg'lar riddled that old punt and sank it under him and one of my pellets kitched him right acrorst his backside. Poor young feller! He looked like a hot-cross bun for weeks afterwards.'

That was the end of that and the young man returned to London sadder, wiser and poorer and convinced that wildfowling was not all that books had made it out to be. The locals watched him with a sigh as his sports car roared up the fen road: they would miss the free beer.

Puntgunners shooting each other, usually by accident but sometimes, in the case of village rivalries 'accidentally-on-purpose', was a more frequent occurrence than one might have imagined for such a solitary sport. Many years ago, when I was out on the tide with nothing but the curlew, the wigeon whistles and a mean north wind for company, I too was involved in a mishap which might have been serious. The punt was a sliding shadow, a mere grey blur on the water, making towards a great stand of curlew which ran on a forest of twinkling legs on a mud bank a hundred yards ahead.

I had a mighty single-barrel 4-bore on board loaded with 5oz of shot. I was nearly close enough, for curlew are wary birds to approach; almost before I was ready, they were up with a wild clamour of silver whistling. 'Whoooomph', a yard-long flame seared the moon haze and the echo of the black-powder explosion rolled over the creek and faded across the mist-drenched marshes.

Birds were splashing about in the shallows and as I hurried forward, I was paralysed by an agonised yell and burst of profanity from the far side of the spit. 'What the hell – yew've bloody well shot me: cor blast, I'm killed,' and much of the same, all to the accompaniment of a rattling of oars and splashing of water as my victim hurriedly left the scene.

I recounted the tale later in The Fish inn, but the old gunners said I need not be over-concerned. 'Yew warmed his backside, I reckon, but that don't s'inify: he aint dead yit.' The door burst open at that moment, and an ashen-faced local burst in. 'I bin shot,' he gasped. 'I was in my

little punt creepin' up on a great herd of curlew: I was just about to pull the trigger when a great gun goes off in my face with a yard of blew flame and a pound of shot whistles past my head so close I can feel the wind of it. I'm lucky I wasn't killed dead.'

I think this chap must have been accident-prone for the following season he was rowing downstream when he rowed smack into a gunning punt moored near the bank. The gun was cocked and the jolt 'jarred her orf'; the charge blasted straight into a tarred dinghy tied up next door, 'that blowed the top strake straight orf and set the boat alight: that burned just like that little old boy's Christmas tree. The recoil lifted me like a balloon: my backside was so sore I couldn't sit down for a week.' When the owners of the punt and the dinghy respectively discovered the mishap, the lad was given even further cause for not being able to sit down in comfort.

I had a punt gun, the first I ever owned, which I fired into a paddling of pochard on the Bedford washes one winter. The metal was old, rusty and tired. When the gun went off the hammer and a chunk of metal about the size of a Swan Vesta matchbox to which it was attached, broke away from the action of the gun and knocked a hole in the combing of the punt. You could have put your fist through it. A few inches further back and it would have taken with it a sizeable chunk of my head, and this tale would never have been told.

Quite often, a punt gun was likely not to go off at all. A foul touch hole, damp powder, poor-quality caps or a gun which had been left loaded in the shed for ten days were the most frequent causes. The real danger, however, was that of a hang-fire, whereby the spark smouldered and spluttered in the nipple, eventually creeping down to the main charge. That made it possible for a gun to go off some minutes after the trigger was pulled, much to the surprise and discomfiture of the gunner. It was especially peeving to fire into a nicely bunched paddling of mallard and have nothing but a flash and a click for your pains. The wary fowl would have heard and seen this disturbance and made good their escape, so that when and if the gun went off, it discharged its load harmlessly onto an untenanted sheet of water.

Tom was minded to go duck shooting, but his gun had stood in the 'washus', loaded, for five years, and what with his missus boiling the copper twice a week and the place full of steam, the black powder was caked as hard as a rock. Come duck-shooting time, Tom took the gun, crept up to the lode and there he saw a nice paddling of fat, September mallard not thirty yards away.

Tom primed the gun with new powder, seated a cap, squinted down the barrel, said his prayers and pulled the trigger. The gun gave a hiss like an angry snake or a kettle approaching the boil. Without a second thought, Tom 'hulled her in the lode' and ducked down behind the bank. He was not going to risk 'gittin' blowed up', as he put it, adding darkly, 'The owd gal was nigh on a hundred years old and the metal in the barrel was like icing sugar. She weren't worth ten bob.'

The mallard had, of course, long since departed while the gun sank in the turgid waters of the lode. Just as 'she' hit bottom, 'she' went off, blew up underwater and killed a great company of eels which had gathered there to feed on the submerged carcase of a dead sheep. Thus the exercise was not a total failure, for Tom gathered the dead and stunned fish in a sack and sold the lot for thirty bob.

In my student days I built my first proper gunning punt. My previous punt the *Mallard*, flat-bottomed and square-ended, had been useful enough and in it I enjoyed some notable adventures. On one never-to-be-forgotten day I was poling along the floodwaters having as my armament a gigantic single-barrel 4-bore which Will Kent had loaned me, along with ten of the huge, red cartridges loaded with BB. Will knew that an impressionable lad would learn fowling sense from a spell with such a weapon and that my ardour for big guns would soon be cooled after I had lugged that monster up and down the marsh a few times. He was right of course, for I could neither swing the gun nor even lift it properly, while carrying it for any distance over mud or snow was purgatory. There were times, especially in thick snow, when I contemplated hiding it in the nearest willow and returning for it after the thaw.

Each time I fired it I was knocked down backwards, bruised, battered and further disheartened. Not a bird fell, not a feather was dislodged and by the end of the season, with two cartridges left, I was fed up with the whole enterprise. The gun had a small hole drilled in the stock; this was to take a light breeching rope so that the gun might be used as a miniature punt gun. At least when the gun was in the boat I was not carrying the thing, and there I was, in my square-ended washing tub, poling dejectedly towards the great osier bed on the very last day of the season. After this final, token expedition, Will could have his gas pipe back, and welcome.

I was on the point of rounding the corner to join the open channel of calm water which ran between the two osier beds. Through the thinning edge of the corner stalks, I could see that the channel was full of mallard. They were still sheltering there after a windy night, for there was no duck to be seen anywhere else on the marshes. In a moment I was down, flat on my belly in the bottom of the boat. The momentum of my last, strong push on the pole was more than enough to take her past the corner. As luck would have it, the stern swung round in the right direction to point the stern and also the muzzle of the gun up that crowded avenue of duck.

I had the advantage of surprise; the birds looked at me for a moment of incredulous silence and with a roar they were up on threshing wings, dripping paddles and a white foam of broken water. The thunder of their wings was echoed by the roar of the punt gun which I had aimed in roughly the right direction and snatched the trigger. I could hardly have missed, and with a big 20oz gun I would have made a heavy shot. As it

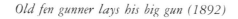

Old fen gunner lays his big gun (1892)

Fenland idyll; a goose, a brace of mallard and a gun. Results of a stalk on the washes

was, the 5oz of BB, backed by a tightly tamped sheet of the *Daily Mail* and a handful of fine-grained black powder, all painstakingly loaded by Will on his kitchen table, went humming like a swarm of hornets on its way.

Mallard splashed and bounced on the pewter ripples and when the smoke cleared, I counted six birds down, floating still and lifeless on the surface. Here an orange paddle waved feebly, there a dead bird rotated slowly as the breeze caught an upflung pinion. Hardly able to believe my luck, I paddled rapidly up to the birds, fearful lest they miraculously recover and make their escape. Six mallard, all stone dead and every one a drake in the fresh paint of full winter plumage.

Life suddenly became beautiful, flooded with *couleur de rose.* I lay the birds in a tidy row on the thwart, heads under wings in the way the proper fowlers had. That way I could admire them properly. I punted back downstream, rippling sweetly along with the wind and the current at my back, my heart a singing bird and my head several sizes too big for my woolly hat. I forgot the ease, the luck, the opportunism and outrageous set of circumstances which had led to my good fortune. In my mind, I was now a fully fledged, proper wildfowler and more than equipped to hold up my head with the hard men of Welney or the Oxlode gunners.

The timing of this stroke of luck was perfect. Before it I was depressed by my failure with the 4-bore and was quite prepared to throw in the towel and abandon the fowler's life I had coveted. After the event, I was more determined than ever to become an expert wildfowler, just like the old marshmen whose romantic and adventurous lives I so envied. I hurried back to Will Kent's cottage where it dreamed among the frosted willows, rushed breathless into the fenman's treasure house which was his barn, and blurted out the incredible success which had befallen me. He gazed at me with his piercing eyes and said laconically, 'Yew done all right, boy.' From him, that amounted to lavish praise.

I knew that the old punt was not right for proper puntgunning so I set my heart and my modest, student purse on a proper, grey, rakish gunning punt on which I could mount the big gun. I saved up and bought from my friend Ken, a famous Lincolnshire puntgunner and wildfowler, his second-best punt and gun. The outfit was delivered by Knowles, the Doddington haulage firm, who had placed the punt on sacks of wood chippings to save her from jolts on the journey. She was a twenty-two footer, a full sea-going punt, painted that deadly off-white which is almost pale grey, the hardest shade to see against the horizon of a grey dawn.

I spent a happy summer stripping off the old paint, stretching new canvas across the decks and replacing one or two suspect timbers. I reached autumn with her in good shape and ready for any adventure and the worst the weather could do to her.

Experimenting with the big gun was, to say the least, interesting. Will Kent could have, in a few moments, shown me what to do, but I did not care to reveal my ignorance and was fired by the chance of finding out for myself. The fact that we had been given a powder-and-shot measure, a crudely cut-off cow's horn with a wooden block in the end, was probably the unconscious saviour of our lives. By adhering strictly to its rule-of-thumb measurements we managed to avoid a fatality, but only just. We charged the gun good and tight, put a cap on the nipple, tied a long cord on the trigger and stood well back. Gallantly I gave my sister Katherine the honour of pulling the cord while my fellow-experimenter David Robinson and I hid bravely behind the oak tree in the garden.

At a signal from me, Katherine pulled the string, the cap flashed, there was a monumental explosion which rattled the window panes of every house in the street, and brought most of the villagers to their front doors. Poor Mrs Robinson, David's mother, heard the boom as she came out of the High Street grocery. She knew full well what it was and feared that she would see her beloved son no more and hurried round to the vicarage garden to view his shattered remains.

In fact, no one need have worried, as the experiment was a qualified success, for the 16oz of shot hurtled over the lawn, over the shrubbery and straight into the pigsty roof. As luck would have it, the building was unoccupied at the time, but a section of pantiles 6ft square collapsed and fell with a musical tinkling to the ground.

The gun had proved its soundness, but now to improve its performance; this, after all, is the real meat of research. The old gunners quite rightly believed that the longer the shot hung together, the better the range and the later the pattern developed. Accordingly we wrapped the shot into a paper parcel, well secured with lengths of Sellotape. The theory was that the deadly package would leave the barrel as a single missile and, after a few yards, the shot would begin to break free of the constraints of the paper and Sellotape and produce a dense, long-range pattern.

The makers of Sellotape need look no further than me for a testimonial to the amazing strength and adhesive properties of their product. At the time my faith was weak. We had been forbidden to experiment further in the garden, so we retired to the churchyard, lashing the gun to the last gravestone on the left which overlooked a wide green meadow. We fired the shot parcel, but it failed to burst through the tape. We saw the black speck hurtling away like a cannon ball and, for all I know to the contrary, it is travelling still, probably somewhere up in orbit. David and I lived in terror for the next few days, closely scanning the local newspaper and

listening for gossip of horses or cows suddenly being struck dead as though by a thunderbolt, or of a local citizen being decapitated in the High Street of the next village. No such reports were heard, but we decided forthwith to greatly reduce the potency of the shot wrapping.

When we advanced to our second punt gun – an altogether more sophisticated weapon, detonated by a blank .303 rifle cartridge loaded with fine-grain black powder firing a blast of flame straight into the main charge – misfires became things of the past. We were to have many adventures in this punt, but few heavy shots since that is the way of puntgunning. The adventure lies in taking a frail craft onto dangerous waters in the worst possible season of the year. It is the challenge of cold so bitter that even an old hand can be physically sick after a bout of returning blood circulation known as 'the hot-aches'. The reward for all the brutal hard labour and the risks is the most thrilling excitement to be felt in any field sport: the stealthy approach, the hundred and one things which can spoil a stalk, the pounding heart and mounting anxiety as the possibility of a shot grows with every creeping yard.

Then when, possibly six times in a good season, the great gun booms to deadly effect, all the hardships and bitter disappointments are forgotten in a moment. The puntgunner and his partner are men at peace, and if they might choose the moment in which they were to die at their happiest, it would be when they are gathering two-score of wigeon, lying out on the mud.

He sees things vouchsafed to few of his fellow men. None save longshoremen or inshore fishermen see the dawns spread as though for their private delectation across an eastern sky. Who else might do as we did on one cold, Lincolnshire dawn, and stalk to within twenty yards of a feeding spoonbill, a white ghost from Holland, striding on stilt legs and dibbling for crustacea in the shallows? Who else would have the company of not one but two pipits settling in the punt, exhausted after their migration and actually pecking crumbs of cheese from our sandwiches? Who else might have been stalking a great company of wigeon, only to have them rise inexplicably twenty yards too soon and then see a peregrine swoop like a blue-black bolt of lightning through the thick of them and send one spinning down to thump dead on the mud?

When punting in tidal waters it was amusing to stalk the common seals of the Wash and see how close to them we could creep. We would note the spot where one dived, hurry to the place as fast as we could work the poles and chuckle at the look of mild surprise on his round face and liquid, brown eyes when he popped up again within yards of the punt. He would gaze at us for a few moments, close his nostrils and simply sink from sight like a lead weight. Seals are, by nature, curious beasts and sometimes they would come close to have a look at us. They are said to be fond of music, and that king of Wash punters, Lawrence Thompson, would sing to them (carols at Christmas, of course) and the seals would cluster round to hear what I guess was a fairly tuneless chanting.

Much of the best shooting literature has been written about puntgunning. Sir Ralph Payne Gallwey was a master at capturing the slumbering lust of the crawling tideway and, in their own way, shooting men from Col Peter Hawker to Peter Scott have expressed, as few can do, the magic, the challenge, the excitement, the disappointments, the wettings, long waits, hazardous runs for home as a storm approaches and the wild adventure of the sport.

Sadly, punting has fallen from fashion. Once a way of making a living for a poor marsh dweller, it became a sport for the gentleman adventurer with the necessary means to pursue it. Public opinion, even among shoulder gunners, raised question marks over the morality of shooting numerous birds with one shot. They cared not a jot about shooting many birds with many single shots, wounding some of them and missing a great many more. A punter wounded and lost very little: his large shot and efficient system of collecting the cripples, coupled with the wide open spaces in which he operated, resulted in very few 'runners'. He would have shot far more birds in a season if he had gone out on the muds with his 12-bore shoulder gun.

Together with this illogical swing in public opinion, the guns themselves, few of them made during this century, began to deteriorate to the point of danger. As fowlers became busy men who could snatch only a few hours at a weekend to follow their sport, the necessary time-commitment required for puntgunning was no longer available. Today there may be half a dozen regular puntgunners round the coast, but few more. I doubt if there will be any by the time the present generation of children become adults.

I am fortunate and grateful that I had the opportunity to sample the sport in its dying years. Ken's old punt, although lovingly refurbished by me, had already suffered eighty years of hard work on the coast and its life could not be prolonged indefinitely. The time came for a replacement, a time which coincided with the publication of a fascinating little book by that noted sportsman–naturalist Colin Willock, entitled *The Gun Punt Adventure.* I decided to build my own gunning punt, selecting the best design features from the traditional Payne Gallwey models but using modern materials. Marine plywood, for example, is light, waterproof, easily available and was not invented when the old punt builders were wrestling with their Sitka spruce, elm, oak and western red cedar. Modern wood glues are superior to the tar and pitch which was all that the old timers had available.

The result was, as schoolteachers tend to write in school reports, 'fairly satisfactory'. Colin had erred slightly on the side of safety, never a bad place to be for amateur puntgunners, but the result was a punt which was rather too broad in the beam for my liking. For all that, I had some exciting adventures in the one I made, out on the peat-stained flood waters where the pretty pintail dibbled in the floating weed-seeds, swans sailed like faerie boats and wigeon settled in packs. However, its rather 'tubby' appearance proved that, a century-and-a-half ago, Sir Ralph Payne Gallwey had designed a series of punts which had reached perfection. His punts had evolved to do precisely what was intended of them in a manner as safe as possible for the punter. There was no further improvement that could be made.

I have written that punting could be a hazardous pursuit and some of these tales emphasise the point. Mishaps could occur for the most mundane or unexpected reasons. I was punting cheerfully up the Bedford washes, pausing occasionally to glass the reed-fingered floods ahead in the hope of seeing the familiar cluster of black specks which meant duck. All was well until I ran across the top of a gate post a few inches under the water. Such are the ways of flat-bottomed boats that she rode over it as gently as a drifting feather, reached the point of balance and stuck. Nothing I could do might free me: I clung perilously to the stem and then the stern; I tilted the punt at a dangerous angle but remained firmly anchored to the spot. I might have been there today or until the floods receded had I not, after a desperate hour of pushing and pulling, taken off most of my clothes, slipped into the chilly water and eased off the punt by hand.

It was a minor incident, perhaps, but had the ice floes of January been bearing down on me, or a rough sea got up, or the shell-thin bottom of the punt been holed, it would have been a very nasty incident indeed. The weather was mercifully mild, but it was a chilly experience and would doubtless had made an amusing spectacle, had there been anyone there to see it. Submerged fence posts, especially the rusty, angle iron stakes favoured by washland farmers, were death to punts when they lurked like a hidden coral reef just below the ripples. I have seen the bottom of a motor boat completely ripped out by such a one. The 'foreigner' from the town who had sought to desecrate the wild desolation of our marsh by running a motor boat up it deserved all he got: he never came again.

The new punt was also useful as a sneak boat, a floating platform from which to shoot, or providing the means of crossing the floods to a dry eminence or willow holt where I could stand out, while the landlubbers moped, shotless on the banks or round the shoreline. I did cheat and use a tiny two-stroke motor, a little J.A.P. boat impeller bolted onto an oaken block on the stern, just powerful enough to push us along gently at walking speed without disturbance and with very little noise.

There is a law about pursuing wildfowl from a powered vessel and it does not do to shoot while actually steaming along. Such terms seemed inconsistent when applied to my little machine, but the law is the law. Accordingly, I used the motor simply to travel to my intended area of operation; on arrival I unbolted it and stowed it beneath the deck. This gave me the advantage of a greater potential shooting area, and also bestowed a few extra ounces of power if I decided to bring home for firing a load of driftwood, or any other bulky flotsam. The motor was never used with the big gun, of course, but I doubt if the ghosts of the old gunners would have approved of the practice of using any form of power other than human sinews. I could never quite shake off the needle of conscience which pricked me every time my little J.A.P. spluttered into life.

Thus I spent my formative years, out in my lean, grey punt lost in the willow-clouded distances. I crossed and followed flooded green lanes, ancient tracks which had, in long-forgotten summers seen the glint of bronze eagles as Roman legions passed; Dutch drainers in their long, leather boots, sheep stealers, fowlers and reed cutters had also known those tracks. There redshank nested in spring; there in the brooding wilderness the harriers still beat over, the mallard flighted in from the far stubbles and peewits wept in the green dawns. It was a place of wet smells, a rare blend of damp reeds and marshes, a fishy smell with sometimes a hint in it of sweet turf smoke from a distant cottage fire.

Pheasants fly up to roost with a great cackling into the buckthorn and pollards. Far above, under the rising moon, is a sibilant whistle and whicker of wings as a flight of wigeon passes, urgent on business of its own. Far off, elm-crowned and lonely on the eminences, stand the humped jumbles which were the villages, each with its great church tower rearing high above the rookery and safe from even the greatest flood.

Light fades: lights of distant cars flash briefly as they turn the sharp corner of the marsh lane. The water looks black and ripples coldly as the knife-edge prow carves it. Then I touch bottom, swishing onto the grass of the marsh edge, back to prosaic normality and a mile to cycle home on my father's old college Hercules.

Decoys and Shoulder Guns

In my life I have had the great good fortune of knowing two decoymen. The art of 'playing the pipes' of a commercial, working duck decoy was widespread when there were hundreds of decoys peppered all over the country, many of them in East Anglia. At a time when meat was expensive or unobtainable, it was a proper thing to harvest the flocks of wildfowl in a more efficient way then the fen gunners, for all their fire power, could manage.

A duck decoy was simply a pond, usually man-made, situated near a main flightline or where wildfowl were likely to be common. At intervals round the pond were a series of netted arches, running away from the open water, narrowing as they went and curving off so that from one end the other could not be seen. The mouth of the pipe was wide enough to drive a coach and horses through, but the other end was a long keep net, narrow enough to be encircled by a man's arms. An aerial view of a decoy pond would resemble a wheel, the pond proper being the hub and the pipes running off it like curved spokes.

Round the pond and along the pipes were ranks of reed screens, sunken trenches and banks so that the decoyman could approach the pond at any point and spy on the birds while remaining quite unseen. The decoymen believed that wildfowl had an acute sense of smell, so they arranged things so that, no matter what the wind direction, the 'coyman could make a secret approach. The pond and the surrounding area was usually densely wooded and kept strictly private. No poacher, flower-picker or courting couple dared enter the decoy wood for it was protected by severe penalties. There was, and probably still is, a law which forbade the firing of a gun two miles upwind and one mile downwind of the decoy. In hard weather the pond would be fed with corn and the ice broken and slid in sheets out onto the bank.

Mallard enter the decoy entrance

The result of this loving effort to provide shelter and complete peace and quiet was to make the decoy a favourite haunt of wildfowl. This inevitably brought others and still more to swell the numbers until the pond became a sanctuary for most of the birds in the vicinity. By the time some of them discovered that they had made a mistake it was too late to communicate the information to the others.

The whole principle of the decoy depended on the blend of curiosity and aggression which wildfowl exhibit when they catch a glimpse of a fox: their instinct is to swim towards it, making a great fuss and drive it off by mobbing it. The decoyman relied on this instinct to make his bags. For the purpose he kept a dog – similar to a fox in colouring and size – which he trained to a high degree to lure the birds to their doom. Spying on the pond through one of the screens he would see which pipe mouth had the greatest concentration of birds near it. Approaching that spot via his secret channels of communication, he sent his little dog to slip over a low reed screen so that the birds were afforded a brief glimpse of it as it dropped out of sight.

All the duck saw was a quick, furry red animal which slid into and out of sight with the smoothness of a well-executed conjuring trick. If all went according to plan, the mallard set up a strident quacking and swam towards the spot, arousing other duck and drawing them in the same direction until most of the birds on the pond were swimming with them, like so many toy boats pulled on strings.

The 'coyman, still invisible behind his screens and holding a smouldering peat turf near his mouth to conceal his scent, moved down a few yards to the next jump and sent over his little dog again to provide another fascinating glimpse. If the duck seemed reluctant or had not spotted the intruder, he might send the dog over a number of times in the same place until he had the duck moving smoothly towards the mouth of the pipe.

Working his way slowly down the pipe, showing the dog at regular intervals, the 'coyman drew, as with a magnet, the fowl down the pipe. The duck, keen on seeing off the fox, did not notice that the pipe was narrowing nor that it began to sweep round a gradual bend so that they were now out of sight of the main pond. Still the dog, commonly and traditionally named Piper, appeared always a tantalising few yards ahead, its owner invisible behind the screens while the duck, oblivious now to all but that red, scurrying shape, pursued it even more eagerly as they scented a victory.

Then came the crucial moment, for the duck were well down the pipe, round the bend and the warier ones would soon begin to feel a sense of claustrophobia. Leaving his dog sitting demurely near the screen over which it had just jumped, the decoyman ran back, swift and soft-footed, to the entrance of the pipe. There he emerged from behind his concealment and ran back up the pipe, waving his arms and flapping a handkerchief. The duck found their retreat cut off: in panic they sprang, bouncing off the roof netting and flying low in a jumbled pack towards the narrow end of the pipe. At last they piled into the giant keep net at the end: the 'coyman slid a wooden board behind the last of the tightly packed mass of fowl. Then it was simply a matter of untying the cord at the end, taking out the duck one at a time, wringing their necks and stowing them on his 'coyman's flat barrow ready for taking down to the cool, stone-built game larder which lay a short way off in a damp and shady part of the wood.

The perfection of this method of harvesting lay in its simplicity, its beautiful application of one of the laws of Nature in using the instincts of the birds themselves to bring about their downfall. No shot was fired, no bird once caught lived to tell the tale and alarm the others, birds left on the decoy pond and not drawn into the pipe with the others, remained unconscious of the fate of their companions and completely unaware that anything untoward had taken place. The decoyman could return an hour later and try for them or, in a busy season, take new parties of fowl which

A decoy pond was kept deathly quiet

had dropped in in the meantime. There was no close season on wildfowl, so the decoy could be worked at any time of the year. A landowner who installed a decoy was assured of a regular income, far more than he would have received from scrubby barley or a few thin sheep kept on the same acreage.

The duck were hung in the game larder. There is one still to be seen at Nacton decoy in Suffolk, a decoy run and worked until recently by the Wildfowl Trust. Force a way through the nettles, put your shoulder to the door and, once your eyes have become accustomed to the gloom, you will see row upon row, rank above rank of rusty hooks upon which the 'coyman hung his catch. At floor level is a series of drain pipes through the wall so that, in especially hot weather, the stone floor could be flooded with cold water – a primitive refrigeration system. Even on the hottest summer day the interior would have felt as cool and airy as a cathedral nave, for those old-time builders knew what they were about.

The duck were taken piled high on the barrow or in a pony cart to the nearest station and were on Leadenhall Street market by next morning, for in the days of no deep freezers or cold stores speed of delivery from producer to consumer was all-important. Even so, there can be no doubt that some of the birds reached the kitchens of the London well-to-do in rather a 'high' state.

The 'coyman at Nacton was, for many years, Don Revitt, an expert at his craft, living in the quiet cottage in the shadow of great oaks, but no more than fifty yards from the nearest of his ponds. The duck he caught were more fortunate than their ancestors for they were ringed and released to research the movements and migrations of these fascinating birds. Nacton was especially well known for its pintail catches and, in the hungry old days, had been responsible for sending many thousands of them to market. Most decoymen inherited a family tradition, the tricks and secrets being passed on from father to son, often through many generations. Don Revitt is a slight exception, since it was his wife's family who were the Nacton decoyers. Don's father-in-law, a man who at ninety could put to shame many a younger chap, was the last of the line. The old gentleman could be seen up a ladder repairing a pipe, his netting needle flashing to and fro, or swinging a scythe in the bankside nettles with a vigour which belied his years.

Wildfowl changed their habits and even their age-old flight lines. The silting of estuaries, local drainage and the creation of huge, new reservoirs to serve the thirsty populace meant that the birds came in ever-decreasing numbers. In the end, the decoy was taken over by the Suffolk Naturalists' Trust and worked only occasionally for demonstration purposes. Don, his wife and family, not forgetting Piper, upped sticks and moved down to the fens to Welney to look after the Wildfowl Trust reserve. Thus one of the last decoys came to an end, and its attendant family dispersed.

My other decoying friend is Tony Cook who works the Wildfowl Trust decoy at Peakirk in Borough Fen near Peterborough not far, as the duck flies, from the site of the great mere at Whittlesea. Tony catches the duck for ringing and no longer for stacking high on the dreaded market barrow. He is one of the last two decoymen, following in the footsteps of the famous Williams family who ran the decoy for many generations. Annie Williams, sister of the late 'coyman Billy Williams, is still alive and sprightly in the old 'coyman's cottage. A nonagenarian and full of tales of the old days, she was much happier 'playing the pipes' than playing with dolls. Decoy folk seem generally to have been long-lived.

Borough Fen decoy is an ancient one with records going back as far as 1670. In that year permission was given to draw water from the River Welland to flood the pond. There is evidence, however, that it was in operation before that and needed the extra water just as a top-up, owing to the increasingly effective drainage of the surrounding fen. It was a Mr Williams who, acting on behalf of the Earl of Lincoln, made that application. One of the family, Andrew (1692–1776), for sixty years decoyman at Aston Hall in Shropshire but who learned the craft at Borough Fen, was given this striking, wry epitaph:

Here lies the Decoyman who lived like an otter,
Dividing his time betwixt land and water;
His hide he oft soaked in the waters of Perry,
Whilst Aston old beer his spirits kept merry.
Amphibious his life, Death was puzzled to say
How to dust to reduce such well-moistened clay;
So Death turned Decoyman and 'coyed him to land,
Where he fixed his abode till quite dry to the hand,
He then found him fitting for crumbling to dust,
And here he lies mouldering as you and I must.

The Perry was the river which fed the decoy. The local decoyman was no rough fen slodger, but a pillar of respectability and an important man in the community: he was responsible, single handed, for earning more revenue than the rest of the parish put together.

The decoy was a logical progression from the duck drive, in which great flocks of young and old fowl in eclipse plumage – and therefore flightless – were driven into nets stretched across the far side of the mere. As long ago as 1432 there is a record of a gang of wild fenmen, half-starving and desperate, taking about 600 fowl from the Abbot's decoy at Crowland Abbey. As for the sheer size of the haul, almost 3,000 mallard were taken in one drive near Spalding, 4,000 were taken at Deeping Fen, and in 1720 another 3,000 were caught in a single sweep.

The decoy proper was obviously a much more efficient, regular and predictable device; duck drives were seasonal, opportunist affairs, demanding of manpower and liable to go wrong.

Sir Ralph Payne Gallwey once researched and mapped decoys and in 1886 published a book, now extremely rare, entitled *Book of Duck Decoys*. He recorded the fenland decoys which then speckled the East Anglian map, but which now reveal themselves as no more than shallow depressions in the great fields or in common place names such as 'Decoy Farm', 'Decoy Field' or 'Decoy Ground'. The efficiency of the decoy can be indicated by a few statistics. In 1816 the Holme Fen decoy took 3,000 in seven days and over 15,000 in the season. The bag was measured by the dozen. Richard Skelton once took 30 dozen birds a day for three consecutive days, well over a thousand head.

Tom Williams hired and worked the prolific Lakenheath decoy and cleared £700 profit in a single year. He sent a ton of ducks to London twice a week when the decoy was at its peak of productivity. A local keeper said in 1878 that he once saw fully 3,000 fowl sitting outside the decoy in the adjoining fen, 'waiting for those inside to be taken to make room for them. The decoy was so full that it looked as if one could not prick a pin in anywhere.' At its peak, this decoy took 15,000 duck in a season and only declined when the local land was drained and farmed and a railway line built nearby created a regular and intolerable disturbance with passing trains. Tom Williams was 109 when he died through falling in a freezing dyke with a sack of ducks on his back.

The final, devastating record to indicate the sheer enormity of fowl taken comes from the Ashby decoy. In thirty-five seasons it accounted for nearly 100,000 birds comprising 48,664 mallard, 44,568 teal, 2,019 wigeon, 285 shoveller, 278 pintail and 22 gadwall. The best year was 1834–5 when 6,357 birds were taken. Consider those figures in the light of the great number of working decoys – the small Lincolnshire village of Wainfleet had no less than five – and it paints a picture both of the enormous number of wildfowl in the fens at the time and of the stupendous catches taken and sold. In fact, the duck decoy was for 200 years a very important element in the rural fenland economy.

The life of the fen decoyer, living his watery life in pursuit of fish and fowl, is shown in a snatch of doggerel by William 'Antiquarian' Hall. A true fenman, living in a turf hut in the swamp, 5 miles from the nearest school or church, he had a flair for versifying which marked him out from his fellow fowlers and fish spearers. He wrote and had privately printed in

Tony Cook of Borough Fen sends Piper over the jump (left); *The trammel net where decoyed fowl ended their journey and, once, their lives* (right)

1825 the extremely scarce *A Chain of Incidents relating to the State of the Fens from the Earliest Accounts to the Present Time*; a long title, but it cost a shilling a copy, obtainable only from the author.

> Born in a coy and lived in a mill
> Taught water to grind, and Ducks for to kill;
> Seeing coots clapper-claw, lying flat on their backs,
> Standing upright to row, and crowning of jacks;
> Laying spring nets for to catch Ruff and Reeve,
> Stretched out in a boat with a shade to deceive.
> Taking Geese, Ducks and Coots with nets upon stakes,
> Riding in a calm day for to catch moulted drakes;
> Gathering eggs to the top of one's wish,
> Cutting tracts in the flags for decoying of fish.
> Seeing Rudds run in shoals 'bout the side of Gill sike,
> Being dredfully venom'd by rolling in slake:
> Looking hingles and sprinks, trammels, hoop nets and teamings,
> Few persons, I think, can explain all their meanings.

Crude, short on scanning and primitive verse it may be, but 'Fen Bill' Hall has, in those few lines, captured the essence of the fenman's activities. The allusion to grinding water refers to the wind drainage pumps which clacked round unceasingly for a century. Coots 'flat on their backs' refers to the defensive attitude struck by coots when attacked by harriers; 'crowning of jacks' was stunning a small pike which basked on the surface; his boat with the 'shade to deceive' is the fringe of sedge which he used to camouflage the freeboard of his punt so that the fowl would mistake him for a mass of floating vegetation as he made his approach. 'Moulted drakes' were caught by driving them into funnel nets as I have described. As for being 'venom'd by rolling in slake', there were serious risks of blood poisoning if a fenman fell into the 'slake' or stinking mud which accumulated in stagnant dykes.

His catalogue of nets and traps includes 'sprinks', a corruption of the horsehair noose or 'springe' used to catch waders; Shakespeare refers to 'springes to catch woodcock'. A trammel is the detachable, giant keep net at the business end of a decoy pipe.

All the decoys have passed away save those worked by Tony Cook and Don Revitt. No wonder I am proud of my friendship with these two men. Both are richly endowed with the skills of their art, and though their secrets will probably die with them that should not be for a long time yet as they are still young. The old decoys and 'coymen have gone, the former just marks on cornfields, identifiable only by aerial photography to show where hundreds of thousands of wildfowl were once caught. Carrots and potatoes grow where the will-o'-the-wisp once capered over steaming morasses and the phut-phutting of tractors and the drone of combine harvesters fill the flat silences where once the wildfowl rose with a sound like distant thunder.

To the modern fen fowlers such places and events are not even memories, but half-understood rumours, tales from the lips of old fen tigers and things gleaned from the dusty writings of historians. There is still excitement, adventure and the old thrill in fowling today, by no means diminished by the fact that the numbers of wildfowl are a shadow of what they were when the decoys took that amazing toll. A few years ago I had observed a gaggle of feeding pinkfooted geese using a fen stubble, so I begged permission of the farmer and decided to try for a shot at them.

The dawn seemed to be an unconscionable time a-coming. The fowler tends not to be prone to lie-ins, but too often is up earlier than necessary, unable to sleep with his head full of clanging battalions of grey geese, and anxious lest he miss the chance of a shot. At the first shriek of the alarm I was up and dressing rapidly, layer upon layer of down-filled waistcoats, long-johns, scarves and waterproofs until my comfortable girth had assumed Pickwickian proportions. It was a cold morning, but the ancient gunners had none of the advantages of such warm clothing. Breakfast, another luxury often denied to the old-time pro, had been bolted with feverish haste, with half a cup of hot coffee poured down the sink: no delay was to be tolerated as I was impatient to be off. The journey to the goose field was a race against a deadline which was purely imaginary and self-imposed. I took hair-raising risks on the icy bends and flouted goodness knows how many elements of the Highway Code on the way. The old gunner walked, cycled, punted or had his boat moored near his back gate.

When at last I pulled into the layby, breathless and flustered, I realised how dark it really was. There was not even the usual pre-dawn glow which picks out the major landmarks, for the great willow by the dyke and the distant carr were still shrouded in an inky blackness which intensified as the car lights clicked off. The engine hissed and ticked as it cooled and I sat there collecting my thoughts, allowing my pupils to dilate and ears attune to more subtle sensations than the roar of a hard-pressed petrol engine. I braced myself to open the car door and admit the inrush of cold air which I knew was waiting outside. I took the plunge, faced the icy blast, pulled on long boots, drew the gun from the slip, whistled up the dog and stumbled off into the night.

The wildfowler must be able to adjust to extremes of temperature which he will experience within minutes of each other. He is cold when he rises from a warm bed, thaws out over breakfast, is uncomfortably hot on the car journey, cools down when the door opens, then his temperature rises to fever pitch as, well-muffled, he plods across the marsh. He reaches his hiding place and settles in to find that, in ten minutes, his teeth are chattering. Apart from taking off layers of clothing and putting them back on a few minutes later, there seems to be no answer to the problem.

I found my place behind a blasted thorn which would have made a good stage prop for a production of *Macbeth* and crouched down to wait. My six goose decoys, smudges of pale grey against the murk, bobbed and weaved on their pegs. They would provide the reassuring flash of white and hint of movement which the skeins would see.

Although it was far too early for the flight – if flight there was to be – I did not begrudge the morning my lost hour in bed. It is far worse to arrive just in the nick of time with fowl already on the move as you are setting out the decoys or dragging the gun from its slip. Then you are flustered and ill-prepared and, what is more, you have not had the time to absorb the atmosphere nor to allow the sweet tingle of anticipation to build up since that is what much of the thrill of wildfowling is about. If success were to be measured purely on the size of the bag, it would be a sorry sport.

It is a long night which has no dawn and at last some watery light leaked over the flat fen: the old willow and the carr were now visible as lowering hulks; the stubble was no longer grey and grubby, but touched with a silver glow.

Some gulls passed high overhead, with sharply angular wings, cold cruel eyes and harsh mewing cry. They flew like geese in lines, echelons or great vee formations. Early gulls are a useful test of a gunner's hide, for their keen eyes miss nothing, and the sight of your upturned face or a careless movement sends them sideslipping your position or tossing themselves up and away as they see you there below. A wise fowler will take advantage of this warning to improve his cover so that, by the time the geese arrive, he will be better hidden.

Then there was a distant burst of goose music, a sound which no matter how often you hear it, never loses its power to stir the hairs on the back of your neck and send a shiver down your spine. Those great, grey birds will always thrill, amaze and mesmerise me. Their wings have borne them, many times perhaps, down from Iceland, flying too high for human eyes to see as anything but black specks, navigating unerringly over the tumbled oceans, through storm, fog and blizzard, gossiping and crying wildly as they travel the unmarked highways like some ancient Vikings. It is the challenge of trying to see, hear and possibly shoot one which drives fowlers to travel many expensive miles, equip themselves with all the necessary gear and suffer considerable physical discomfort and, on the saltmarsh, actual personal danger.

Now that familiar cry brought instant recall of the thousands of times I had heard it from my boyhood; there came memories of the rusty, single barrels of youth, the hundreds of miles of motoring, wild scenery and desolate flats of thirty years of wild-goose chasing.

A party of fifteen appeared from the east. I called them and they replied: 'Pink-wink,' I cried; 'Wink wink wink,' they answered. We chattered and 'oggle-goggled' as that noted Wash fowler Ken Morrel described their strange, buzzing gabble, and they set their wings to the

decoys. Nearer and nearer they came; now they were in line with the top of the hawthorn, just visible through the black twigs. In five seconds they would be overhead and planing in. I lay like an old fox in the long grass and then leaped up onto one knee, levelling the magnum at the head of the first bird, firing and then swinging onto the second. Two stabs of fire shot up; the skein burst out with a wild clamouring, flared with incredible agility for such large birds, and within seconds were over the far boundary hedge.

But I had one down. I had heard a great thud rather than seen it drop and then, as I gazed wistfully at the departing skein, another separated and I realised that it too was falling, half a mile off by now and many deep dykes away but at least I had a line on it, thanks to a solitary leaning gatepost two fields off. Kenzie my dog had retrieved my first bird, a fine pinkfoot (but aren't they all?) which was, from its small size, a bird of the year. A right and left at pinks with the first chance of the day was enough for anyone. More geese in bigger skeins were now in the air but I let them rest, for how could my feeling of triumph be improved? I stacked the decoys in the dyke bottom, stowed the gun and trudged off in the direction of that leaning, solitary gatepost. I had walked for five or six minutes, casting Kenzie out to right and left when I spotted a distant white speck on the ploughing. A dead gull perhaps, a scrap of polythene, or a blown newspaper? I quickened my pace and there lay my second goose, flat on its back, stone dead, just waiting for me to pick it up. Those two geese were worth to me a thousand fowl tamely slaughtered in one of the old decoys.

I love those wild marshes where the bullocks graze, the gulls mew and the peewits dapple the green. There are wide, still places where the old fen rivers slip slowly towards the North Sea. Herons fish, grey rags in the dykes, and the willows stand in a frieze against the flat horizon while the poplars rustle in the stillness of the November sunshine. Those great levels where you see no man, no house roof and no plough seem a place apart from the twentieth century, a place where time stands still. You are back with the old fen which, at this time of year, is a glaze of gold and orange, a sea of flaming reed beds, an ocean of peat-stained waters and grey floods in the long winters.

On such an evening I picked my way gingerly through the splashes to a reed clump on a little mound where I could hide more or less dry shod. My decoys swam attractively on the sheet of open water nearby. I had not used them for some time and had little faith in their powers, but hoped they would do enough to draw in a few of the teal which had recently come to our shores, driven off the Continent by a sudden cold snap.

I heard them before I saw them, a sharp 'pripp-pripp', and a spring of teal skimmed in from somewhere behind me and landed right among my maligned decoys. They jumped up immediately as they caught sight of the burly shape of yours truly lurking in the sedge, and flew low across my front giving me the chance to knock one down as they fled. The dog had it back in the hide in an instant and showered me with muddy droplets as he twirled his coat; the night was already raw and I could have done without that chilly and unsolicited shower bath. More teal swung round, or was it the same lot? Again my double shot dropped one bird which peeled out of the flock and splashed far out on the water, calling for a long and gruelling swim by the old monster. Who could possibly go wildfowling without a dog?

Then it was wigeon, half a dozen swinging round with a growl and a

A pack of wigeon swings over a corner of ancient marsh

whistle, coming in more confidently as the night closed round me. I got two and lost another which dived in a twinkling the moment it hit the water, never to be seen again. The old fenmen believed that wounded duck dived and seized underwater weed in their beaks, drowning themselves rather than giving away their position to the questing snout of a dog. By the time the mallard, which are always the last to flight, decided to come I was gazing round with dilated eyes trying to see fowl, the whispering wings of which sounded all around me.

Just when I thought I would have to leave without a mallard there was a whistle of wings overhead and a pair of them came over like black witches flying etched against the charcoal-grey sky. Two easy ones, and I swung the gun to take an easy right and left, the drake falling in the hide, narrowly missing the dog and startling him out of his reverie.

That was it, and with teal, mallard and wigeon warming my back through the canvas of the game bag, I splashed off, feeling my way with my long stick. It would not do to walk over a flooded dyke all alone and on a cold night. A herd of bullocks met me on the high bank: they blew fragrant steam at me and chewed a drowsy cud. Somewhere high above me, under the pinprick stars, a mallard chattered gently and, as I dragged to the ill-fitting gate and re-tied its binder-twine fastening, a wigeon, somewhere far away on the river lifted his head and whistled, 'wheeoo wheeoo'.

By God, but I love this sport and this place!

By no means every outing produces a bag. One which does not is certainly not to be written off as a disaster, for there is always something new to see, a fresh lesson to be learned and the excitement of the ambush or the pursuit is undimmed whether or not it ends in a tangible result. To those who demand something in the bag to show for all their trouble, I say you will never be wildfowlers which is a sport as much for philosophers and naturalists as the hard men from the coast. In autumn there are mushrooms to be found, a log of driftwood to be gathered or a perfectly sound bucket, handle and all, lost by a summer angler and carried down to you on the floods. Even those without handles, and I admit to those being in the majority, may be made serviceable by means of two holes and a short length of rope.

I once heard of a goose shooter coming off the marsh with a 12lb fresh salmon to console him for a blank flight. The famous Solway professional fowler, Peter Blackburn, once of the Wash, was leading his small party of guns off the marsh one morning. The geese had passed them by either too high or too wide, but they had made a stirring sight as they went clamouring by in great waves against the apple-green and salmon-pink of the dawn. Peter was some way ahead of the others when they were amazed to see him suddenly stop in his tracks, unbuckle his gun slip and, with desperate urgency, drag forth his weapon. The rest believed that he had seen a party of latecomers, geese left on the tide after the rest had departed and only coming in at this advanced hour. They dropped like stones into the nearest creeks, but were surprised to see him cram in a cartridge and take aim at what appeared to be the toes of his boots.

There was a shot, eruption of water and Peter leaped down into the creek which had been concealed from his companions and emerged, wet and breathless, clutching a shining bar of silver by the tail. The fish had swum into the creek at high tide and remained there when the water had receded. Sharp-eyed Peter had seen it and, making due allowance for refraction, had given it an ounce-and-a-half of goose shot to deadly effect.

There have been several other instances of fish being shot but the creature must be close to the surface if the shocking power of the pellets is to have any effect: they lose their velocity almost immediately on striking the water. A hundred and thirty years ago, in the last hard winter of Whittlesea Mere, the skaters spotted a huge pike swimming slowly beneath the ice. It was clearly starved of oxygen and in a parlous

state. A fenman skated back to a hut on the edge of the mere and returned with an axe. The spectators had followed the movements of the fish during his absence and were able to point it out to him. He delivered a mighty blow on the ice just over the pike's head. Stunned, the fish rolled over, belly up. They cut a hole through the ice and dragged forth the monster. It weighed 32lb, a good fish even for that great water. The fish was cut up on the spot and divided between those present.

Even a blank morning is no loss, but part of the rich pattern of the fowler's life, and an experience to sharpen those days when he does manage to make a bag. There are times, however, when appalling conditions can spoil some of the excitement while still providing a challenge of a different sort. Two such nights of many stick in the mind. The first one was fog bound, for a dense pea-souper had blanketed all the eastern counties that mid-November. I had planned to go up to the coast the following morning early, and go I would for it was my proud and foolish boast that I never cancelled an expedition on account of the weather and that I was never late.

The fog was so thick that I *was* late having hugged the grass verge at crawling speed for 50 miles. On a normal morning I would have arrived far too late for flight, but the fog had kept the geese out on the sand bar

Even today a fen farmer uses a punt on his watery domain

for longer than usual, as they can see no better in it than we humans. I found the sea wall and struck off across the green, intending to go only a hundred yards out and wait. The geese would be low, and to go out further would be a dangerous waste of time with a making tide and my compass forgotten. I had walked almost far enough when a long grey bank loomed up ahead of me. It was the sea wall and I had walked in a complete circle, in the unshakeable belief that I was heading out towards the sea. I turned and set off again, but exactly the same thing happened: it was like Harris in the centre of Hampton Court Maze for I was quite unable to get away from the bank.

I did manage at last to put it out of sight behind me and settled down, feeling rather shaken, and resolving never again to forget the compass.

I could not see my hand in front of my face. At long last the geese did come, buzzing like so many bees, lost and anxious with no landmarks to guide them, but I could see not a feather of one although they must have passed low over my head. I made the error of firing at the swooshing of their wings, but I did not score. I hurried back to the sea wall, stumbling on it more by luck than judgement for, having had such a hard task to leave it behind me, now I could not find it again. I was a relieved man to feel at last its tussocky grass beneath my feet.

It was a bad morning: a bad journey, an irresponsible shot, a nasty scare, a vital piece of equipment forgotten and not even the satisfaction of seeing the birds or the unfolding of the dawn. It was also a day of tragedy, for later I discovered that on that marsh on that very morning, two young chaps were cut off by the tide and drowned. They also had gone too far out in the fog, had become disorientated by that clammy white blanket and wandered about this way and that until the creeping tide first cut them off and then overwhelmed them. When the bodies were recovered by the RAF the next day, it was found that they had tied themselves together by one wrist each with a scarf, in order not to be separated as the water rose about them.

It must be a fearful death to feel each little wave lapping further and further up your body while you flounder this way and that seeking escape but, in the fog, not certain whether you are not heading further out to sea. One can feel only deep sympathy for the families of those poor lads, and the disaster brought home to me how close was my own escape and how I was saved by pure good fortune. Never again did I venture onto a tidal marsh in any weather without a compass, for I might set off in good visibility but a sudden sea fog could swirl in in half an hour and leave me completely lost.

Funny stuff, fog, since by cutting out familiar landmarks it affects your sense of distance as well as direction. I set off once in dense fog to pole the punt from Sutton Gault up to the site of an old marshmen's pub, The Jolly Bankers. I was making good time pushing strongly and making the bows purr through the iron-grey ripples. My pole work was impressive to behold, and I regretted that there was no one there to witness it. I had long passed where I guessed my first landmark to be, a huge willow which stood alone and visible for miles around in the middle of the wash. I began to peer ahead looking for the iron bridge which marked my destination, for surely I must be close now. To my amazement there was my willow looming up. This time I had not been travelling in circles, but had travelled only a third of the distance I had imagined.

The other eminently forgettable day was in snow. I was far from home flighting duck coming to a flash in the evening. The west was piled high with oily yellow clouds heavy with snow and the first flakes plopped onto my shoulders almost as soon as I had squatted down in the reeds. Several duck came in a sharp flurry at last light but by then the snow was falling heavily. The black coat of the mighty Cassius had a wide shelf of it from the roots of his ears to his tail, making him look all the blacker beneath. Eventually the snow had covered all the hollows and cloaked the rushes in white and my eyes were screwed up tight against the swirling flakes.

It was time to go home and it was the hardest hour's walk of my life. If anything the snow was thicker than ever and I floundered on like Captain Scott on his last desperate push from the Pole. There were times, and I laugh now to think of them, when I actually wondered if I was going to make it. I fell in concealed holes, put both feet in a hidden dyke and half walked, half waded through the drifts. I considered leaving the gun and the heavy bag in some hidden cache so that I could come back for them after the thaw. I was never so glad to see anything in my life as the dim light on the road bridge flickered through the blizzard.

Not all fowling is rosy dawns and heavy bags.

·Fowler's Moon·

Deep down in the fen peat amid the fossilised pelican bones and wolf tusks, the last remnants of more ancient fen dwellers, there lies another marvel. Mention the word 'bog-oak' to a fen farmer and he will scowl and purse his lips, mindful of broken plough shares, ruined machinery and the immense labour of dragging them out with chains to prevent further damage. At various periods between 4,000 and 70,000 years ago the whole of fenland was a great forest of mighty trees, deep rooted in the gault clay and growing through the peat. In the earliest times, East Anglia was connected to the Continent, but the land sank, allowing the inrush of the North Sea.

At different times the climate changed as successive minor ice ages had their effect on Northern Europe. At one point the sea rushed in and flooded the great forest and salt water was as deadly to trees then as it is now. The forest giants died and stood, gaunt skeletons as far as the eye could see. Then came a mighty gale, the force of which can be only guessed at, but it came from the south-west and hurled down that great forest, and the millions of trees lay where they fell, all facing north-east. The peat gradually built up, covering the trunks with a layering many feet trick. Preserved by the peat, the older ones part way to becoming coal, the trunks lay beneath the swamps and meres until the fens were drained. The peat shrank as the water table fell, erosion took an annual toll of the topsoil and gradually the monsters of the ancient forests once more lay exposed to the light of day. Stained red, black or dark brown by centuries in the peat, some of the trunks are many yards in circumference and up to 80–100ft in length. Lumped together by the general description bog-oak, the trees were oak, elm, Scots pine, yew, hazel, alder, willow and sallow, although oaks predominated. The proximity of the trunks to each other, and their great length (some of them grew up to 70ft before throwing out a branch), suggests just how dense the original forest must have been.

When first exposed, the wood is soft, drying to flaky layers on the outside, but remaining for many months close grained and moist in the middle. Gateposts and rough bridges across wide dykes were occasionally made from it, but in a treeless country it is mostly used as firewood. It has to be sawn when first dug up and left to dry in the sun. It burns with a fierce red glow, gives off a steady heat and leaves a delicate, ochre-coloured ash when spent. Some fenmen would carve the freshly dug bog-oak into walking sticks or stick handles which, when dried and polished, looked and felt like the best-quality ebony.

Farmers have good cause to curse them, for a plough touching a bog-oak on the way down the field buckles the implement like butter. As the trunk might lie at a uniform depth across the field for another 80ft, there is nothing for it but to assemble a team of men, tractors, chains and saws until the monster can be hauled out and dragged to the headland. In many fen parishes a giant pile of bog-oak in a tumbled heap is such a frequent feature of the landscape as not to be worthy of comment. To this day, new trunks are hauled out, often in short pieces, and added to the heap. The advent of the power-driven chain saw has meant that the wood may be more easily cut up for firing. In the old days it would blunt a handsaw in 5 minutes and it was too hard to have a 6in nail driven into it without bending. I have a precious store of it, precious because it is a finite resource, and when the last piece has turned to ash there will not be any more, so I burn it only at Christmas and other high spots in the calendar.

Other remains of the great forests emerge with the bog-oaks. Bones by the barrowload were carted off and thrown on rubbish tips or sent, by the more perspicacious, to museums. The Celtic short-horned ox, Irish elk, mammoth, wild horse, cave lion, woolly rhinoceros, wild boar and narrow-toothed elephant all roamed the fens once upon a time, as did the reindeer, lemming, musk sheep, bison, wolf, and brown bear. These marvels now are not even memories, but mere fragments of broken bones stored in dusty ossuaries, the only proof that ancient fenland was a playground for creatures which outlived their time on earth.

One does not associate the fens with the business of mining. Curiously enough, though, it did once enjoy a mining rush which saw labourers flooding into the flat lands, stakes contested, fortunes made and lost and a wave of short-lived excitement to match anything that happened on the Klondike. It was the coprolite digging industry which caused the boom. Coprolite is the fossilised dung of prehistoric dinosaurs: it makes excellent chemical fertilisers, superphosphates which have a powerful effect on growing crops. John Ball, the Burwell miller in the 1850s, owned a small parcel of land outside the village and his turnips grew much better than those of his neighbours. Being an inquisitive chap, he dug down in the greensand and discovered a number of round, hard fossils. The local doctor ground them to powder in his mill and treated it with acid to make fertiliser.

The discovery of the first gold nugget in the Yukon could not have caused a more startling effect. Geologists discovered that the coprolite strata lay near the greensand ridges in Cambridgeshire. A man with coprolite on his land was suddenly rich and he imported 'foreign' labour to dig it out and used the new railways to transport it away. Rents were

Bog-oak jumbled in a farm gateway. Wolves and beavers roamed when these trees were alive

astronomical, De Freville paying £150 for 2 acres of diggings in the village of Harston.

The mining was hard and dangerous pick-and-shovel work, the labourers wearing iron spikes or creeping irons on their boots to keep a grip on the slippery slopes of the workings. The practice of undermining caused many miners to die in cave-ins, owing to negligence and a complete absence of any safety rules. The problem was such that Fred Barlow, the Secretary of State for Agriculture, wrote to *The Times* about it. Some greedy farmers neglected their land and failed to clean their dykes just in order to take a quick profit from their coprolites.

The boom was quickly over and by 1904 there was only one coprolite pit left, that at Potton in Bedfordshire. Phosphates were now being imported in enormous quantities more cheaply than they could be mined at home, and in any case the most accessible Cambridgeshire seams had been worked out. In the dying days, the diggers lost 6d per ton of coprolite they handled. The processing plants were abandoned and fell derelict, the army of labourers who had brawled so lustily with the locals, invaded the Upware Republic for drinking and fighting matches, and assailed the virtue of the village maidens, all departed, many of them to go as 'navigators' on the railways.

The legacy was left in the shape of improved waterways and better roads, for the industry depended on its links between producer and buyer and saw to it that channels of communication were improved. Village populations were enhanced by new blood, for some of the workers married locally and stayed behind after the collapse. Aerial photographs show the chequered patches on the fields which were the sites of the old workings, while here and there in the green heart of the fens lies a reed-fringed pond to show where once workmen shouted, and horses and carts plied to and fro.

I had the shooting on a pond which had been an old coprolite working. There was little save some grassy mounds to show that it was man-made, for the coot clanked on it, moorhen flirted their white tails in the shadows and mallard and teal sat on it during the day. Their quacking could be heard two fields away on a still day. Many a night I hid in the green sword blades of reeds, my ears full of their harsh clashing but sharp pricked to listen for the whistle of approaching wings or a distant mallard chatter. Like most fen ponds, it was a place of quiet and mystery. It was not difficult to imagine the scene a hundred years ago. The excavation then would have been dry earth with jumbled piles of blue gault clay, duck boards laid in tracks to provide a grip for men and horses, and tools stacked in casual piles.

The workers would have been a rough lot, velveteen waistcoated, moleskin breeked, with red stocking caps, short clay pipes and dyking boots. The accents of Ireland, Scotland, Tyneside and Nottingham would have mingled in a throaty burr, with a shout now and then from the 'watcher' whose job it was to stand on top of the working and watch out for signs of a cave-in, in which case his warning cry gave the underground workers time to scramble clear. It is not difficult to imagine the echoes of that bustle in the whispering and rustling of the sedge when you are there, alone with your thoughts on an October evening.

The farmer put forward the theory that the pit was over-stocked with great pike which were taking an unacceptable toll of the duck and making them wary of the place. I had seen no evidence of this, but he was full of tales of predatory monsters like freshwater sharks which his farm labourers had seen basking on the surface. Accordingly I made arrangements to have the pond netted: angling would not be allowed because of the disturbance it would cause the duck.

The great day arrived and a team of netsmen, complete with yards of corked and weighted net, a huge aerated water tank for holding the catch, a collapsible rowing boat, a Land-Rover and an electro fisher for good measure, reported for duty. The boat moved slowly across the pond, the man in the stern slowly paying out the net. He reached the far bank and the rest of us, like a tug-o'-war team, hauled away. A man on the bank piled the dripping folds: it was not until the last moment when the bag end was drawn out that we would see the extent of our catch. The moment arrived.

The net was empty! I state the fact baldly since it calls for no amplification. We dragged that pond from left to right and up and down just in case a tightly packed shoal had hidden in one corner, but apart from a handful of tiny roach, the pit was as good as fishless. So much for rumour, and yet another pike legend of a local monster of undreamed-at size and unguessable weight was shattered and disgraced.

The duck, however, were more real for they could be seen by anyone with half an eye as they swung through the towering smoke clouds of an autumn stubble fire and set their wings before dropping down onto the glassy surface where they dibbled and preened.

I was up well before dawn one October morning, dressed and booted, my old magnum, with which I have shared many a flight, in my hand. The coprolite pond was not really a magnum place: an ordinary game gun would have done just as well, but the mental link between a magnum and wildfowl was a strong one. It was still dark as I parked the truck at the end of the green lane, an ancient by-way which had seen pass some curious pedestrians in its time. I swished through the dewy grass and through a mist which had settled in the hollows and which clung heavily to the cobwebs shrouding the roadside thorns. The coprolite pond was an island of thicker mist which coiled and smoked from its surface. The cluster of self-planted willows loomed grey, the feather heads of the reeds were heavy, drooping and full of moisture.

An early woodpigeon cooed throatily, a muffled 'quaack quaack' came from the pond; a moorhen spoke once, sharply, and a teal whistled softly. It is always a problem for a fowler to approach his intended hide and find the duck already there. What should he do: take the easy chance they offer as they spring but give the rest a bad scare and ensure that they never return that day; or should he exercise restraint and show himself to drive them off in the hope that they will come back in dribs and drabs half an hour later? A bird in the hand is worth two which might or might not come back, but I decided on the policy of restraint. Walking boldly up to the pond and whistling loudly as might any innocent farm labourer on his way to work, I put up the duck which sprang in a long string from the shadow of the reeds, leaving behind them only a few coots and the spreading ripples of their own departure.

I stood for some time watching the water, semi-comatose as I was after my early rise, and then stirred myself enough to spread my canvas bag on the wet grass and sit with my back to a half-rotted willow stump, facing the paling eastern sky. Almost immediately there was a sound as of the tearing of sheets of newspaper as seven teal came from behind, raced their reflections over the water, flared over the far bank and came back in a right circle over my head. Caught completely by surprise, I was scrambling to my feet as they presented themselves and my rapid, single shot resulted only in the birds exploding like a star shell, each one rocketing up and away at breathtaking speed. Those shots who claim the driven grouse swinging round a contour as the hardest bird to hit, can clearly have had no experience of flaring teal by a Cambridgeshire pond in the half-light of a misty, moisty morning.

Now I crouched rather more alertly, not wishing to be caught napping for a second time, while a pale, brassy sun rose and the mist thinned. The sky overhead was already a delicate China blue; clearly it was going to be a hot day. Four mallard came, distant dumb-bell shapes in line astern, but they made a great circle and departed. Pigeons began to coo and croon from the willows, flying from branch to branch, climbing steeply, clapping their wings and almost stalling in mid-air in their curious courtship flight. Should I shoot one or two? Such is another hard decision for a gunner, though not so in the old days in the fen when fowlers shot at every bird of any species which ventured into range. The driven-partridge man who sees a passing pigeon before the drive is properly under way, the goose flighter confronted with a pack of approaching mallard or a wigeon shooter who sees a passing snipe are each faced with the same problem. The firing at the lesser quarry in each case might disturb and divert the more noble game which just might be coming a minute or so behind.

I had exercised restraint once already and my bag was empty. I chose an easy pigeon as it crossed in front, gave it 2ft of lead, swung and fired. It came clattering down on the pond, a squirt of white feathers drifting slowly to catch and trickle on the bankside elders. The bird splashed into the water and Drake retrieved the soggy bundle of cotton-wool feathers, such a miserable and unprepossessing thing that I immediately regretted having fired. I decided to shoot at no more pigeons unless they would fall on dry land.

The echoes of my shot had barely died away when a party of eleven mallard came from in front, making to top the great willow on the bank. I sat as still as a stone, glaring up under the shade of my hat brim and waited for them to reappear from behind the fronds. This time I made no mistake, but nipped up smartly and fired two measured shots at the first two birds to appear silhouetted against the sheen of the sky.

One collapsed and fell, the second, hard-hit, separated and angled down towards the far side of the field. Leaving the dead one to lie where it fell, Drake and I hurried after the runner which, after a short search we found in a clump of old cow parsley. To my surprise I discovered that the bird, though fit and well in every other respect, had only one leg, the other being a perfectly healed stump close to the body. Wildfowl have marvellous powers of recovery from the most horrific injuries. I once heard of a barnacle goose which made a perfect recovery and lived to a great age after having the top of its skull shot clean away.

I put this oddity in the bag, wondering idly whether a roving pike, stray pellet or deformity from birth had caused the loss of its leg, and what the problems for a one-legged duck might be: presumably it had to work hard to avoid swimming round in circles. We hunted for the dead bird and, another surprise, it was pure white. It was no albino, but a domestic call duck that had gone wild and joined the roving life of its wild cousins in preference to a tedious existence anchored on a farm duckpond. It was a curious right and left, and to have picked, by pure chance, the two oddities from a pack of apparently normal, healthy duck must have been a considerable coincidence.

I walked home across the stubble, back to the ill-defined end of the lane. On the way I found a great patch of mushrooms, those strange, twilight fruits of mild, damp autumns. I gathered them and took them home for breakfast, since they were fresh and free from the dreaded mushroom-fly larvae. As I gathered the firm, white domes, I wondered idly if it might, by chance, have been the horse of one of the old coprolite diggers which first spread the spores, for they say that you find mushrooms only in fields which were once used by horses.

I grew tired of begging permission of the village farmers to shoot over their land. In my youth, the wide fen was a free-for-all as no single farm of scattered fields was worth shooting on its own and few fen farmers then could see the sense in spending their weekends and spare time tramping about in wet sugar beet of which they saw more than enough from Monday to Friday. Permission was easily obtained and for me, the

A goose down, but a big mouthful for even this big dog

parson's son, there was rarely any demur to my request to 'have a walk round'.

As the pheasant population increased and shooting became a more popular sport, there was more competition. Only the great expanse of the lonely Bedford Levels remained free, and even there some shooting groups were quietly buying washland and restricting access. It calls for no meteorologist to tell a fenman when the wind is changing; I decided to buy my own little patch so that, no matter what happened in the future, there would be a small portion of that marsh which I could call my own.

My ear was to the ground and I knew well several marsh farmers and their disposition. When one of them retired and sold up I was able to obtain his little 10-acre holding, a low-lying, fenny patch, right under the main flightlines, quick to flood and slow to lose its water, so that in a dry season there was always a splash there to hold a few teal and snipe. The wild marsh pheasants roosted in the clumps of rush and there was no telling what might fly over or spring from your feet at any moment. The land was not expensive as land goes, costing as it did about £35 an acre. Its low value was due to its unsuitability for grazing cattle

Shortly after, the 11-acre wash next to it was for sale and, reducing my bank balance to nil, I bought that too. It included the small holt of gnarled leaning willows which I had known as a playground since childhood. It was a good feeling to walk to the horizon on wild marsh and know that, while every square inch of it belonged to someone, that someone was far away and not jealous of his possession. Far better was the feeling when the piece upon which I stood belonged to me alone and could not be taken away.

In times of flood, it was good to punt across it and note the shaggy fringes of the boundaries poking above the water. In high summer we had picnics in the bee-buzzing holt and the children, as they grew up, clambered about in the branches, made camp fires, fried sausages and pitched tents. I even managed to let the grazing, full of 'fegs' and rushes though it was. My tenant was a man who believed in good, rough grazing for big, rough bullocks and his herd of fierce crossbreeds turned themselves into slab-sides of beef after a summer spent on greenery which grew more quickly than they could eat it. Each time I ventured onto the marsh, they came thundering up, flying their tails and snorting their aggression. In fact, they were simply being inquisitive, but it took a brave man to stand calm and still as they stampeded across the marsh towards him.

It was a magic place of plover-wailing autumn mornings, swirling pike in the dykes, frog spawn, willows misty pale in the distance, whispering stands of Norfolk reed and hovering dragonflies. In winter its character changed completely as the shining floods spread over the levels, the wildfowl poured down from the north and the haunting music of a thousand wild swans and ten-thousand wigeon filled the cold dawns.

Would that I had a pound note for each time I have tramped up Washcart Way which runs alongside the Old Bedford River up to my little marsh. I have crunched through ice, floundered through snow, waded knee-deep through flood water and skidded over a perilous skin of chocolate-brown mud. In all its varying moods the washes had a special charm, each season bringing its own birds, colours, scents and sounds. I loved them all, but it was flighting the duck which gave the special thrill. So many dawns and dusks stick in the memory, so many lonely vigils under the moon or when a sharpening frost turned every reed blade to ice and the wigeon packs sounded close enough to touch.

For an unbroken run of thirty years I have shot duck there and any changes in the scenery have been unnoticeable. There is the same riot of rush, nettle and water dock on the drove side, the same dilapidated bridge, the same old dyke dug by those ancient Dutchmen who thus contrived to move the sluggish waters out to sea.

It has remained thus for three hundred years so maybe it is unreasonable to expect to see many changes in the last thirty. I parked my cycle (and, in later years, my car) by the same elder bush, once a sapling but now big enough to cast a giant shadow. My antennae would

twitch suspiciously for signs of change but such a gradual and imperceptible thing as the growth of a tree is acceptable, for Man has had no hand in it save, perhaps, in failing to cut it back. I would ease out of the car, stretch my legs and sniff the remembered scents: old potato haulms, a hint of stale stubble smoke, water weed and overblown vegetation, not one of them the sort of perfume which Dior might care to bottle but, when subtly blended, they form an evocative aroma, eloquent of the sad theme of autumns in the fens.

On this particular day I walked the 50yd up the drove to the old bridge, its peeling paint and bent bars in much the same state of disrepair as always. As I set my foot upon it, there was a roar of wings and eighty mallard sprang with dripping paddles from the water not a dozen yards away. Quacking hoarsely, they reformed into a coherent pack, swung out over the field, strung out and slowly vanished over the horizon. I watched them until the black pin-pricks faded to invisibility.

It was clear that they had been using this length of dyke for some time, for white feathers speckled the water like daisies on a vicarage lawn, the freshest ones still lying fluffy and upcurled where they had been newly preened. I walked along the low marsh bank and saw that the whole stretch had been similarly used, whereas the other side of the bridge, a place more favoured in past years, seemed not to have been visited at all. The decision where to ambush the birds, if and when they returned, was made for me. As it still lacked three hours to nightfall, Drake and I settled down in the reeds on the gentle bank and watched the sun slide down until it balanced delicately on the topmost twigs of the distant willows.

No duck showed, which is unusual. Early in the season the sky is usually full of them seaming the far skies like a sewing machine run amok, but there were other birds to catch the eye. Swallows and martins speckled the burning bowl of the heavens; a kestrel hovered, pigeon flighted over the dead poplar, a carrion crow cawed stridently, the sedge warbler reeled his mechanical song and somewhere a moorhen croaked. Little rustles showed that water voles had accepted me as part of the landscape and were busy with their evening business. Over the water dragonflies, some blue and some brown, hawked for insects. One big brown one patrolled a 20yd beat back and forth in front of me. I watched it divert to hit a mosquito, miss it, swing round for a second attempt and take it with an audible snick of its jaws. More power to its elbow, thought I, for our big fenland mosquitoes are formidable biters. A large squadron of them hovered over my hat; occasionally, like a space invader, one would detach itself and zoom in for the kill, pulling up short as it caught a whiff of my Jungle Formula insect repellant.

Thus I could recline at ease, safe from insect attack, blending with the scenery and awaiting whatever the evening might produce. It was at precisely 7.55pm (I looked at my watch), that five black specks, not midges, not swallows, not pigeon, hurried into view and, without so much as a preliminary circuit, dropped their paddles and cupped their wings for a landing. This was too good to be true, and my two careful shots, taken at 20yd at steady mallard, missed with an absolute completeness. I shook and rattled the next cartridge in my belt – definitely some shot in there! The duck vanished more quickly than they arrived and an uneventful quarter of an hour saw the light fade and no further birds show.

Then more came, a small party followed by a huge lot, 200yd behind it, and once more I made a mess of things. The gun was at my shoulder and I was aiming a fairish shot while knowing full well that the proper thing to do was to wait, allow the flock to circle, disperse, and come in in small lots as is their custom. Why does one do these things? Even as my finger pressed the trigger I knew I was wrong and another double miss and the scaring of the whole pack was no more and no less than I deserved. Drake gave me a hard stare and even raised a black eyebrow at this inept performance.

Next, a single bird answered my chattering call and came straight in to my feet: thank goodness it fell with a splash and so opened my score for the evening. Then I got one out of the next two, followed quickly by a right and left, all three birds falling on the far side of the dyke and retrieved by Drake with the unhurried assurance of a dog of nine summers who knows exactly what he is doing. Then I called in another singleton. It had intended to pass me by but, at my strident 'Karr, karr, karr', it jammed on its air brakes, set its wings, turned back on its track, gave an answering chatter and planed in. It fell with a mighty splash which showered me with pondweed.

With three brace of mature mallard for my eleven shots, slung by their necks and not stuffed anyhow into the bag, I felt that the night had, after all, turned out to be one to remember. With more duck still keen to land in the gathering darkness I left, content but conscious as much of another year having passed and of a new season freshly begun. If we seek changes, we must seek them in ourselves and not in the outward manifestations of our favourite haunts. The fens remain much the same, but the sportsmen age, alter, shift their tastes and opinions, and too often blame the fact not upon themselves, but on the things they find around them.

The modern fens are now producing crops second to none in quantity and quality in the whole of England. In the 1930s the land was of little value, for agriculture was in a parlous state of depression, one from which it was to recover in a spectacular fashion but at the time the future looked bleak. Adrian Bell described in that rural classic *Corduroy* how he bought a Queen Anne house and 200 acres of land for hundreds rather than thousands of pounds.

At that time the fen farmer would gladly sell his land to anyone who would pay his drainage rates. Some farmers gave up the struggle and emigrated, taking with them the deeds to their worthless acres and throwing them into the middle of the Atlantic. There are today several land parcels of doubtful ownership which have been absorbed for so long into neighbouring farms as to constitute a legal right to possession.

The war and the 'War Ag' saw to it that wasted land was drained and put into full production. Farmers who failed had their land confiscated and farmed by those who could do the job. An excellent book by that famous fenman Alan Bloom, entitled *A Farm in the Fen*, describes the reclaiming of part of Adventurers' Fen. The author dragged out great bog-oaks which had not seen daylight for thousands of years, dug dykes, and the smoke of burning hassocks once more drifted over the fens, as it had done in the times after the Dutchmen left. The true fenmen had as little time for the 'War Ag' as had their ancestors for the 'furriners' who came in to dry out their shining marshes. Many fenmen, war or no war, preferred their local marsh to remain as it was, and, as already mentioned, the drainage of Wicken Fen was especially resented.

Land prices are a different matter today. A 1,000-acre block near Wicken Fen could once have been yours for a few hundred pounds: such a farm was sold in the 1980s for £2¼ million. I wonder what the fen tigers would have thought about it. Land which is so expensive needs to be well farmed if the expenditure is to be deemed worthwhile. Fields have been made as large as possible, drainage dykes made to run underground and the few native hedges removed. The ancients knew little about the dynamics of turbulence and the strange ways of wind, but at least they knew from which direction it blew and the effect it had upon their land. In a dry April, a sudden gale would lift the tiny particles of sooty soil and blow it in a great cloud across the flat landscape. With it would go freshly drilled carrot seeds, while tiny sugar-beet seedlings would be dislodged or cut to ribbons by its abrasive action. Most serious was the loss of the peat or silt which formed the topsoil.

Somewhere beneath it, be it feet or inches away, lies the thick blue and yellow clay in which nothing would grow. On the day that the last remnant of topsoil blew to the four winds and the clay appeared, the richness of fen farming would be lost for ever. Shrinkage and erosion have had an extraordinary effect on fenland. We have seen how high the lodes now stand above the land with which once they were level. When it was built, the old vicarage at Prickwillow had a front door which opened straight onto the path. Today the same door is reached only after climbing eight stone steps, one of which was added each time the land shrank a little more round the foundations. A few decades ago, the experts attempted to measure the shrinkage of the fens, so they buried a long iron pole vertically in the ground at Holme Fen, not far from the old mere bed at Whittlesea. When it was placed there, its top was level with the earth: today it protrudes 18ft above ground level.

The old farmers appreciated this and set their rows of poplars, belts of willows and elder spinneys to take the cutting edge off the prevailing wind and protect the precious soil. Their grandsons needed larger and larger fields to justify their gigantic machines, so the shelter belts were pulled out. Subsequent erosion saw them searching afresh for a solution. Claying was tried, a system of diggings not unlike coprolite workings from which the deep-lying clay was dug out and mixed with the light

An 8-bore, a goose and two labradors; a morning on the flooded marsh

topsoil in order to bind it. The latest solution is to plough in rows of straw between the lines of seedlings to prevent a fen 'blow' making a start. Others sow quick-growing seeds like barley or radishes between beet rows to protect the plants until they have become established.

The wise ones are replanting trees and spinneys and allowing their dykes to grow rough coated. 'Blows' did not occur where fields were small, the headlands bound in by reed growth and the wind interrupted by thick clumps of fen trees. The modern fetish for clean, weedless fields with geometrically cut dykes, shaved and scraped clean at regular intervals, created a desert upon which the dry warm winds of spring leaped with delight.

Some say that claying, planting straw and replacing the old spinneys has all come too late: the clay will win in the end and fenland agriculture will collapse. Some of the older farmers advocate giving the Bailiff of Bedford a free hand: reflood the marsh as it was flooded for centuries and revitalise the land. The floods would need to be left for a generation if they were to do any lasting good, but they would re-swell the peat, settle a new layer of topsoil and rest the land from its exploitation by hungry man. 'That'll come back agin one o' these days, yew see if'n it doant,' thus old Charlie Benstead who stood at my side on the lode bank gazing out over mile upon mile of waving corn growing where the bittern used to boom. 'T'weren't natural to drain these here old fens, and one day the water'll be back agin – dew yew see if I'm wrong.'

The old man did not see it in his lifetime and we continue to defy gravity and several other laws of nature in keeping the land dry, but who can predict the next century's events? 'Water,' as Charlie would sagely remark, 'that's funny old stuff,' and I knew that, at that moment anyway, he was not referring to its qualities as a beverage.

The fen farms with the spinneys, belts and rough dykes were the ones for the shooter. Today the fens are as famous for game shooting as once they were for wildfowling, for wild game birds love the wide, loamy acres and the temperate climate. They cannot manage without shelter for nesting and protection from the vicious Arctic winds which sweep across East Anglia uninterrupted from the North Sea. Fen farms which make such provision are perfect shooting country. Classic game shots bemoan the lack of hills and hanging oak woods from which testing birds may be shown, but they speak with no first-hand knowledge. A wild cock pheasant flushed from the sugar beet on a windy day and heading for the distant rampart of the dyke bank, curling wickedly, tail fluttering and wings a blur is a target good enough to present to the best shot in the land and not feel ashamed.

I have the shooting on a 1,000-acre block of black fen, bounded on one side by a quiet lode, once a hive of activity now a dreaming, green-banked water, and the River Cam which winds like a lazy snake across the great plain.

In spring when the fields are bare, sandy scars wind here and there across the land showing where once the old, untamed waterways ran in the days – not so long ago – when a great marsh swept across towards Wicken, and the fen knew more of boats and eel fishermen than it did of tractors and ploughs. The land is farmed to the height of modern efficiency, with yields which would make envious a farmer of higher, heavier land. However, our enlightened farmer is also keen to preserve what he can of the old plants, insects, birds and beasts, so he allows some corners to grow rough and spray-free so that warblers may nest. Clumps of willows and spinneys of newly planted, mixed trees occupy other corners and the banks of the river and the dykes are a tangle of loosestrife, alive with butterflies and a-buzz with bees. These miniature habitats are of great value to game birds and the other elements in the food chain, from raptors to sawfly larvae, which relate to them.

In the rivers great pike still swirl in the shallows and shoals of great bream and dusky, jewel-eyed tench lie fanning their fins in the cool depths. When first we took the shooting, the farm had been exploited to the extent that every square inch of soil held a carrot seed or a grain of wheat; no nettle to hold a small tortoiseshell butterfly was allowed to bloom, every reed was close cropped as soon as it showed a green shoot. Feral cats, rats, crows and a precarious population of game birds were all that might be found by even the keenest naturalist. The ghost of old Houghton, the eccentric but immensely knowledgeable local botanist, a man who wore a hat made of the skin of a hedgehog and who knew these marshes like his own hall, would have surely been uneasy at the decline. No bittern thundered in the reedy nights, no harriers, otters, kingfishers nor duck loaned magic to the quiet mornings.

The farm changed hands, my friends and I took the shooting and a new policy set out to redress the imbalance. We started a programme of thinning out the vermin, decimating the crows, stoats, weasels and foxes which had held undisputed sway. The result was that nesting game had a far better chance of rearing broods to maturity. The farmer planted the rough corners and allowed others to run riot so that the quality of the habitat improved, giving room for nests and protection from both prying eyes and the cruel easterlies of winter. The third element, without which no shoot may flourish, is some feeding of game birds in the hard weather. Long periods of frost and snow lock away the food supply of most birds. The wildfowl have the instinct and the strength to migrate to milder places; pheasants will wander to the warmer woods on higher ground, but song birds and partridges are not wanderers and remain close to the point where they were hatched. The establishing of a few feeding points with a broken bale of straw and a sack of corn scattered upon it, will fan the flickering spark of life in many birds, and not only game; it will hold them to the spot and help them arrive at the following spring in good physical condition for the hard work of nesting.

The result of these policies was spectacular. The farm looked better, with eye-catching clumps of bushes and singing reeds to break the monotony of the landscape. Insects returned and with them the birds, so that the grasshopper warbler reeled his song in the shadow of the thorns; the sedge warblers chattered, reed buntings, nightingales and most of the finches brought their own shred of magic back to the fens. Kingfishers nested under the overhang of the banks, the harrier beat across the stubbles once more; foxes and even badgers could be glimpsed in the gloaming. The game birds multiplied so that the bags on shooting days increased every year for seven years. The size of the bag may bear little relation to the enjoyment of the day or the quality of the sport, but the increase left us in no doubt that the farm was a better place in many ways, without the cropping being affected. The story of this shoot and what we did, month by month, to build it up is told in my book *The Do-It-Yourself Gameshoot*, published by David & Charles in 1983.

I became very attached to this farm and spent a good deal of my time there. My two boys learned to stalk and shoot rabbits with a rifle, we flighted duck on the river and made it a point of honour always to leave the place a little better than we found it on each visit. Planting a sapling, setting a rat trap, trimming a few nettles from a ride or even collecting a handful of litter all qualified, and the cumulative effect of such small actions was spectacular.

My favourite place was the river wash, a place of impassable riots of water dock, rush and rough grass in summer, full of duck and moorhen nests and redshank belling their cries across the water meadows. In winter the grey waters rose and spread over to the floodbanks and in our gutter boots we would splash out across the shallows to a dry spot, make a rough hide from handfuls of bleached rush, and wait for sunset and the arrival of the duck. There was that magic moment, which all evening flighters will know, when the light has all but gone and, although there is no sight or sound of a duck, somehow you just know they are coming. The very air is highly charged with a tingle of volts which tells you clearly that something is about to happen. You shift your position, easing your cramps, and feel your safety catch to make sure it is still there. Then you see them, a cluster of hock-bottle shapes coming purposefully upstream: you hear the whicker of wings, a muttered duck voice, and then The Moment is upon you.

After it is all over and black night has fallen, you make your way back to the looming high bank, feeling with your feet for the hidden potholes while behind your back cluster the ghosts of the old fen, the monks, soldiers, raiders and humble fen fowlers and fishers who have walked or boated along those ancient ways long before you. I do not fear their shades, for I feel that just by being there and enjoying the places they knew, I have something in common with them. On especially glum nights this thought does not prevent me from pulling up my coat collar against their cold whisperings and hurrying to my little van hidden near the elder clump, rather more quickly than I might in broad daylight.

At the far end of the farm lies a quiet, neglected and overgrown little wash, less than eight acres, but choked with reed and even in the dryest summer, soggy underfoot. I fell in love with this little patch, spoke to the farmer and he agreed to sell it. Not being a wealthy man, I was obliged to sell some of my little holding on the Bedford washes in order to finance the venture, for there is a limit to how much one may reasonably invest in unproductive tracts of bog.

On my new wash I intend to reintroduce some of the vanishing fen plants, set a few willows and dredge out the low places to form flashes of open water. Frog spawn and grass snakes will follow and there will be eels and a few pike in the deeper holes. No whiff of spray ever contaminates the air thereabouts and the place is quiet and lonely. I have great hopes for its future and intend to enjoy it on many levels. Pheasants roost there in winter and duck drop in from the distant stubbles. It will become a tiny fragment of what parts of the undrained fen were like.

Unless such things are done by more people, a vital and fascinating part of England will have been overwhelmed by the modern, agricultural gorgoroths and the marshes, will-o'-the-wisps, the animals and birds will be matters only for the dusty pages of old books.

Days and Nights on the Fen

A fen slodger turned up on the washes armed with a mighty muzzle-loading fowling piece which had been bequeathed him by his grandfather. The weapon had not been fired for thirty years and woodworm and rust had corrupted it to the point of danger. A fellow gunner regarded the piece with a rare blend of awe, disbelief and contempt. 'That's a masterful gret owd gun you've a got there. I'll lay yew half a crown yew dussent shute the owd gal orf, bor, and git that little owd redshank down there on the mud.'

The owner said nothing, but with an air of dignity outraged, he charged his piece and crept like a snake to the foot of the bank and bellied up through the teazles. He poked the long brown barrel through the grass and glared down over the fat foresight at the redshank running unconcernedly on the mud. 'Neow, yew little beggar, that's eyther yeow or mey, mate,' he remarked, and fired.

Later on, swathed in bandages, from his hospital bed he was to report: 'She blowed her snout orf, alright and gied me a clink o' the skull – but I got the 'shank, and me half dollar; Yis Yis.'

I know how he must have felt, for my early outings with the sexton's crazy 12-bore placed me at risk of a similar or a worse buffet. It was a rickety piece and I still wake in a cold sweat at night when I recollect just how dangerous it was. Only one hammer cocked, and the action was so loose that the brass head detached itself from the cardboard tube of the cartridge in the moment of firing. I shot several sitting pigeons with it and it gave me a start, so I am grateful to that nameless 'farm gun' for that, if for nothing else.

My next gun was bought for £20 from the head shooting man of the village, Mr Fred Ibbott. Fred was a mighty shooter and fisher, and with his companion Fred Holt, they made a formidable couple of bag fillers. Fred Holt was a harness-maker who lived in a two-roomed cottage in the High Street, and many an hour I spent in one of his well-worn and comfortable armchairs, listening to his shooting wisdom and watching his little labrador Bess fetching his slippers, pipe and newspaper more quickly than the wife he never had. I still treasure my first game bag made by him from double-stitched binder canvas. Countless times has it been filled, and it is a tribute to his workmanship that it has stood the test of so many decades. My son uses it now, just as I did when I was his age.

It was Fred Ibbott who produced the gun which cost me my complete savings from a whole season I spent helping with the harvest. The gun was not the ideal weapon for a beginner, being a fully choked Winchester 1897 pump-action 12-bore; he threw in a dozen cartridges of loads and brands long forgotten, collectors' pieces they would be today, but I fired them off all the same.

It was, in many ways, a frustrating gun, since the full choke made close-range shooting a chancy affair. The cock pheasant, a jewelled pasha, blundering up in a blaze of gold, red and black, near enough almost to touch, was easily missed with a fully choked barrel, while the flickering snipe was even more safe from danger. It came into its own with flighted mallard or geese when my 'bang clank clang; bang-clank-clang' became my trademark among the fowling fraternity. Our finest moment together was when I shot five mallard in five cartridges when I blundered upon a large pack of them resting in a fen drain.

Such moments were rare, for the tight choke together with the lack of balance made the gun unsuitable for a tyro, but it taught me several lessons which were useful later on and, of course, if I could shoot with that gun, I could shoot with anything. When I was invited on the local farmers' end-of-season cock shoot, where convention expected an

orthodox side-by-side shotgun, I borrowed one from a kind farmer friend. I was surprised at how well I could shoot driven pheasants and partridges with this open-bored, cheap, hammer gun. My struggles with my own gun and long apprenticeship at mallard in the half light constituted a handicap the removal of which made a great difference.

The gun I really wanted belonged to George Carr, the foreman of the fen farm where I worked in my summer holidays. It was a plain, double hammerless Belgian gun looted during the war. It was never fired during the five years that I knew of its existence, but I could never persuade George to sell, which was a pity, for the gun suited me perfectly.

Fred Holt made me one of his patent gun carriers for cyclists. This comprised a deep hook which fastened onto the handlebar pillar and a leather strap round the pole of the saddle. The gun barrel lay snugly in the hook and the hand of the stock fitted into the strap. It would not jolt out, even over the worst bumps and, lying as it did along the crossbar of my father's 1930 Hercules, it did not get in the way. Thus, with the yellow labrador Ajax – a mighty warrior – loping by the back wheel, the gun in its cradle and my canvas bag on my back, the whole of the fen was mine to explore. We would ride out into the distances, hide the bike in an overgrown ditch and set off, a direction chosen and a route selected, ready for what the Fates might send. No matter how far I walked, for in those days we were careless of boundaries, I never reached the end of that great expanse of land. I might leap dyke after dyke and struggle through the jungle of willow herb, bramble and fat hen on the forgotten by-ways and see no human being but only the occasional ramshackle farm

building to show where they had been. A distant gang loading sheaves or the trickle of blue smoke from the exhaust of a tractor were infrequent encounters.

If I had timed things properly, I ended the day at a place where mallard might drop in at last light. The wild dykes are perfect for them, safe nesting places in summer, a-buzz with insects and secure bases from which to mop up ears of corn missed by the gobbling combines. While the early hours of an autumn morning have a magic all their own, the duck tend to spring in one or two large lots giving you only a shot before they depart for the day. In the evening they return in smaller groups, giving more sport for less disturbance.

On a typical, golden evening there was time to smoke a leisurely pipe and scan the skies through my binoculars. A thin piping nearby proclaimed a brood of a dozen well-grown pheasant poults on the weedy side of the drove. Near them a tiny patch of uncut corn, missed by the combine in the corner of the field stood yellowed, drooping and over-ripe. Ajax made a beeline for this patch and pushed out a mangy fox which had been lying there within yards of me as I sauntered about. My rapid double shot coincided with his reaching the reedy run of the dyke. I reloaded and ran to the spot but the dog was there first and dragged out an old vixen quite dead. She had been living on duck and pheasant for many a long year and, as there was no hunt within forty miles, I had no compunction about bowling her over.

After this adventure, the flight was something of an anti-climax, but I crouched down in a dyke near the drain; my horizon was reed heads and a forest of purple loosestrife. Faint clickings and rustlings came from within their fastness; mosquitoes swarmed about my ears, so I squirted my insect repellant and puffed so strongly at my briar that I gave myself a headache. The main drain was speckled with white down and the tussocks were downtrodden and soiled, so I knew the birds had been using this stretch, but it was to be a long wait.

When it did come, the flight was short, sparse and late.

At very last light there was a heart-stopping, guttural chatter from the heavens and the hiss of wings. Two mallard dropped from the burning dome of the west. I bided my time, sat upright at the last minute and dropped the first but missed the second. My reedy screen made for bad marking but Ajax had it at last. I had just taken delivery when a longish single bird came and I missed it neatly with both barrels. Almost on its tail came four more: I allowed a longer lead this time and one fell, crashing down within a yard of the dykeside. With a brace in the bag and senses pitched as finely as fiddle strings, I awaited the rush which now must surely come. It did not materialise, but one final duck, an easy one which virtually hovered above my hat, splashed down in a mighty eruption of water, but Ajax could make nothing of it.

I could hear him in and out of the water, working both banks, investigating every clump of rush and stirring up the mud. He was a good fenland, bag-filling dog and he knew his work and covered the ground within 50yd of the fall, even working out onto the boundaries of the field. Now it was almost dark and we had a long way to go over unfamiliar country so, reluctantly, I called him off. We plodded back along the bank and had almost reached the end of the field when there came a hoarse quacking from the water and a single bird was up on a flurry of wings and invisible against the black curtain of falling night. This might well have been my lost bird as I had not heard another one land. Such recoveries from a glancing pellet on the head are by no means unknown, but we had our brace to add to the three brace of partridge and a hare, so we could return with heads held high.

It took half an hour to find my bike, for cloud had covered the dim glow of the stars and I lost my bearings. At last I caught a dim gleam of chromium plate and slowly we made our way along the maze of droves over the flat lands until we began to climb gently up towards the lights of the village. Later in the week, my mother cooked the bag in a mighty pie with onions, runner beans, baked potatoes and fresh mushrooms; that was a real fenman's, hunter's pie, if you like.

I shot my first goose almost by accident. I have shot many since, but the first is the first and indelibly remembered for that reason. My bike had skidded perilously on the frozen puddles, but at last I was safely at the marsh bank, sliding to a halt in the lee of the derelict barn and hiding my machine inside the door, near where a broken-down Suffolk wain stood dreaming of better days.

Booted and armed with a long-barrelled single magnum 12 I stood shivering and felt the bite of frosty air in my nostrils. Ajax had already run the 2 miles from home and now he skittered and danced, a pale ghost in a monochrome landscape.

I heard the distant bark of a farm dog; a mallard quacked gently and a wigeon whistled. It was time to go, tinkling and crunching through the filigrees of ice left by receding flood water, stopping every so often, hissing the dog to silence, holding my breath to listen intently before trudging on. I reached my favourite place by a hunch-backed willow stump which seemed, at any moment, about to topple over into the floodwater at its feet. The stretch of open water beyond it was as black as a puddle of ink beneath a half moon as white as a cleanly cut segment of apple. With a splash and a grunt of alarm a string of mallard sprang from the water and became instantly invisible against the star-studded sky.

I waded out and set my six decoys bobbing on the water, old, wooden veterans, which had seen many a duck killed over them and also, to judge from the pellet holes, from among them. I draped some brown, frosted grass, flotsam from an earlier flood, onto the rushes to thicken my cover. Even behind this flimsy screen I must have cut a fearful, black figure hunched there in the gloom. When the duck flew over, I might have blended more successfully. Ajax quivered at my knee, his pale coat blending perfectly, and we both scanned the skies like old-time air-raid wardens. The gun barrel was blisteringly cold and the frost began to sap all the feeling from my ears and nose. I rubbed these extremities to make sure they were still alive and was just in the act of doing so when there was a flicker of wings and a silvery whistle across the pale of the dawn. A small knot of wigeon flashed across the curtain of cloud, vanished, re-appeared and with a whoosh, there they were on the water. The real birds distinguished themselves from my decoys by relaxing and, like clockwork toys, began preening and dibbling. The nearest cock was not ten yards away; he put up his head and whistled with surprising loudness, wheeeooo–wheeeooo . . . Ajax's eyes stood out like the proverbial chapel hat pegs as he gazed in quivering disbelief at the sight.

Stubbling mallard; a sign of autumn

The sun had now edged above the rim of the far bank and the Christmas-cake landscape lost some, but not all, of its ghostliness. Two mallard passed, a very possible chance on my left. As I peered round at them and half-shifted the gun, my wigeon sprang and flew with a growl and a whistle. My finger was on the trigger, but I did not fire. To have broken the solemn stillness of the scene would have been a sacrilege, rather like shouting in church. I left them for another day, but vowed to return in proper fowling weather when the gales swept the marshes and roared in the withy beds. I could not find it in my heart to knock them down when they had settled so trustingly close to me.

But what of that goose? I was tramping back along the marsh track, ready if a snipe or one of our little wild marsh pheasants should either spring unexpectedly from the rushes, when I heard a distant bugling in the sky. There, far away and steady as a constellation, flew a line of ten geese. How distant and remotely untouchable they seemed: if only they would come over and give me half a chance. Not much hope of that, for, by their height and steady course, they knew just where they were going and were hardly likely to fly near me, one tiny dot on miles of untenanted marshland.

But that was precisely what they did. For no apparent reason, those whitefronts turned at right angles, lost height and, still going strong and not intending to land, came straight towards me. Had I myself flown up and guided them, they could not have come with greater precision over that clump of reed behind which impromptu screen I had dropped on one knee.

Ajax sat as good as gold where I had dropped him in the open, his pale coat blending perfectly with the icy tussocks. On and on came the birds: surely I would miss; might they turn at the last moment and save me that humiliation? They might not. The gun found the shoulder, finger the trigger while my eye ranged through that leading, wide black shape . . . forward . . . forward . . . bang!

There was an appreciable pause, just long enough for the brain to say 'missed' and beg for a second chance, but it was all right. There was a 'phrutt' of pellets striking tough pinions and, suddenly shrunken, my bird was falling for what seemed a full minute but could have been only a few seconds, and the second bird in line − not the one at which I had aimed − thumped with a complete and heart-stopping finality onto the frozen grass.

That was a Christmas I shall never forget.

Things did not always go so well. On another day a gale was tearing at the poplars, sending the tenacious last clusters of leaves streaming like giant snowflakes across the road and into the dykes. The washes had flooded earlier than usual that year and I lay in the banktop grasses and scanned the water through my binoculars. Wigeon, mallard and teal speckled the water among the regular herd of Bewick swans. I took the glasses from my eyes, and then I heard it, the unmistakeable gabbling of grey geese.

Knowing the ground as well as I did, I spotted a gaggle of about seventy greylags, preening and splashing on a patch of floodwater on the far side of the wash. I worked out a stalk which would keep a dense fringe

of osiers between me and those sharp eyes, but keeping silent while wading through ankle-deep water was not so easy. I could tiptoe along in reasonable quietness by choosing where to place my feet, but there was no way I could convince Ajax that it was not more fun to slosh along through all the deepest places. Painfully slowly and by means of a back-aching stoop, we reached the rushes nearest to the geese and, still undetected, collapsed to recover our breath.

I parted the rushes with my fingers. The pewter gleam of the water was speckled with black specks of duck; here and there the ghostly outline of a swan drifted wraithlike while, beyond them all, the geese sat. I was in line with the main flightline so I had a better-than-average chance that they would pass me within shot, so I settled down to wait in as much comfort as 6in of water would allow.

There was a muffled chattering and a string of mallard came whistling past. At any other time I would have had a shot, but with the geese so near, I was not prepared to risk disturbing them. Then, with a roar, the wigeon were up, strings of black beads laced across the deep-blue curtain of the eastern sky. They came from my splash and from others beyond it in eight or ten huge lots and again, some of the stragglers offered chances but still I resisted, pinning all my hopes on the remote chance of a goose.

The spectacular duck flight was over; it was broad daylight, and my barrels were clean. Cock pheasants crowed and flighted out from the distant banks and onto the farmland to feed, but still the geese remained, perfectly happy where they were, in among the swans and not moved by the urge for early departure which had affected their smaller cousins. I waited on, cramped and uncomfortable, well past the time that most respectable folk would have cleared away the breakfast things. I began to think desperate thoughts such as trying to stalk nearer along the flooding dyke, sending out the dog as a diversion or even throwing a stone, but none of them was necessary.

With a sudden crescendo of clamouring, the greylags grouped, faced the wind, ran a few, quick paces and with a threshing of wings and clarion burst of music they swung round and came past me. How big and black they seemed head on. My thumb was on the safety catch and they beat on, but now tacking slightly to pass me on my left. I managed a crouching run to bring me a few yards nearer, but still the flightline veered away from me. I flung the gun to the shoulder and swung past the leader. How far were they? Fifty yards perhaps? The second it took me to aim told me that they were all of that and more, possibly sixty or even seventy. A stray pellet might have knocked one down, but that is not the name of the game. I held my fire and slowly lowered the gun.

Long after they had gone, I stood there gazing mournfully at that empty patch of sky which they had so recently endowed with that special kind of magic that only grey geese can give.

Inland encounters with geese were rare, so that each one was a memorable occasion. The goose shooter had to seek out the mudflats and sandbars of the coast of Norfolk or Lincolnshire if he was addicted to their special appeal. Some fen gunners even made the long trek to the Scottish firths and estuaries where grey geese are as common in winter as they were on the fens before they were drained.

The silver ribbon of Vermuyden's great level is still much the same as it has been for 200 years. The wildfowl of the fens have drawn into that last major watery strip and the area is now one of the most important wetlands in Europe. I mentioned earlier that the Wildfowl Trust bought a series of washes at Welney and placed them under the stewardship of one of the old fen skaters and puntgunners, Josh Scott. On the principle that a poacher makes a good keeper, Josh did an excellent job of protecting and enhancing the reserve, feeding the Bewick's swans in the hard weather and welcoming thousands of human visitors a year with his earthy blend of folksy bonhomie.

Josh Scott feeds the swans on the Wildfowl Trust Reserve at Welney on the Bedford washes

Josh did not entirely abandon the old life, but cut a few reeds, just to keep his hand in, and passed his summers doing his old job of shepherding the wash cattle. One concession to changing times was his use of a powerful trials motor cycle for herding the beasts, a method rather more efficient than shanks's pony. Josh's old punt and his famous punt gun 'Bacca Jack' were honourably retired from active service and displayed in the Wildfowl Trust buildings at Welney, and no doubt they make an interesting puzzle and a conversation piece for visitors. Josh takes Bacca Jack to country shows, and at unexpected moments during the afternoon there is a searing flash of flame and a cloud of smoke as he gives a demonstration firing. Fortunately, he omits to load any shot on these occasions. Nothing could be more of a contrast to the sort of life to which the old gun was accustomed, out under cold moons on the washes, than the summer afternoons at this or that stately home, the crowds of people, children with candyfloss and the distant echoes of a brass band beneath the beech-trees' shade. It is easy to imagine being put out to grass in a less pleasant manner.

I return home today having spent a day bobbing up and down in a boat fishing for trout on Grafham Water. I reflected, as I did so, that this man-made lake with its 11 miles of bank is situated in the old county of Huntingdonshire, not far from the site of the last of the fen meres which we drained in the 1850s. Grafham Water was created to supply the needs of the thirsty East Midlands and it cost millions of pounds to create, almost as much as it had to drain Whittlesea and reveal the biggest English pike and that monstrous eel.

Modern reed cutting; still a rich harvest but no more scythes

Modern fen farming; intensive and high-powered. Does it leave room for the old creatures of the ancient fen?

It is such an irony, and a comment upon Man's petty schemes and aspirations. Grafham also holds great pike, although possibly not a 52-pounder – yet – and coarse fish of great size and incalculable numbers shoal in summer in the shallow bays. Doubtless there are great eels there, down deep in the shadowy holes. As at Whittlesea in the old days the lake is a pleasure ground, not for aristocrats in their sailing launches, but for modern dinghy helmsmen and wind surfers. No more trimmers set for pike and perch, but rod and line, fly-only anglers of the new middle classes whip the water for stocked trout. The large copper, swallowtail and blue butterflies have not returned, but in winter a great host of wildfowl speckles the surface and a lucky birdwatcher might see an osprey fishing in one of the quiet bays.

Thus, there is once more a great lake in the fens and it has attracted to it some of the old water birds, but the conference centre, sailing lodge, nature trails and jet fighters from the nearby air bases speak of the twentieth century. The old wildness and sense of Nature holding sway will never be recaptured, and they were two of the most powerful features of the old fens of Guthlac. Grafham is very much under the control of Man who holds the water behind a great, concrete dam, pumps it in or out as required, supervises the activities and collects the money.

It is the best that we can do, for civilisation has come to mean the taming and organising of the wild places, the removal from them of even the hint that Man is not the master there, for to be alone in a desolate place makes him feel threatened and generally ill at ease. He is happier where boundaries are marked with fences and the unknown places mapped and made safe.

The old fen fowler/fisher did not require such reassurance, but accepted the boundless miles of waving reed, meres, rivers, swamps, mosquitoes and the sad, wild crying of the birds as his natural world. He adapted to it and became part of it without ever wishing to change it or even dreaming that it might, one day, be possible.

·Finale·

It was evening. The smoke of stubble fires drifted across the plain as when Lars Porsena marched on Rome and laid waste the farms as he passed. I was coming home across the fen, my bag heavy with partridges and one unlucky cock pheasant which I had hunted from field to field before he would show himself. When at last I cornered him in an elder thicket and he erupted in a whirr of black and gold, he was quick to place the scrub willow between us, but not quite quick enough. Even so, it was a lucky pellet which caught him, for he flew up and up vertically on quick fluttering wings and when he was seventy paces high, he set his wings and, gently as thistledown, he floated down to the reeds where I found him neatly spread, eyes demurely closed in death. These 'tower birds' are the result of either a pellet in the brain or the lungs, but I was lucky and pleased to bag him no matter where he was struck.

My face and arms were reddened and tingling after a day of golden October sunshine; my baggy corduroys a mass of burrs, teazles and the cotton-wool fluff of redshank weed which grew thickly on the site of the old Fenland Flier railway line. One foot squelched uncomfortably to show where I had failed to clear a 7ft dyke, but just fallen short and filled a boot with black dyke water, liberally laced with duckweed.

The western sky grew rosier by the minute and the blood-red balloon of the sun swam down, painting the streaks of cloud as it went. Overhead there was a great rushing sound of wings and a cacophony of whistling and chattering as tens of thousands of starlings flew over towards their roost in the great reed bed. I have seen them in wavering soughing banks half a mile long and a hundred yards deep, sweeping in with a roar of wings like the rush of waves on a shingle beach. They damage acres of valuable thatching reeds, the sheer weight of their numbers breaking the slender stalks and the accumulation of their ammoniac droppings poisoning the ground. No bangers, flares or scarecrows can keep them off.

Hot, uncomfortable, raw from the sun and with the bag strap digging into my shoulder, I marched on towards the distant willow where I had left my cycle. For all that, I was at peace with the world. Let the traffic jams build up on the hot tarmac roads on the way home from the coast; let the drivers fret, fume and inhale the exhaust fumes, while children in the back seats bickered and whined. Within cycling distance of my house lay all the escape that I needed for I was spared the need to emulate the majority of my fellow countrymen and follow the crowds who took their squalor with them up to the nearest seaside town.

I was surrounded by stubbles, some with piles of jumbled straw bales on them, fields of dark-green sugar beet and the brown stripes of potato land, the haulms beginning to die back as the wheel of the seasons rolled on. They blended into a not-unpleasant scent, the whiff of water mint from the dykes and even the hint of black ooze and sweet stubble smoke each contributing a vital element to the bouquet. From far and near partridges were chirruping as they prepared to jug and I saw a covey, whirring brown dots, flying out of the far end of my field and onto the next as I came tramping along.

Far away, towards the sun, a long string of mallard flew high and handsome coming whence I knew not and going – who knew where? Maybe their distant ancestors flew under that same sun when the fens looked very different and that red glow was reflected in a million red ripples on some great mere.

Old fen 'slodger', once a familiar sight

I approached the great bank, the claim to immortality of the Adventurers and the Dutchmen who risked everything to carry out their great enterprise. Here had they carried the first spits of earth in baskets on their heads. A little further on stood the new diesel pumping engine continuing the task which Vermuyden began; but nearby, in a clump of dank elders, under a tangle of dead nettle stems, I knew there lay the remains of one of the old drainage wind pumps, which once clacked round cheerfully for decade after decade until the job became too much for them. A long-eared owl nested in that spinney, so the last vestige of the derelict gave harbourage to one of the old woodland fen birds.

I hurried on, sniffing the scents, feeling beneath my feet the rich dusty peat. At the end of the field lay a jumbled pile of bog-oak like a giant's heap of kindling, fragments of ancient trunks dragged out the previous spring by the tractors and waiting to be taken away and sawn up for firewood. I wondered what birds flew in fenland skies and what animals stalked the primeval forests when those black logs last grew leaves.

The very land upon which I now walked was once the bed of a great mere, rimmed with miles of whispering reeds, full of brown gnome bitterns and bearded tits. Had I stood there 200 years previously my head would have been 6ft under water. Pike big enough to give a twentieth-century angler nightmares would have hugged the bottom or lain like sunken logs beneath the lily pads awaiting the next meal. Shoals of tench

Out on the flooded washes, and rewarded for the effort

and bream would have drifted past, white-mouthed, lazily gaping. Above, on the surface, the blue darrs would have hawked for insects and harriers and ospreys swung in the thermals, drifting over autumn skies which nowadays only rarely see the shadow of their passing. Grebes, coots, moorhens and great rafts of tufted duck and pochard would have blackened the surface.

The water and the birds were long gone and the ground I trod was worth £2,000 an acre, not a bad price for the bed of a lake. Raiders, mercenaries from many lands, holy men, crusaders and plump abbots had once sailed those winking waters; kings had been rowed by teams of lusty oarsmen and no doubt gazed with approval at the church towers of Barnack rag which, half-completed, reared up above the sedge-thatched cottages, marks that the new God had, at last, come to the 'hideous fen'. In winter the skaters would have glided and hissed past on their bone runners, their faces aglow from the blend of alcohol and cold air.

On I plodded, until a glint of water caught my eye. I knew the place well, an old coprolite digging which once hummed to the raucous shouts of the cheerful, imported labourers who were to leave their indelible mark on both the fenland landscape and its people. The place has become a donnish pleasance for latter-day explorers to whom the fens and its curious histories have, overnight, become matters of fascination. The rough old men who dredged out the precious coprolites would have given them short shrift as 'bug-hunters' who could not give even a bird its proper name but 'needs must keep a'spoutin' that owd Latin all the time.' Only the most practised eye could detect the site of their hard labour, but the silent pond with its fringing band of *Phragmites* was the most conspicuous testament to their presence and their eventual passing.

Two fields later and I was onto a tract of land known as Decoy Farm. The place was well named, for here, a century ago, Farmer Jenyns, a famous naturalist and county squire, dug a decoy pond to capitalise on the myriad duck which darkened the dawn skies with their passing. That decoy took 10,000 birds each year for two decades until local drainage caused the birds to move away to more secluded places where the hand of man was unknown. The great pond is now no more than a shallow hollow in the peat, while all vestiges of the pipes, screens, 'coyman's cottage and the appendages necessary to such an operation have completely vanished. Thick, green sugar-beet leaves cloak the spot. The 'coyman's old barrow, upon which he must have carted the best part of quarter of a million wildfowl to the railway station, is now an exhibit in the local museum.

Nearly there, and night was falling. The sharp, delicate bark of a fox pricked my ears and had me hefting the reassuring weight of my gun. On my left, amid the tangle of nettles and enclosed by a thick fence of willows – once the stakes for a hen-run, but now well-rooted and mature trees full of hollows for little owls and starlings – was the site of a ruined cottage. It fell in the Black Winter of '47 along with many another outlying holding when the waters burst through and gave the cottagers a night of terror and misery, sending them clinging to their roof trees and chimney stacks until rescue arrived. One could only recall that, well within living memory, the Bailiff of Bedford had returned to claim his own. The human misery is in no way properly recorded by that ragged chimney stack, those crumpled remains of walls and the scatter of broken slates beneath the cow parsley. A short while ago, children screamed in those bedrooms as they heard the fearsome roar of the great flood coming nearer by the moment, the desperate squawking of the hens and whimpering of a half-drowned farm dog still tethered to his floating kennel. The people had gone – lost, drowned or saved and moved to a safer habitation – but their stories lay in those pathetic ruins.

So, it was back to father's old cycle. I would give the duck a miss this evening, but only because no sure spot presented itself. I hauled the machine from amid the keks (cow parsley), slid my gun into Fred Holt's patent gun carriage and pedalled slowly up the fen towards the village and the comforts of the home fire. Ajax loped by my back wheel, a pale ghost beneath the paler moonlight. Together we traversed safe ground, ground which it would have taken a fenman of even a century before a week to have crossed on his stilts. The road at last began to rise and take us into the safety and companionship of the village. I passed the pub on the left, Stan Robinson's farm on the right – the fen farmer who gave me much of my shooting – past the Post Office, the baker's, the butcher's and the row of old Dutch houses, relics of the drainers, and marked with the distinctive gable ends. Then I came to the dark, lowering monolith which was the church, built in the fourteenth century by godly men for whom no labour was too great.

So home, and I lay the cycle under the porch and hung the birds on the row of nails placed for that purpose under the eaves of the shed. Next the dog, and I took him down to his run for his well-earned supper. As he munched, I leaned on the garden fence and gazed through the rising fog, out at the old fen. No will-o'-the-wisp, no marsh gas, no ghosts, no hordes of deadly stinging flies came to plague me, but I felt they were all there, biding their time until they might come again, for it is not too late for Nature to claim her rights and take back the fens for her own.

I had leaned there for long enough in the chill, and with a sigh, I turned to make my way back to the old vicarage to clean the gun.